FAMOUS VISITORS

TO

JEFFERSON COUNTY, ILLINOIS

EARLY YEARS 1819–1919

HOWARD JOE ASHBROOK

ISBN 978-0-557-50733-7

Front Cover: Images of John A. Logan and William T. Sherman by Glenn Moreton

Back Cover: Image of Carrie Nation by Glenn Moreton

PREFACE

I began this research with the goal of making a list of famous people who came to Jefferson County. Soon the objective became one of writing an article or even a book because the list grew very long, and there were so many interesting stories attached to these visits. Although certainly not a comprehensive history, hopefully the information can give the reader an idea of the political, religious, entertainment, and sports picture in the county over this time period. It is also my hope that the book will to some extent fill a gap in southern Illinois history. Jefferson and surrounding counties in the middle of southern Illinois have been overlooked by writers of regional and Illinois histories. In addition my purpose is to show how local history integrates with state and national history. The "famous" people who came to Jefferson County were often part of a state or national trend or movement. Teachers may be able to use this information to help students understand and enjoy history. If students see that the state and national figures they are studying came to their own town or county, maybe they will think of them as more relevant.

Deciding who should be included as "famous visitors" was sometimes very easy (Lincoln, Roosevelt) but often was a judgment call. There were two basic questions that had to be answered. The first question— Was this person famous?—was not always easy to answer. My decision was to include those who were well known at least state-wide. They could have been famous at the time of their visit but not so much today. Or, they could have been little known then but well known today. Either would qualify. Practically speaking, this means that in the political world—governors, members of the United States Congress, presidents, vice presidents, etc.—were included but (with some exceptions) not mayors, state legislators and other state officials. For military leaders they had to be generals or someone of lower rank who had achieved a national reputation. For religious and entertainment figures they had to be nationally known. For sports figures usually the qualification was making the Hall of Fame for their particular sport. Sometimes a group came to the county and was included because the group was famous (the Apache Indians) even though the individuals were not.

The second question—Were they visitors?—also was sometimes difficult. I did exclude famous residents of Jefferson County because they were not really visitors. Here again some judgment calls were made. Zadok Casey and L. L. Emmerson were excluded because they lived in Mt. Vernon most of their lives. Walter B. Scates was a more difficult decision. He lived in Jefferson County in the 1840s and 1850s but moved away. Living in the county for about twenty years was enough to exclude him. Robert G. Ingersoll on the other hand lived in Mt. Vernon only about one year. So he was considered a visitor and was included.

Sources for this book are incomplete, especially for the early years. Local newspapers only began publishing in the 1850s. They were weekly newspapers, and very few issues remain today. The first daily newspapers were produced in the 1890s, but there are gaps here as well. So for the earliest years I had to rely on court records, local histories, and other sources to find the visitors. This means that many people could have been missed. An effort was made to check from multiple sources, but this was often impossible. In some cases the newspapers would report that someone would be in Mt. Vernon "next week," but the following papers could not be checked because they are missing. I tried to indicate that it was possible the person cancelled or for some reason didn't come.

Court records are also incomplete. Jefferson County Circuit Court Record Book C (1844–1849), E through J (1853–1868), and others are missing. The Supreme Court began work in Mt. Vernon in 1848 and the records are mostly complete. But as with the circuit court records, they can only tell about famous judges or attorneys.

Local and regional histories have some information on famous visitors. There are two main local Jefferson County histories (Perrin, 1883, and Wall, 1909) that are very helpful. But they were telling the history of the county and were not focused on famous visitors. Also, they were written for readers of their time and assumed they knew the events of the years just prior to the book's publication. As a result there are many gaps here as well. In recent years Thomas A. Puckett's books, *Mt. Vernon: A Pictorial History* (1991) and *Mt. Vernon Remembers* (2000) have also been very helpful. Some regional histories such as George W. Smith's *When Lincoln Came to Egypt* (1940) were helpful. But Smith often used oral sources, and it was not possible to follow-up on his information. It is unfortunate that more local leaders did not leave papers, letters, or memoirs.

An attempt has been made to show the reader where these famous visitors went while they were in the county. This was complicated by several factors. Many of the roads, railroads, places, and towns have been re-named or have ceased to exist. On April 5, 1900, Mt. Vernon changed the system of naming streets and numbering the buildings, homes, lots, etc. From that point all streets running north and south were to be "number" streets and all streets running east and west were to be "name" streets. This required changing the names of many streets. Here are some of the key changes:

- Vernor Street became Second Street.
- Marion and Bullock Streets became Third Street.
- Lee Avenue became Fourth Street.
- Park Avenue became Fifth Street.
- Spring Street became Sixth Street.
- Breckinridge Street became Seventh Street.
- Green Street became Eighth Street.
- Washington and Watson Streets became Ninth Street.
- Union Street became Tenth Street.
- Casey Street became Eleventh Street.
- First Street became Twelfth Street.
- Second and Franklin Streets became Thirteenth Street.
- Third Street became Fourteenth Street.
- Fifth Street became Fifteenth Street.
- Benton Avenue and Edgewood Street became Sixteenth Street.
- Chance Street became Seventeenth Street.
- Tildon Avenue became Eighteenth Street.
- Bunyan Street became Broadway.

Businesses, schools, churches, and many other organizations have changed names and locations over the years. For example, the First Methodist Church was on Eleventh (Casey) Street when Lincoln was in Mt. Vernon in 1840 but later moved to Twelfth (First) and Main. The Jefferson County Fair was in east Mt. Vernon during Civil War times but by 1906 was located in south Mt. Vernon. The Mt. Vernon Chautauqua had at least five locations around town. Hopefully with this explanation, maps, and information in the text, the readers can decipher the places where celebrity people visited. I will use "modern" street, place, and organization names unless otherwise specified.

I would like to thank the following people (in no particular order) who have helped me with this project: John Howard, Linda Short, Jack Flood, Glenn Moreton (for the sketches of John A. Logan, William Tecumseh Sherman, and Carrie Nation plus much information), Rebecca Brewer, Polly Dulaney, Tom Puckett, George Kuhn, and the staff at Brehm Memorial Library. Of course there were many others too numerous to list. Thanks to them as well.

TABLE OF CONTENTS

Chapter IV - The 1880s and 1890s

Chapter V - The Progressive Era 1900–1919

List of Illustrations

Chapter I

Chapter II

Chapter III

Chapter VI

CHAPTER I

The Earliest Years

George Rogers Clark

Even before Illinois became a state and Jefferson County existed there was a famous visitor to the area. In February, 1779, during the American Revolution, George Rogers Clark and his men passed through the land that would become Jefferson County. No one knows the exact route of the expedition. John Wall, who produced an early county history, wrote that they crossed into Jefferson County near the southwest corner, passed by the area where Waltonville now is located, camped south of Mt. Vernon at Rogers Ford where Route 37 crosses Casey Ford, and left the county into Wayne County near Kelns Skillet Fork.[1] Others suggest a more northern route through Grand Prairie and Rome Townships.[2] Regardless which path they took, all sources agree they passed through Jefferson County.

Clark and his approximately 175 men were part of the Virginia militia. Their goal was to capture the British forts north of the Ohio River and secure the area for the American side. On July 4, 1778, they captured Kaskaskia, and on February 9, 1779, they left on the more than two-hundred-mile trek through the wilderness to Vincennes. Clark and his men surprised the British and captured the fort at Vincennes. It was one of the greatest victories of the Revolutionary War. Unfortunately for Clark he was never to achieve greatness again. He died in poverty in 1818.

Mt. Vernon, the county seat of Jefferson County, was founded in 1819 by a few families in the middle of the wilderness in southern Illinois. No rivers or roads connected Mt. Vernon to the rest of society. The Goshen Trail, running from Shawneetown to Edwardsville, missed Mt. Vernon. So at first very few people—famous or not—came to the town. Famous visitors such as Lafayette (1825) or Charles Dickens (1842) traveled along the Ohio and Mississippi Rivers and stopped at towns such as Shawneetown, Cairo, and Cahokia.

During the 1820s and 1830s roads were built north, south, east, and west to connect Mt. Vernon with near-by counties and towns. The most important road connected Mt. Vernon to the Goshen Road, which went through Jefferson County from southeast to northwest but missed the town by a number of miles to the east. This new road joined the Goshen Trail north of Crenshaw's Corner in Moore's Prairie in the summer of 1821. It gave travelers on the Goshen Road the opportunity to take a shorter, better route through Mt. Vernon on their way north and west.

Mt. Vernon began to grow slowly with businesses, churches, schools, a courthouse, and a jail. But Mt. Vernon, like other "frontier towns," was wild and wooly at times with drinking and brawling common. Here is how one woman described conditions: "But Saturday was always a lively day. Races and shooting matches were now carried on with the frenzy of intoxication, and oaths, knives, clubs, guns, and whisky were kept going with an energy and a gusto that were truly appalling."[3]

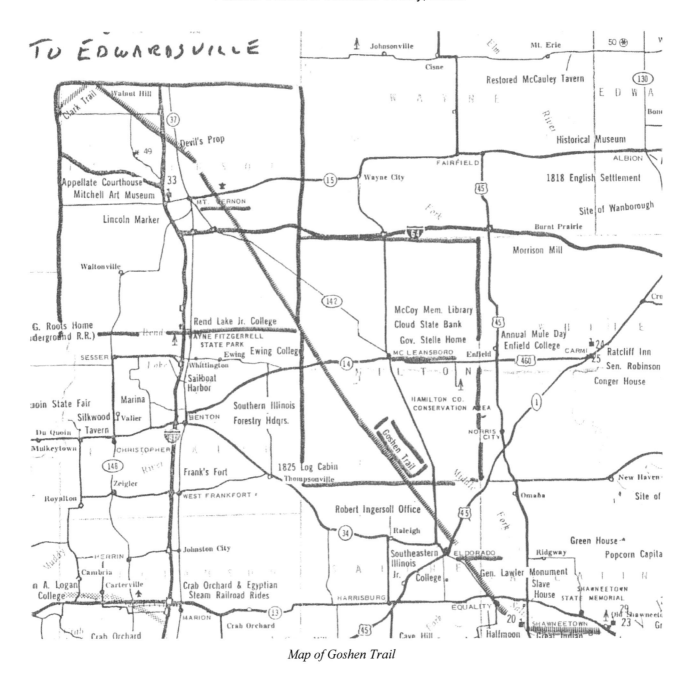

Map of Goshen Trail

Even if some important person had come to Mt. Vernon or Jefferson County in the 1820s or 1830s, we might not know about it today. Mt. Vernon's first newspaper, the *Jeffersonian*, wasn't started until 1851, and very few of those issues remain. Many newspapers followed, but none of them remained long. The first daily newspaper for Mt. Vernon was the *Daily Register* in 1892. Thankfully, there are other sources.

The Delaware Indians

The first notable visitors to Jefferson County were the Delaware Indians. They arrived in 1819, camped on Horse Creek about eight miles from Mt. Vernon, and remained until late 1820. The Delawares had signed treaties giving up their land, and small groups were slowly moving west with stops in Ohio, Indiana, Illinois, and Missouri on the way to Oklahoma. The group in Jefferson County was very friendly and invited the white settlers to visit them. The Indians treated their guests royally, refusing to eat their meals until the visitors had finished. Early records indicate this group of Delawares numbered about six hundred. However, a book about the Delawares, *The Delaware Indians: A History* by Clinton A. Weslager, states that in November of 1820, 1,346 Delawares from Indiana were taken across the Mississippi River by the ferry at Kaskaskia, Illinois. Perhaps the group from Horse Creek joined those from Indiana on their way west.[4]

Early Governors

According to Jefferson County Circuit Court records and local histories, two very important political figures were in the county in the early 1820s. Thomas Reynolds was the circuit court judge in November, 1822, October, 1823, and May and October, 1824.[5] He was chief justice of the Illinois Supreme Court from 1822 to 1825. Later he was in the Illinois House of Representatives and then moved to Missouri, where he was elected governor in 1841. Tragically he committed suicide in 1844, leaving a note that stated: "I have labored and discharged my duties faithfully to the public, but this has not protected me from the slanders and abuse which has rendered my life a burden to me. I pray to God to forgive them and teach them more charity."[6]

John Reynolds, nephew of Thomas, was presiding judge in the circuit court in May of 1823.[7] As a soldier in the War of 1812 he earned the nickname "Old Ranger." He was a member of the Illinois Supreme Court from 1818 to 1825, and the Illinois House of Representatives in the 1820s, 40s, and 50s. He was elected governor of Illinois in 1830 (with Zadok Casey of Jefferson County as lieutenant governor). In 1834 he was elected to the U.S. House of Representatives. Below are sketches of the courthouses of 1819 and 1823.

Sketch of Jeff. Co. Courthouse 1819

Sketch of Jeff. Co. Courthouse 1823

Peter Cartwright

In the fall of 1824 Peter Cartwright (1785–1872) came through Jefferson County on the Goshen Road. Cartwright was one of America's most famous early frontier preachers. He was a Methodist minister known for "fire and brimstone" sermons and occasional physical confrontations with drunken rowdies at his camp meetings. He held camp meetings all over Illinois that drew fifteen to twenty thousand people and continued for several days at a time. One famous story, which Cartwright denied in his autobiography, told of a fight between Cartwright and the famous Mike Fink. Cartwright was a founding member of the Methodist Illinois Conference, helped found McKendree College, served in the Illinois legislature, and in 1846 was defeated by Abraham Lincoln for a seat in the U.S. House of Representatives.

Cartwright, who was raised in Kentucky, decided to move his family to Sangamon County, Illinois, partly to flee from the institution of slavery. On the way north a tragic event took place. While the family was camping, a tree fell and killed Cartwright's daughter, Cynthia. According to Cartwright: "Just as day was appearing in the east, the tree at the root of which we had kindled a small fire fell, and it fell on our third daughter, as direct on her, from her feet to her head, as it could fall; and I suppose she never breathed after." She was buried somewhere in Hamilton county, probably near Cartwright Chapel southwest of McLeansboro. Again according to Cartwright: "My teamster and myself fell to cutting the tree off the child …, drew her out from under it …, and moved on about twenty miles to an acquaintance's in Hamilton County, Illinois, where we buried her."[8]

Upon entering Jefferson County the Goshen Road passed by Crenshaw's place (formerly Andrew Moore's cabin in Moore's Prairie), which was a camping ground for emigrants to "Sangamo country," and a location where wandering ministers stopped and preached. According to Perrin's *History of Jefferson County*, "it was no uncommon sight to see a hundred wagons in a single company going north" during this

4

time.[9] After Crenshaw's place the Cartwright family most likely took the branch road into Mt. Vernon. In any case the Cartwright family reached Sangamon County on November 15, 1824.

Cartwright Monument

Early Attorneys

Many important people worked as attorneys in the Jefferson County Circuit Court in the 1830s and 1840s. In March of 1836 Illinois Secretary of State A. P. Field appeared in the circuit court. He was defending a client accused of sodomy or as the records put it, "infamous crime against nature."[10] Field was also a member of the Illinois legislature and toured with Abraham Lincoln in 1840 to promote the Whig cause. Shawneetown attorney, Samuel D. Marshall, had many cases in the courts during this time. He was state's attorney for Jefferson County from 1837 to 1846. He was also a good friend of Abraham Lincoln. [11]

Another Shawneetown attorney, John A. McClernand, appeared often in the Jefferson County Circuit Court in the 1830s and 1840s.[12] On May 26, 1847, he wrote a letter from Mt. Vernon to Abraham Lincoln asking for his help on an appointment.[13] McClernand and Lincoln were both members of the U.S. House of Representatives at the time. McClernand had defeated Zadok Casey for a seat in Congress in 1842 and served from 1843 to 1851. Hamilton County attorney, Samuel S. Marshall was elected prosecuting attorney for Jefferson County and other counties in 1846.[14] He was elected to the U.S. House of Representatives and served from 1854 to 1858.

CHAPTER II

The 1840s and 1850s

During the 1840s and 1850s Jefferson County was slowly growing and developing. Politically the county was dominated by the Democratic Party. Two Democrats, Zadok Casey and Stinson Anderson, competed for support. The only real question was which Democrat would win office. The Whigs—and later the Republicans—didn't have much of a chance. Even so, Lincoln and other Whigs made an effort in Jefferson County in 1840. Nationally the political trend was the rise of the "common man." Jefferson County participated in that by strongly supporting westerners like Andrew Jackson. Unfortunately this period also saw the developments that led to the Civil War. The arguments over slavery from some very famous people were heard in Jefferson County.

Economically the biggest development was the railroad-building craze. Plans for the route of the Illinois Central Railroad, which would cross the state from north to south, were heatedly debated. Local officials worked diligently, but they failed to have the railroad come through Jefferson County. Even so, the new railroad (completed in the mid-1850s in southern Illinois) came close enough to bring famous visitors. The most positive development for Jefferson County was the placement of the Supreme Court in Mt. Vernon in 1848. The court brought many well-known attorneys to the area over the years of its existence in Mt. Vernon.

Abraham Lincoln and John A. McClernand

Politics brought Abraham Lincoln and John A. McClernand to Mt. Vernon in August and September of 1840. Lincoln, of course, needs no introduction or explanation of his claim to fame. He was elected to the U.S. House of Representatives in 1846 and to the presidency in 1860. But in 1840 he was a thirty-one-year-old, politically ambitious Springfield attorney who came to southern Illinois campaigning as a Whig elector for William Henry Harrison.

McClernand, later famous as a Union general in the Civil War, was a member of the Illinois House of Representatives in 1840 and was elected to the U.S. House of Representatives in 1843 and 1859. He was defeated for speaker of the house in 1860 partly because of his "moderate" views on slavery. He supported Stephen A. Douglas and served as one of his campaign managers in the 1860 presidential race. McClernand came to Jefferson County as an elector for Democrat Martin Van Buren to debate Lincoln in the hotly contested Tippecanoe campaign. According to *Lincoln Day-by-Day* (the authoritative source on Lincoln's daily activities), the debate was probably on August 28, 1840.[15] Since the Jefferson County Courthouse had partly collapsed in 1839, and a new one was not completed until 1841, the Methodist Church (west side of North 11th about the middle of the block) was used as a temporary court and was to be the site of the debate.[16] McClernand gave his speech during the noon recess.

Lincoln, who was to speak in the afternoon, was turned away by the Democratic sheriff, Bowman, and judge, Scates. So Lincoln gave his talk in front of the Kirby Hotel, now 117 North Tenth. He stood on a goods box and kept the audience laughing and swearing for an hour or two. Many Mt. Vernonites, including Harvey T. Pace and his son, James M. Pace, aged fourteen, attended the debate. According to Judge William T. Pace, son of James M. Pace, McClernand wore a long blue coat decorated with brass buttons and was very neat in appearance. He spoke with great force and vigor. When Lincoln spoke later at the hotel, he was somewhat careless in his appearance. Lincoln remarked that McClernand was so impetuous that the buttons on his coat resembled snapping turtles.[17]

Methodist Church 1835-1854

Kirby Home

Lincoln and McClernand left Mt. Vernon but returned to debate again during the week of September 21, 1840. Although no local sources describe the speeches, the Springfield newspapers were following the debates. The Springfield Democratic newspaper said that the Whigs spoke of going to the South "to enlighten the ignorant loco focos of that benighted region." They titled stories "Further News From the Missionaries" in describing Lincoln's visits to the southern counties. In a column dated "Mt. Vernon, October 3, 1840," the *Illinois State Register* printed a letter signed "Patriot," which described the Lincoln tour from the Democratic Party point of view. Among other things it said, sarcastically, "…we are no longer to walk in ignorance and darkness—" since "—the junto of your place have kindly taken our case under consideration, and sent us one of the 'long nine' of Sangamon to shed the light of whiggery around us." The writer described the debate in Mt. Vernon in this way:

Lincoln Tour Article

At Mt. Vernon, Mr. Lincoln again addressed the people, and was listened to with attention; possessing much urbanity and suavity of manner, he is well calculated for a public debater; as he seldom loses his temper, and always replies jocosely and in good humor, — the evident marks of disapprobation which greet many of his assertions, do not discompose him, and he is therefore hard to foil. Col. McClernand was called on, and responded to the call. He was more logical and argumentative than his opponent— His forte being more in the power of reason and depth of research than in those amusing anecdotes with which Mr. Lincoln strives to delight, if they fail to convince, and the citizens of Jefferson will long remember his exposition of modern whiggery, and his defense of the true Democratic principles.[18]

Lincoln and McClernand were back in Mt. Vernon on September 30, 1840. This time they faced each other in the courtroom rather than in the political arena for a case called *Holt v. Dale*. Jefferson County Circuit Court records show that Lincoln, along with a man named J. P. Hardy, were attorneys for John Dale.[19] The case was an appeal by John Holt, represented by McClernand and well-known Shawneetown attorney, Henry Eddy, over a justice of the peace decision to award twenty dollars to Dale.

Holt, apparently a good citizen, was an early resident of Casner Township. Except for this case his name only appears in the old court records as a juror for the first murder trial in Jefferson County history. He and the other jurors found the defendant guilty, and Judge Scates ordered him hanged. A gallows was built, but a pardon arrived from Springfield just in time to "disappoint one of the largest crowds that had ever assembled in the county."

Lincoln's client, John Dale, on the other hand, had a very different past. The state brought John Dale to court three times in 1836 and 1837 for disturbing the peace, fining him one hundred dollars. Dale seems to have had a running feud with two other families as they sued and counter-sued for destroying property and trespass. Meanwhile the state sued Dale's wife, Cynthia, for "fornication and adultery." After this Cynthia Dale sued for divorce from her husband. (His attorney was John A. McClernand.) In 1838 John Dale sued his wife for divorce, and it was granted in 1839.[20]

9

The judge in *Holt v. Dale*, Walter B. Scates, ruled that the justice of the peace was wrong and that the defendant, Dale, should return the twenty dollars to the plaintiff, Holt. Lincoln had lost the case. Walter B. Scates had been Illinois attorney general in 1836 and was a justice of the Illinois Supreme Court from 1841 to 1847 and 1854 to 1857. Other than the Illinois Central case in Mt. Vernon in 1859, this circuit court case may represent the only documented court appearance by Lincoln in southern Illinois.[21] Many years later on March 21, 1865, shortly before his death, Lincoln wrote to then General Walter B. Scates, "If you choose to go to New Mexico and reside, I will appoint you chief justice there. What say you? Please answer."[22] Scates respectfully declined.

Holt v. Dale

As of the date of this writing, many Lincoln sources state that Lincoln was in Tremont, Illinois, rather than Mt. Vernon on September 30, 1840, for a case called *Kellogg v. Crain*. However, in this case Lincoln had four co-counsel, including his associate, John T. Stuart. There is only one document dated September 30, 1840, in *Kellogg v. Crain,* and it is a court order that states "on motion of plaintiff's attorney" without giving any attorney's name. The only two documents in this case that have Lincoln's name on them are a court order and an "amended replication," both dated April 21, 1841. It is clear that one of the other plaintiff attorneys was in court in Tremont on September 30, 1840, while Lincoln was in Mt. Vernon for *Holt v. Dale*.[23]

John A. Logan

John A. Logan (1826–1886) was another famous visitor to Mt. Vernon. In the 1850s he was elected prosecuting attorney of the judicial circuit including Jefferson and the counties to the south.[24] As a result he moved from Murphysboro to Benton to be more centrally located. He was elected as a Democrat to the Illinois State House of Representatives in 1853 and to the U.S. House of Representatives in 1858. He was a general in the Civil War and received the nickname "Black Jack" because of his dark hair and eyes. He was described by a friend thusly: "He was a natural soldier. His shoulders were broad, his presence was commanding; with swarthy face and coal black hair, and 'eye like Mars', to threaten and command, he was every inch a warrior. There is no question that General Logan was the greatest volunteer officer of the Civil War."[25] After the war he was elected as a Republican to the U.S. House of Representatives (1867–1871), and the U.S. Senate (1871–1877 and 1879–1886). He was nominated for vice president of the United States in 1884 on the Republican ticket with James G. Blaine.

Certainly John A. Logan was in Jefferson County in the 1850s and 1860s. But was he in the county in the early 1840s? Jefferson County history books all tell of a famous horse race in 1841 or 1842 featuring a fifteen-year-old John A. Logan as the jockey for his father's horse, Walnut Cracker. He was up against a horse, Polly

Ann, owned by former Lieutenant Governor Stinson Anderson of Mt. Vernon and ridden by his sixteen-year-old son, William. The race was a big event that drew people from a hundred miles around with many men betting all they could on their favorite. Although he was favored to win, Logan and his horse lost the race.

Both of the main Jefferson County history books (Perrin and Wall) have the race in Murphysboro. And an August 12, 1885, *Mt. Vernon Weekly Register* account states: "It was to take place on Logan's farm, on the track where Murphysboro now stands." However, a January 23, 1895, *Mt. Vernon Daily Register* article titled "Twas Run in Mt. Vernon" says the race took place in Mt. Vernon "just south of John Gibson's present residence." There is a Captain John Gibson listed in the 1893 Mt. Vernon City Directory at 610 Shawnee Street. So although unlikely, perhaps the famous race was held in Jefferson County.

Lyman Trumbull

Lyman Trumbull was another important early visitor. Mr. Trumbull was an attorney from Belleville, Illinois. He was a member of the state legislature in 1840. Later, he served as Illinois secretary of state and state Supreme Court judge. He was one of the Illinois United States senators from 1855 to 1873. He served on the Senate Judiciary Committee and is most famous for sponsoring and helping pass the Thirteenth Amendment abolishing slavery in the United States.

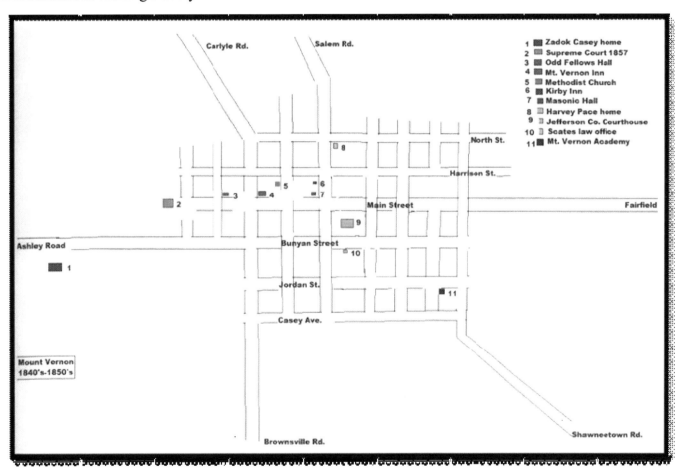

Map of Mt. Vernon 1840s–1850s

In 1848 Mt. Vernon became the seat of the First Grand Division of the Illinois Supreme Court. The Supreme Court building, now known as the Fifth District Appellate Court, was not completed until 1857. So lodge halls and other places were used until that time. From about 1848 to 1853 the Odd Fellows Hall (north side of Main Street about two lots west of 12th Street) was rented for seventy-five dollars per year. The building was a two-story, box-shaped structure of heavy wood construction built about 1847 on land donated by Zadok Casey.

According to an article by John A. Wall in the April 22, 1914, *Mt. Vernon Weekly News:* "Abraham Lincoln, Stephen A. Douglas and many other prominent legal lights transacted business in the Supreme Court in this room." The old hall was torn down in 1914. From about 1853 to 1857 the court was located in the Masonic Hall over Joel Pace's store at the corner of 10th and Main Streets. The first term of the Supreme Court convened in December, 1848, with Lyman Trumbull as one of the associate justices. He remained on the court and thus in Mt. Vernon when the court was in session from 1848 to November, 1853.

Traveling to the Supreme Court in Mt. Vernon in the 1840s and early 1850s before the Illinois Central Railroad was not easy. In 1893 former Chief Justice John Dean Caton described his first trip to Mt. Vernon in 1848. He and Judge Treat left Springfield on a Wednesday expecting to arrive in Mt. Vernon on Saturday. This was December and they immediately ran into a blinding snowstorm. The roads were filled with snow ten inches deep, but they reached Carlyle on Saturday night. After replacing a sick horse they drove their buggy on to the home of a wealthy farmer about fourteen to eighteen miles from Mt. Vernon. They were turned away because the lady of the house was having a tantrum. It was pitch dark, cold, and raining. Caton remembered that, "…one of us had to get out and wade through the mud in front of the horses and with our feet feel where the road was and see if there were gullies on either side, and so we plodded on for more than three hours, copious rain falling all the time, and the cold wind increasing in violence."

After finding shelter at midnight in another home Caton and Treat moved on toward Mt. Vernon in the morning. Caton wrote: "We pursued our way slowly but diligently through the muddy forest road, and reached Mt. Vernon soon after noon, where we found Judge Trumbull, who had arrived before us." They took a room at Grant's. (The Mt. Vernon Inn on Main Street was owned by the Grant family and later the Anderson family.) Here they drew lots to determine who would get the three, six, or nine-year term. Judge Treat drew the nine-year term and thus became the first chief justice under the Constitution of 1848. It had taken Caton and Treat four days to reach Mt. Vernon. But they held the first Supreme Court session under the new Constitution, and soon the railroads would make traveling to Mt. Vernon much easier for future judges and attorneys.[26]

Sidney Breese

Sidney Breese (1800–1878) was in Mt. Vernon from 1848 to 1859 and on many other occasions. Breese probably lived in Mt. Vernon from 1848 to 1850 since he was the law partner of local attorney, Lewis Casey.[27] As an attorney he appeared before the Supreme Court in Mt. Vernon in November of 1849, 1850, 1851, and 1852.[28] On September 26, 1850, he attended a "rousing" railroad convention in Mt. Vernon that was presided over by Zadok Casey. The purpose of the meeting was to have the Illinois Central Railroad built through Jefferson County. Breese, William S. Wait, and Stephen T. Logan (Lincoln's law partner) were appointed as a committee to confer with Governor French.[29] Later, Breese was in Jefferson County many times as a member of the Illinois Supreme Court when it was in session in Mt. Vernon. On November 18–19, 1859, he was one of the judges who heard the famous Illinois Central case when Lincoln and George McClellan were at the Supreme Court.

Sidney Breese was a member of the Illinois Supreme Court from 1841 to 1842, and from 1857 to 1878. He was elected to the U.S. Senate and served from 1843 to 1849. He was defeated for re-election to the Senate by General Shields, the "hero of Cerro Gordo" in the Mexican War. Shields' main appeal was his war service as a wounded veteran. Some wags at the time joked that the bullet, which wounded Shields, passed through him without great harm but killed Breese a thousand miles away. Breese was elected to the state legislature in 1850, but his main public service was as a judge of the Supreme Court. Perrin's *History of Jefferson County* lists him along with Lincoln and Douglas as the three greatest men in Illinois history.[30] Illinois Supreme Court Justice Albert Watson of Mt. Vernon wrote: "I have of course seen and known in and about our court houses mainly men and some women of distinction, some of local, some of state wide, and some of national distinction; of these I choose to mention two, namely Miss Clara Barton…, and Sidney Breese, for many years a very distinguished judge and the shining light of the Illinois Supreme Court."[31]

Early Supreme Court Attorneys

Many well-known attorneys came to the Supreme Court in Mt. Vernon during the late 1840s and 1850s. Ninian Edwards, son of Governor Ninian Edwards, and brother-in-law of Abraham Lincoln, was at the court in November of 1849.[32] Gustave Koerner, a Lincoln friend and later lieutenant governor of Illinois appeared before the court in November, 1849, and in the 1850s.[33] John A. McClernand was at the court in November of 1853.[34] John A. Logan had cases before the court in November 1853, 1855, and 1858.[35] Robert G. Ingersoll, later known as "The Great Agnostic," came to the Supreme Court in December, 1854, to be examined for admission to the bar.[36]

Abraham Lincoln

The Supreme Court drew two very famous people to Mt. Vernon during this time. Wall's *History of Jefferson County* states Mt. Vernon "became to a degree the political headquarters for southern Illinois." Wall further reports: "Among the many who came were Abraham Lincoln and Stephen A. Douglas, who afterwards in 1858, publicly discussed what they then talked to a more select circle..."[37] John A. Wall knew about this first-hand since he was a "waiter boy" at the old Mt. Vernon Inn where he listened to Lincoln and Douglas and blacked their boots for their appearance before the Supreme Court. In a lecture in 1920 Wall stated: "These great men were very chummy with this orphan boy (Wall) – especially Lincoln – who personally gave me good counsel and advice ..." He also said that in the presence of the other lawyers Lincoln handed him a dollar for blacking his boots. This prompted the others to give liberally as well, and Wall was able to buy a pair of "red top copper-toed boots" at Pace's store. These boots were the first he ever had and made him feel "as big as the lawyers themselves."[38]

Wall was born in 1836, orphaned early in life, and indentured to the Anderson family who ran the Mt. Vernon Inn in 1841. He worked at the inn until August of 1851 when he went to work for the *Jeffersonian* newspaper. Then in 1853 he began to work for the Illinois Central. If Lincoln and Douglas were discussing issues in Mt. Vernon that they later discussed in the 1858 Lincoln-Douglas debates, the time period was probably 1848–1851. The War with Mexico of 1846–1848 brought new western land to the United States and new arguments over slavery in the territories. And of course the Illinois Supreme Court came to Mt. Vernon in 1848.

John A. Wall

Lincoln and the Dorman Case

Dorman v. Lane (later *Dorman v. Tost*), which was a lawsuit about an inheritance, was one Supreme Court case that might have brought Lincoln to Mt. Vernon. In the March term of 1849 the White County Circuit Court ruled for Lane, and Dorman appealed to the Supreme Court. The case came to the First Grand Division of the Supreme Court in Mt. Vernon in the November term of 1849. But on November 20, 1849, attorney Robert F. Wingate told the court of the death of John Lane, asked that J. C. Yost (Tost) be substituted for him, and per agreement of the parties, asked for a continuance of the case to the next term. (John C. Yost was John Lane's son-in-law. His name is misspelled as L. C. Tost on the Supreme Court documents.) The case remained in Mt. Vernon and on November 15, 1850, the parties appeared in court with an agreement, which asked that the continuance be revoked and the case be removed to Springfield "December next."[39] In the Supreme Court opinion, which Lincoln later won for the Dormans, it states: "During the pendency of this suit in the court, at Mt. Vernon, Lane deceased, and L. C. Tost, as his administrator, was substituted in his stead; and by agreement of parties the venue was changed from the first grand division (Mt. Vernon) to this division (Springfield)."[40]

It seems likely that Lincoln would have come to Mt. Vernon for the Dorman case. He had been the Dormans' attorney since 1842, and the case was in Mt. Vernon in November of two years. His good friend and co-counsel, Samuel D. Marshall, in an April 20, 1849, letter told Lincoln how important the case was to him and urged him to give it his utmost attention. He wrote that he "had more interest in this case than all the business put together to which I ever attended," and pleaded: "Please think of this and write at your earliest convenience. Don't do as you did before. This is a great matter with me." Later in the letter he confessed that he was not "acquainted with either the practice of the Supreme Court or the mode of taking up suits …"[41] Clearly Lincoln was committed to the Dormans and would want to help his friend, Marshall, if at all possible. But Lincoln's co-counsel, Marshall (Shawneetown) and Wingate (Mt. Vernon), lived closer to the Mt. Vernon Supreme Court, and Lincoln's name does not appear on any court document until December of 1851 in Springfield. So, the question of Lincoln's appearance in Mt. Vernon for the Dorman case must remain open at this point.

Lincoln and Zadok Casey

Casey v. Casey was another case that may have brought Lincoln to Mt. Vernon. This case began in 1844 when Aaron Piggot of New York died with a will leaving a large estate to his wife, Sarah. She died the same year intestate but on her deathbed said she wanted the entire estate to go to Zadok Casey, a friend and relative. (In his *Recollections of Jefferson County and Its People* Adam Clarke Johnson reported that "Aaron Pickett of New York" was Zadok Casey's uncle.) When Zadok Casey arrived in New York, he found that the courts had ordered that the estate should be divided between eight closer relatives. He traveled around the country, found the eight heirs, and bought their inheritance rights. One of the eight heirs, Robert Casey of Tennessee, upon finding that the value of Sarah Piggot's estate was about fifteen thousand dollars, retained Mt. Vernon attorney Richard S. Nelson and threatened to sue, alleging that Zadok Casey had defrauded him of a rightful inheritance. Apparently Nelson offered Zadok Casey a compromise proposal for him to pay Robert Casey one thousand dollars to settle out of court. In a letter to Nelson dated June 26, 1848, Zadok Casey, who was in "Washington City," replied: "I can make no such compromise as you propose. I cannot give your client $1,000, nor 1,000 cents, nor one thousandth part of one cent."

Zadok Casey

As a result of this rejection, Robert Casey sued Zadok Casey, one of the most famous men in Mt. Vernon history (one of the "founding fathers" of the town, elected to the state and national legislatures, and elected lieutenant governor of Illinois), in the Jefferson County Circuit Court on March 23, 1849. The case had eleven hearings over three years until September 23, 1852, when Judge Samuel S. Marshall ruled in favor of Robert Casey for $1,294.47 (his one eighth share of the estate) plus interest for a total of $1,759.04. Although the attorneys listed for Zadok Casey were Walter B. Scates and Robert F. Wingate, a 1929 Mt. Vernon newspaper article claimed that Abraham Lincoln also appeared for him in the circuit court in September of 1852. The headline states, "Lincoln Appeared in Important Suit in Circuit Court." The article reports that the fact that Lincoln was one of the attorneys in the September term "will be news to practically everyone except attorneys who have had occasion to know of the suit …" It further states: "There was nothing remarkable in the subject matter of the case in which Lincoln appeared as counsel in Jefferson County, an inheritance being involved." However, Lincoln's name could not be found in the 1852 court records.[42]

Lincoln Circuit Court Article

Zadok Casey immediately appealed the circuit court decision, and the case came to the Southern Grand Division of the Illinois Supreme Court in Mt. Vernon on November 8, 1852. Again Zadok Casey's attorneys were Scates and Wingate. They presented a document listing eight errors, which they said the Jefferson County Circuit Court made in the case, and they asked for a reversal. But on November 23, 1852, by agreement of the parties the appeal was moved to the December, 1852, Supreme Court term in Springfield. It is unclear exactly when Lincoln agreed to take the case. He could have been involved in the Jefferson County Circuit Court case or the appeal in the Mt. Vernon Supreme Court, although no documents support this. But there is no doubt he was one of Zadok Casey's attorneys in the December, 1852, Supreme Court case in Springfield. Lincoln, S. T. Logan, and Scates are listed for Zadok Casey in the Opinion in *Illinois Supreme Court Reports*. Plus, Lincoln's name is on the documents for the appeal.

The main issues in the appeal were whether Zadok Casey knew the true value of the Piggot estate, and whether he had a fiduciary duty to tell Robert Casey the true value. After reviewing the testimony of the executors of Aaron Piggot's estate, the testimony of Mt. Vernon residents Harvey T. Pace, Joel Pace, Noah Johnston, and Tazewell B. Tanner—who had conversations with Zadok Casey about the inheritance—and the testimony of others, the Supreme Court decided that Zadok Casey did have a good idea about the value of the estate. Lincoln, Logan, and Scates argued that Zadok Casey acted responsibly by using his own money to hire an attorney to fight a suit by relatives of Aaron Piggot who were contesting the will, and that he thought whatever value the estate had might be reduced or lost altogether as a result of the lawsuit. However, the court rejected these arguments and also ruled that Zadok Casey had a duty to inform Robert Casey of the value of the estate. So Lincoln lost this appeal from Jefferson County involving one of the most important people in Jefferson County history.[43]

Lincoln, George McClellan, and the Illinois Central Case

Illinois Central v. State of Illinois (November 18 and 19 of 1859) was the most important case that brought Lincoln to Mt. Vernon. The railroad claimed that the state valuation of its property for tax purposes was too high and that it did not owe more taxes for 1859. Lincoln was the attorney for the Illinois Central, and as fate would have it, one of the men who came to Jefferson County with him was George B. McClellan, vice president of the railroad. Later, of course, McClellan was the commanding general of the Union Army during the Civil War and Lincoln's opponent in the 1864 presidential election.

There is no doubt that the case was heard in Mt. Vernon. There is a letter from Auditor Jesse Dubois to the Mt. Vernon Supreme Court Clerk Noah Johnston dated October 15, 1859, giving him information on the case. There is a subpoena from Noah Johnston on October 25, 1859, to the sheriff of Madison County for Samuel F. Buckmaster to appear in Mt. Vernon to testify in *Illinois Central v. State of Illinois*. There is a subpoena from Noah Johnston on October 25, 1859, to the sheriff of Sangamon County for John Moore and T. J. Carter to testify in *Illinois Central v. State of Illinois*. The clerk's docket for the November term, 1859, lists the appeal of the Illinois Central from the auditor's assessment. The judge's docket from the November term of 1859 in Mt. Vernon lists an appeal of the Illinois Central against the auditor's assessment. Justice Breese's opinion from January of 1860 in a separate Illinois Central case states: "… evidence heard by this court at the last November term of this court held for the First Grand Division, should be considered before the court now here. That testimony was taken on an appeal from the assessment of the auditor as prescribed by law."[44]

Noah Johnston

However, in the last 150 years many have overlooked this case, or doubted that Lincoln was in Mt. Vernon for the trial. How could such an important case be overlooked for so long? The case was heard in the First Grand Division in Mt. Vernon. According to one author, "Everything in this connection was done very quietly." Newspaper coverage would be much less likely in a smaller town than in the state capital. No opinion was issued for the 1859 case in Mt. Vernon, just a decision. The first mention of the case in *Illinois Reports*, the official summary of the Supreme Court opinions, came in the opinion issued on the 1857 Illinois Central debt case decided in the Second Grand Division in Springfield in January of 1860. But this January 1860 opinion was not published in the reports with the other opinions rendered at the same term. It was finally placed in *Illinois Reports* (Volume Twenty-seven) for the years 1861–1862. This volume was published in 1863. Of course the Civil War was dominating the nation's attention in that year.

To add to the confusion the introduction to the January, 1860, opinion states: "The case was originally commenced in the Second Grand Division, but by consent, was finally heard and determined at Mount Vernon in the First Grand Division." That is not true. This case was heard in Springfield. The separate appeal case was heard in Mt. Vernon in November, 1859. There is a note at the bottom of the page saying that the case was heard at a term "anterior to that named in the caption." That is true since both cases were heard before the "1861" in the caption.

Later as historians began to write about Lincoln and his legal cases they were drawn to the McLean County case (*Illinois Central v. McLean County*) in 1856 with Lincoln's gaudy five thousand dollar fee. An Illinois Central Railroad historian wrote in 1950: "The McLean County case and Lincoln's suit for fees in that case have been highlighted by most biographers to the exclusion of many other important services which he performed for the railroad."

THE STATE OF ILLINOIS v. THE ILLINOIS CENTRAL
RAILROAD COMPANY.

ORIGINAL SUIT.

For purposes of taxation property should be assessed at its present value, and
not at its prospective value.

In assessing the value of a railroad, for purposes of taxation, the inquiry should
be, what is the property worth, to be used for the purposes for which it was
designed, and not for any other purposes to which it might be applied?

In such a case, if the property is devoted to the use for which it was designed,
and is in a condition to produce its maximum income, one very important
element for ascertaining its present value, is the amount of its net profits.

This, however, should not be the absolute standard of value. There should be
taken in connection with it, the inquiry, what would a prudent man give for
the property as a permanent investment, with a view to present and future
income?

ALL the facts of this case are fully set out in the opinion of
the Court by Mr. Justice BREESE.

The case was originally commenced in the Second Grand
Division, but by consent, was finally heard and determined
at Mount Vernon in the First Grand Division.

J. B. WHITE, State's Attorney, S. T. LOGAN and M. HAY,
for The People.

J. M. DOUGLAS, and A. LINCOLN, for the Railroad Company.

BREESE, J.* This is an action of debt originally brought
in this court, against the defendants, for taxes alleged to be
due to the State, for the year 1857, by the defendants, and
unpaid.

To the declaration, the defendants have pleaded the general
issue, payment, and set-off for over-payments, on which issues
are made up. It is these issues, and these only, we are called
upon to try.

After the institution of this suit, on the 31st of January,
1859, it was agreed between the parties, that in order to com-

_____
* NOTE. This case was heard at a term anterior to that named in the caption.

People v. Ill. Central RR

Another author suggests that Lincoln, the Illinois Central Company, and the Supreme Court might have been pleased that the case wasn't widely publicized. After all Lincoln was already preparing to run for president in 1860. In December, 1859, he published an autobiography for campaign purposes, and in February, 1860, he accepted an invitation to speak in New York in order to introduce himself to eastern audiences. He didn't want to give Democrats like Stephen A. Douglas, a potential rival for president in 1860, additional ammunition against him. In the 1858 Lincoln-Douglas debates, Douglas had already accused Lincoln of helping the Illinois Central cheat the state out of money due it for his huge five thousand dollar fee.

Similarly, the Illinois Central didn't want politicians using it as an election issue. The judges on the Supreme Court favored the Illinois Central and didn't want to harm its cause. Justice Sidney Breese, an honorable man as were the others in this case, was a bitter rival of Stephen A. Douglas and a strong advocate of the Illinois Central Railroad project. He thought that he, not Douglas, should have received credit for the success of the railroad. He even had this inscribed on his gravestone: "He who sleeps beneath this stone projected the Illinois Central Railroad." So for various reasons the 1859 case in Mt. Vernon remained almost unknown for over one hundred years.[45]

Some people who do not know local history have had doubts that Lincoln and McClellan were in Mt. Vernon at the Supreme Court (now Appellate Court) in the 1859 Illinois Central case. They argued that Lincoln was in court in Springfield on November 18, 1859, the first day of the trial in Mt. Vernon. For years this put a serious burden on local historians who tried to prove that Lincoln was in Jefferson

County. They suggested that Lincoln could have left early on the 18th and by traveling on the Illinois Central Railroad and stagecoach could have reached Mt. Vernon the same day. But it would have been well into the afternoon, and he would have missed the first day of the trial. A 1977 letter from State Historian William K. Alderfer cast serious doubt on this theory: "Given the vicissitudes of transportation in 1859, the long buggy ride, as well as the time he would have to spend eating, sleeping and working at the court—well, the chances of his being in Mt. Vernon on the 19th are very slim indeed."

A 1978 letter from Robert W. O'Brian, director of corporate relations for the Illinois Central, boosted the spirits of Jefferson County historians. In the letter O'Brian noted that the Illinois Central ran regular passenger service or a special train for railroad officials between Decatur and Cairo. Lincoln could have traveled the thirty-nine miles from Springfield to Decatur by stagecoach or "by train on what is now the N & W Springfield – Decatur line." The train trip between Decatur and Ashley (the closest Illinois Central station to Mt. Vernon) was about four hours. Lincoln could then make the sixteen-mile trip from Ashley to Mt. Vernon by stagecoach. Still, this was only proof that he could have come to Jefferson County by late afternoon on the 18th, not that he actually did.

Even as recently as 2008 two of the most important sources for Lincoln's life, *Lincoln Day-by-Day* (Miers, 1991), and "thelincolnlog.org" did not have Lincoln in Mt. Vernon at any time except 1840. Finally, in 2008 researchers looked more carefully at the Sangamon County Circuit Court records and found that they only showed the solicitors were there. Lincoln's name was not listed. William H. Herndon, Lincoln's law partner, could have represented their clients rather than Lincoln.[46] This would have allowed Lincoln to leave Springfield on November 17th. However, doubters continued to doubt. They pointed out that the judge's docket in Mt. Vernon did not list Lincoln as one of the Illinois Central attorneys. Experienced researchers countered that it was not unusual for judge's dockets to omit some attorneys who were actually there.[47]

The evidence that Lincoln was in Mt. Vernon for the Illinois Central case is very strong. The Illinois Central officials specifically hired Lincoln as their lead attorney to defend them in this case that was so important to them. Lincoln's name is on most of the records leading up to this case. He appeared in the Supreme Court in Springfield for another Illinois Central case related to the Mt. Vernon case. He met with witnesses for the case. He corresponded with railroad men about the case. There is a gap in knowledge of his whereabouts from November 17 to 21, which corresponds to a similar gap for George McClellan. Why would Lincoln not be in Mt. Vernon for the trial itself when he did all the work before it?

There are many other reasons to believe Lincoln was in Mt. Vernon for the Illinois Central trial. First, other attorneys were asking him for help in Mt. Vernon. On August 16, 1859, Joseph and David Gillespie of Edwardsville wrote to Lincoln informing him that they planned to appeal a case to the Supreme Court, "and have a decision at Mt. Vernon in time if favorable to the defendant to influence Judge Treat in his decision …." They went on to ask Lincoln to "Please see what can be done …."[48] On November 4, 1859, Edwardsville attorney Michael G. Dale wrote to Lincoln giving information on cases related to the case mentioned in the August 16th Gillespie letter and stating: "Joseph Gillespie will endeavor to be at Mt. Vernon, but his health is such as not to be relied on – He desires you to argue the case …" Dale further asks, "Will you please state if you can attend to the case at Mt. Vernon and please name the day of the term …"[49]

Second, Lincoln was clearly planning to be in Mt. Vernon. In October he filed an appeal of the state's valuation of the Illinois Central property. By filing the appeal in October Lincoln assured the case would be heard in Mt. Vernon because the law required that any appeal would have to be heard "the term next succeeding the taking of such appeal," and the Southern Grand Division term in Mt. Vernon was in November. And in a reply to the November 4 letter of Edwardsville attorney Michael G. Dale dated November 8, 1859, Lincoln wrote: "My expectation is to be at the Mount Vernon Supreme Court, reaching there the 21st of the month. Can then attend to your case if it be not disposed of before."[50] (The date of the trial was changed to the 18th after Lincoln wrote this letter.)

Dr. J. H. Watson

Third, local physician Dr. J. H. Watson often told of sitting on Lincoln's lap as a youngster in a crowded stagecoach from Ashley, Illinois, to Mt. Vernon. Apparently Lincoln took a stagecoach or train from Springfield to Decatur or some other station on the Illinois Central on the 17th. Then he traveled down the Illinois Central line to Ashley and caught the stagecoach to Mt. Vernon. Also on the Ashley to Mt. Vernon stagecoach in addition to Lincoln and the young Watson was George B. McClellan. According to Dr. Watson, Lincoln kept the passengers laughing with his jokes and stories. After arriving in Mt. Vernon Watson ate supper and hurried over to the Mt. Vernon Inn hoping to hear more of Lincoln's stories. He was disappointed to find that although Lincoln was in the lobby, he was in a conference with McClellan and told no more stories that evening.[51]

With all the evidence pointing conclusively to Lincoln being in Mt. Vernon authorities finally agreed. At a September 18, 2008, panel discussion at the Appellate Court John A. Lupton, associate editor of *The Papers of Abraham Lincoln*, announced that he and his associates agreed that Lincoln was in Mt. Vernon for the Illinois Central case, and that Lincoln would be placed in Mt. Vernon on November 18–19, 1859, on "thelincolnlog.org."

The Illinois Central Trial and Its Importance

As previously noted, the trial began on November 18, 1859 at the Mt. Vernon Supreme Court. And it was a trial not just a hearing. Lincoln called ten witnesses —John B. Turner, president of the Galena and Union Railroad Company, Colonel Roswell B. Mason, the engineer who constructed the Illinois Central Railroad, S. H. Clarke, William D. Griswold, president of the Terre Haute and Alton Railroad, Mr. Hall, superintendent of the Galena railroad, Lusian Tilton, president of the Great Western Railroad, J. M. Douglas, attorney of the Illinois Central Railroad, Mr. Smith, auditor of the Chicago and Burlington Railroad, Mr. Bradley, auditor of the Chicago and Rock Island Railroad, and Timothy B. Blackstone, later president of the Chicago and Alton Railroad. George McClellan was not called as a witness. The list included some of the most outstanding railroad men of the state. They mostly testified to the poor prospects for railroads in the state, and that the valuation of Illinois Central property by the state was much too high.

The state was represented by attorneys J. B. White, S. T. Logan (former partner of Lincoln), and Milton Hay (uncle of John B. Hay who became Lincoln's secretary during the Civil War and U.S. secretary of state in 1898). They recalled Col. Mason as one of their witnesses but called only one witness of their own, T. J. Carter, superintendent of the Great Western Railroad. They had subpoenaed other witnesses but were unable to present them because they were under the impression that the trial was to be on the 23rd rather than the 18th and 19th. Carter testified that the value of the Illinois Central must include its future profits as well as its present value. The Supreme Court was impressed with Lincoln's witnesses, and the three justices—Breese, Caton, and Walker —ruled for the company. The Illinois Central did not owe any additional tax for 1859.[52]

The Illinois Central case heard in Mt. Vernon is extremely important for a number of reasons. For Lincoln, himself, it is arguably the most important case in his legal career. Speaking about both the 1857 and 1859 cases in 1950, Illinois Central historian Carlton Corliss wrote: "Curiously, one of the most important law cases Lincoln ever handled for the Illinois Central Railroad, if not the most important case in his entire professional career, went virtually unnoticed by historians and biographers …" Also speaking of both the 1857 and 1859 cases, one author wrote: "Measured by money involved, this service was by far the most important of Lincoln's legal services. Measured by the obstacles to be surmounted, those services were remarkable …"

And of the two cases the Mt. Vernon case was clearly the most important because it determined the result of the Springfield case. Judge Breese said as much in his January, 1860, opinion from the 1857 case heard in Springfield. He wrote: "The case turned upon the second proposition as to the valuation of the property, and on that point it was agreed that the evidence heard by this court at the last November term of this court held for the First Grand Division, should be considered before the court now here." Lincoln's tactic of concentrating on the value of the Illinois Central property rather than the legal interpretation of the railroad's charter worked, and he won the Springfield case based on the evidence from Mt. Vernon.

Appellate Courthouse

As for the McLean County case, often cited as Lincoln's most important case, attorney Charles Leroy Brown wrote: "Many writers have treated this as Lincoln's greatest achievement. It has often been said that the decision saved the company untold millions of dollars. Those who have carefully studied the matter, including many counsel for the corporation, believe otherwise." Also for Lincoln, winning the Mt. Vernon case and other Illinois Central cases meant prestige and money that boosted his political career and helped him become president of the United States in 1860.

For the Illinois Central and the state it was crucial. The U.S. was hit by the Panic of 1857 and many railroads were failing. If the decision had gone against it, the Illinois Central probably would have declared bankruptcy. If that had happened, it would have been disastrous for the state, which was receiving thousands of dollars each year from the company. For the court it was the only time it was ever given original jurisdiction as an assessor of a company's property. Its decision in the case was the law for the next eighty years and beyond.

For Jefferson County and Mt. Vernon it means Mt. Vernon is the site of what is possibly Lincoln's most important legal case. Also, for the people of Jefferson County and Mt. Vernon, it means that they have "the only remaining courtroom in which Abraham Lincoln tried a case that continues to be used to this day in the manner it was used in the 1850s." The Appellate Court, formerly the home of the First Grand Division of the Illinois Supreme Court, was completed and ready for use by 1857 and is still used today. It is located at 14th and Main in Mt. Vernon.[53]

Appellate Courtroom

Other Lincoln Visits

No doubt Lincoln was in Mt. Vernon on many other occasions. There is much evidence in regional and Jefferson County history books. Professor George W. Smith of Southern Illinois University wrote *When Lincoln Came to Egypt* in 1940. Here are some parts of the book that relate to Lincoln and Mt. Vernon: "Lincoln found occasion to come to Mt. Vernon oftener perhaps than to any other city in Southern Illinois.", "A scrap of a legal document shows that Lincoln was 'guardian ad libitum' for two hapless children whose descendants are still numbered by the score in Jefferson County.", "From what one gathers, Lincoln was often a guest at the (Mt. Vernon) hotel which means that he had a goodly number of cases in the courts in the 50's.", and "A Benton attorney says that as Lincoln was returning to Springfield from court in Mt. Vernon, the stage coach broke down…."[54]

Another reason to believe Lincoln was in Jefferson County more often than can be proven is the number of friends and acquaintances he had in the county. Lincoln knew Zadok Casey well enough that when he saw Casey in the crowd at the 1858 Jonesboro Lincoln-Douglas debate, he hailed him as "my friend Casey over there."[55] Lincoln worked with Stinson Anderson in the state legislature from 1838 to 1842. Lincoln served with Harvey T. Pace in the state legislature from 1835 to 1840. They were "warm, personal friends," and Lincoln would often visit the Pace home when he was in Mt. Vernon.[56] A chair from the Pace home, purportedly used by Lincoln, has been preserved. Lincoln served with Noah Johnston in the state legislature from 1838 to 1842 and on a commission on matters relating to the Illinois Canal. Lincoln also knew Johnston as the clerk of the Illinois Supreme Court in Mt. Vernon. In addition Lincoln knew Walter B. Scates from their work in the courts. Lincoln and Scates worked together as attorneys for Zadok Casey in 1852–1853 and opposed each other in the well-known Dorman case. At one point Lincoln wrote that Scates was "… an old personal friend and most worthy gentleman…"[57] These are just a few of the many Lincoln friends and acquaintances who lived and worked in Jefferson County.

Pace Chair

On one occasion while staying at the Mt. Vernon Inn, Lincoln told this story about himself to the visiting lawyers and others. He had to take a stagecoach from Springfield to Taylorville where he had a court case. Lincoln wanted to make a good appearance, so he "greased" his boots, put on his new jean pants and stove-pipe hat, and spruced up generally. Unfortunately, the stagecoach was full and he had to sit on top with the driver. According to Lincoln's story, the driver "reached down in the box and drew forth a raw twist of tobacco, and after helping himself, offered it to me with a 'take a chaw, mister?' I thanked him, I did not chew. After saturating a mouthful of the stuff he puffed it out against the wind, causing it to come back over my hat, pants, and boots – utterly destroying my handsome appearance, but this did not disturb him. He then reached down again and brought forth a flask of red-eye and after treating himself, offered it to me. Again I thanked him, I did not drink. This seemed to confuse him and giving me a queer look with his cock-eye said: 'Mister, do you know what I think of your fellows who aint got no small vices?' 'No, said I.' Then with a glance of disdain, he drawled out, 'I think you make up in big ones what you lack in little ones; and I can tell by the cut of your jib that you are bad after the wimmen.'"[58] Apparently the story was a big hit at the old Mt. Vernon Inn.

Stephen A. Douglas

No doubt Stephen A. Douglas was in Mt. Vernon as well. But the evidence is more difficult to find. Douglas was attorney general of Illinois (1834), state legislator (1836), secretary of state of Illinois (1840), judge of the Supreme Court of Illinois (1841–1843), United States representative (1843–1847), and United States senator from Illinois (1847–1861).

In a meeting of the Supreme Court District Association in 1932, Appellate Clerk R. B. Roe presented a gavel made from "historic wood." He said the gavel was made from a bench at the Appellate Court that dated back to the time when Lincoln, Douglas, Trumbull, Logan, and other "great legal lights" appeared there at the Supreme Court.[59]

John A. Wall reports that Douglas was at the Mt. Vernon Inn in the late 1840s or early 1850s and that he had "blacked the boots" of men like Lincoln and Douglas. Although Wall says Douglas was in Mt. Vernon for a hearing before the Supreme Court, a search of court records does not show any references to Douglas in Jefferson County. However, the search only covered decisions of the court involving Douglas. So he might have been in the county for a case that was postponed, transferred, or undecided for some reason. There was an 1851 case in which Lincoln and Douglas opposed each other as attorneys before the Supreme Court, but this was not in Mt. Vernon.

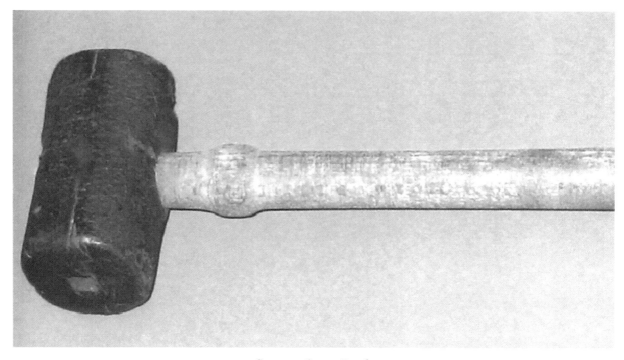

Supreme Court Gavel

Douglas may have been in Jefferson County on one of his many political tours. He came back to Illinois after Congress passed the Compromise of 1850 to combat criticism of the strong Fugitive Slave Law part of the compromise. He also returned, toured the state for two months confronting hostile audiences, and debated Lincoln in Springfield and Peoria after he persuaded Congress to pass the Kansas-Nebraska Act in 1854. So, possibly Douglas came to the county during one or both of those political campaigns. He also ran for president in 1852, 1856, and 1860, and could have been in Mt. Vernon any of those years. Douglas and Lincoln were both in Salem on September 22, 1856, and could have come to Mt. Vernon then.[60] While running for the United States Senate on September 15, 1858, he was in Anna-Jonesboro for one of the famous Lincoln-Douglas debates. Mt. Vernonites William T. Pace and his father witnessed that event. In 1940 then Judge Pace recalled how the two men looked and acted but most vividly remembered the roaring of the cannon.[61] On the trip back north Douglas left the Illinois Central train on September 16 and took a stagecoach to Benton to visit John A. Logan. Douglas and Lincoln were both at the Centralia Fair by September 17.[62] Perhaps he stopped in Mt. Vernon on that occasion.[63]

Robert G. Ingersoll

One of the most famous visitors in the 1850s was a young man who came to Mt. Vernon to teach but went on to become known throughout the U.S. as "The Great Agnostic." This visitor was Robert G. Ingersoll who came to town in 1852 and returned many times. Robert Green Ingersoll (1833–1899) was a well-known lawyer. During the Civil War he was a colonel of a cavalry regiment that he organized. He was the Illinois attorney general from 1867 to 1869 and gained national fame with a well-received presidential nomination speech for James G. Blaine at the Republican convention in 1876. But his greatest fame came as an anti-Christian lecturer questioning the Bible and religion.

Oddly enough, Ingersoll's father, John Ingersoll, was a minister who moved often and came to Mt. Vernon in 1852. In Mt. Vernon John Ingersoll met and later (on August 2nd, 1852) married a Miss Frances L. Willard, a teacher at the Mt. Vernon Female Seminary.[64] She was hired to teach "Young Ladies and Misses" by H. T. Pace of Mt. Vernon who erected the school at 311 North Tenth Street near his home and opened it August 22, 1851.[65] The building was torn down in 1954. But the Central Church of Christ retained a copy of Miss Willard's first examinations from 1852.[66]

Another landmark of early Mt. Vernon is passing from the scene. This century-old building, at 311 North 10th street, is being razed to clear the site for the Central Church of Christ. Erected in 1851 by Harvey T. Pace as a school for young women, the building at that time was in a grove of trees well outside of the main part of town. Mill Willard, stepmother of Robert G. Ingersoll, was the first teacher.

Mt. Vernon Female Seminary

25

Robert Ingersoll, then about eighteen years old, followed his father to Mt. Vernon a few days previous to September 16, 1852. In a letter to his brother Robert wrote: "I can get a very large school and I shall stay if I get a certificate. I am to be examined this afternoon…. I have to be examined by the Commissioner of the County, so that the scholars can have the benefit of the public money." For a young man Ingersoll was very self confident, bordering on arrogant. In the same letter to his brother he described his examination in this way: "There were two examiners both of whom considered themselves particularly smart … One of them … is the present schoolmaster at this place. He asked me all the questions he could think of. I laughed at him and answered them all and asked him if he had any more to ask. He said no and gave me a certificate, and then I came away."

Ingersoll went on to say: "This is a very pretty town of about six or eight hundred inhabitants, and it is finely located, and I think that I shall like to live here." Two additional letters to his brother on September 29, 1852, and January 14, 1853, indicate that Robert Ingersoll remained in Mt. Vernon. In the January 14 letter he reports: "I have toward thirty scholars at 2.50 per quarter and each quarter consists of twelve weeks…"[67]

According to Edwin Rackaway who was a boy in the 1890s, Ingersoll's school, the Mt. Vernon Academy, was still standing then—a little red-brick building on Eighth Street between Casey and Jordan. But, writes Rackaway, it "had degenerated into a bawdy house, and the small fry of the neighborhood (of which we were one), kept close watch on the comings and goings of the citizens who were customers of the establishment." Mr. Rackaway was wrong about this. The Mt. Vernon Academy was a two-story wood building described by Adam Clarke Johnson in his *Recollections of Jefferson County and Its People* as having two "large school rooms – one below and one above – a hall and stairway on the north below, and over these a room for apparatus, etc." The Academy was opened in 1839 and closed in 1854. It was torn down in 1882 and replaced with a red-brick building. This must have been the "bawdy house" that Rackaway saw.

Rackaway also states that two of Ingersoll's students in Mt. Vernon were Jimmy Johnson and John A. Wall. (This was the same John A. Wall who told of shining Lincoln's and Douglas's boots in his history of Jefferson County.)[68] Another of Ingersoll's students was Dr. J. H. Watson. (This was the same J. H. Watson who rode on Lincoln's lap from Ashley to Mt. Vernon in 1859.) Still another of Ingersoll's students was Edward V. Satterfield, who led a group of rambunctious students in an attempt to turn the school building over with a heavy pry. When Ingersoll returned from lunch and caught them, his profane language "turned the air blue for 40 rods in the whole neighborhood."[69] Ingersoll also taught at the aforementioned Mt. Vernon Female Seminary. He is listed as being a teacher there in Adam Clarke Johnson's *Recollections of Jefferson County and Its People* on page thirty-seven. Writing about Pace's Female Seminary, Johnson stated: "Miss Willard, afterwards married to John Ingersoll, taught here; then Miss Chamberlain, Miss Hogue, A. M. Green (Mort), Col. R. G. Ingersoll and others."

Like his father, Robert moved frequently. Later in 1853 he was teaching a "subscription school" in Metropolis, Illinois, where he found trouble because of his religious views. He was boarding in a local home along with some Baptist ministers who asked him what he thought of baptism. He replied that, "With soap, Baptism is a good thing." He was run out of town and had to walk to Marion, Illinois, where his father and step-mother were then living. In Marion he began the study of law in the office of Willis Allen. And on December 20, 1854, as previously noted, he and his brother, Ebon Clark Ingersoll, came to Mt. Vernon to be admitted to the bar.[70] In those days admission to the bar was relatively easy. The brothers had to furnish a certificate of good moral character, submit to an exam in open court, provide liquid refreshments for the officers of the court, and take the oath of office. Ebon Clark went on to become a member of the U.S. House of Representatives in Washington, D.C. Robert moved to Peoria and eventually settled in New York City. But as stated before, he came back to Mt. Vernon on several occasions.

Ned Buntline

About 1853 or 1854 Ned Buntline (E. Z. C. Judson), one of the most famous writers in Nineteenth Century American history, came to Mt. Vernon. He is best known for his "dime novels" of the Old West, which were extremely popular in the Nineteenth Century, and the Colt revolver (the Buntline Special) named after him. Some see him as a colorful, eccentric character who made Buffalo Bill famous with his dime novel and stage play. Others report his many scraps with the law and call him a rascal and worse. In 1846 Buntline shot and killed a man whose wife was having an affair with the writer. The man's brother shot Buntline in the chest and a mob lynched him. He survived when a friend cut him down. Later he was found not guilty with a plea of self defense. In 1849 Buntline instigated the Astor Place Opera House riots in New York City. Twenty-three people died. In 1852 he was indicted for his role in violent anti-German rioting in St. Louis. He jumped bail and fled to Carlyle, Illinois, where he edited a literary periodical called the *Carlyle Prairie Flower*. By 1856 he was back in his home county in New York. In 1869 on a lecture tour of the West on the topics of temperance (Even though he was a heavy drinker.) and Americanism (He had joined the "Know Nothings" in the 1850s.) he met William Cody. And the rest, as they say, is history. He died in 1886.

When Buntline came to Mt. Vernon, he told the locals that he needed a quiet place to rest and recuperate. However, he soon met a local man who had many of the same interests, i.e. editing, writing, drinking, and finding excitement. This young man, Edward V. Satterfield, who was later described as a "remarkable character, the sage of Mt. Vernon," apparently looked like a young Buffalo Bill Cody. He had just graduated from the Mt. Vernon Academy and was ready to "sow wild oats." The two men became friends, took in the local saloon, and looked for adventure.

Here is what one article reports happened next: "The two new friends started out to take in the town and they shook it up in so lively a manner that the occasion has formed a sort of exclamation point in its history. At that time the court house square was covered with brush and was the haunt of rabbits, wild-cats, and skunks. All the dogs, boys and many of the men were drafted into a grand circular hunt. The square was surrounded, the dogs sent in and in a short time the surrounding streets and vacant lots were alive with flying rabbits, wild-cats, skunks and dogs. The air was literally torn into shreds from the yelping of the dogs, the howling and screaming of the boys and men, the tooting of horns, jingling of bells and firing of pistols and guns. The skunks became highly indignant and defended themselves in their usual style, and the result may easily be imagined." Apparently Buntline didn't find the peace and quiet he said he was looking for in Mt. Vernon. He soon left town but never forgot the incident or Satterfield, who, it was reported, became the hero of several of Buntline's novels. It should be noted that Satterfield became an attorney and a justice of the peace. He remained colorful and maybe eccentric, but a solid citizen.[71]

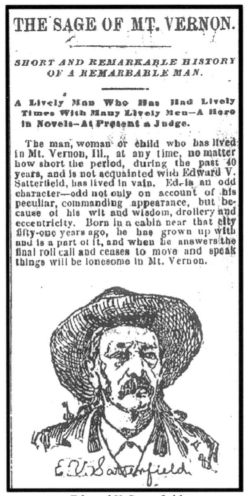

THE SAGE OF MT. VERNON.

SHORT AND REMARKABLE HISTORY
OF A REMARKABLE MAN.

A Lively Man Who Has Had Lively
Times With Many Lively Men—A Hero
in Novels—At Present a Judge.

The man, woman or child who has lived
in Mt. Vernon, Ill., at any time, no matter
how short the period, during the past 40
years, and is not acquainted with Edward V.
Satterfield, has lived in vain. Ed is an odd
character—odd not only on account of his
peculiar, commanding appearance, but because of his wit and wisdom, drollery and
eccentricity. Born in a cabin near that city
fifty-one years ago, he has grown up with
and is a part of it, and when he answers the
final roll call and ceases to move and speak
things will be lonesome in Mt. Vernon.

Edward V. Satterfield

"Uncle Joe" Cannon

One of the last figures from the 1850s was "Uncle Joe" Cannon (1836–1926), the famous speaker of the U.S. House of Representatives. He was a member of the U.S. House from 1873 to 1891, 1893 to 1913, and 1915 to 1922. He was speaker of the house from 1903 to 1911 and was considered by most historians to be the most dominant in United States history. But when Joseph Cannon came to Jefferson County in 1858, he was just a young attorney—long before his political career brought him fame. He came to the Supreme Court in Mt. Vernon and met locally prominent men such as Sidney Breese, William R. Morrison, and Sam Casey. Cannon recalled the visit to Mt. Vernon during a speech at the Mt. Vernon Chautauqua in 1914. He remembered another visit to Mt. Vernon while talking with a reporter on the public square but couldn't give an exact date. He remembered that it was when Tom Casey was prosecuting attorney. Cannon said: "I was getting a man out of the penitentiary, and I had to get the prosecuting attorney's signature to some papers." Casey served as state's attorney from 1860 to 1862 and from 1864 to 1868.[72]

Indian Visitors

A group of Indians visited Jefferson County in 1859. Although they were not famous individually so far as is known, it was always a notable occasion when Native Americans came to the county. The July 15, 1859, *Mt. Vernon Star* reported that about a dozen Indians from Kansas came through Mt. Vernon on the way to see President Buchanan in Washington. The article was critical of their begging, but said: "They were a great source of wonder to the boys, who were much amused at their feats of archery and gymnastics." The article ended with this comment: "No doubt James Buchanan will consider himself highly honored to receive a visit from those lousy mendicants."

Although the Indians were not identified by name or tribe, the fact that they came from Kansas at this particular time may give a clue as to who they were. President Buchanan had appointed a Robert S. Stevens as a special U.S. Indian commissioner in Kansas in 1857. His job was to arrange for the sale of Kaskaskia, Peoria, Piankashaw and Wea tribal lands that had been ceded to the United States in 1854. So it is possible that the Indians who came through Jefferson County wanted to talk with the president about this matter.

CHAPTER III

The 1860s and 1870s

The 1860s and 1870s were dominated by the Civil War and Reconstruction with all the emotion and turmoil affecting Jefferson County like so many other parts of the United States. Many people in southern Illinois came from the South and still had strong ties there. Well-known Jefferson County physician, Dr. Andy Hall, lived in Hamilton County as a boy and experienced some of the bitterness of the times. He wrote about those days in an article in 1961. He told of a company of men organized by John Bagwell, ex-sheriff of Jefferson County, who joined the Confederates and fought at the Battle of Shiloh. Local Confederate sympathizers became part of the Knights of the Golden Circle or "Copperheads." Dr. Hall wrote: "My father, who was a member of the 40th Illinois Regiment, had left my mother at home with six children, the oldest not yet 19 years old. From time to time an old man who was supposed to be one of the ringleaders of the Knights of the Golden Circle would drive by the farm, stop, and holler, 'Hello! Well, I understand the 40th has been in a big battle. A lot of them were killed and some were captured and sent to prison!'" Later, Dr. Hall's mother would find out this was false.[73]

During and after the Civil War the United States was changing economically, politically, and culturally. The industrial economy of the North continued to grow. Railroads were expanding across the country. Other great industries such as steel and oil were beginning to boom. Unfortunately this led to a great period of corruption in politics. Some ex-soldiers became outlaws, and others became politicians. Humorists said you couldn't tell the difference. Politically, the country soon became tired of the reforms of the Radical Republicans and ended Reconstruction in 1877. But a strong anti-drinking crusade started by the women of the WCTU began to make progress. In the cultural area the U.S. became fascinated by a relatively new sport called "base ball." And, of course, the United States celebrated the country's 100th birthday in 1876.

Jefferson County participated in many of these trends. The county obtained its first railroad in 1869 when the St. Louis and Southeastern Railroad, which became the L. & N., was extended from Ashley to Mt. Vernon. This was a huge local event with a big celebration. People packed the train for its first official run—some even riding on flat cars. [74] The local chapter of the WCTU was started in 1878–1879. Soldiers' Reunions were held in Jefferson County in the 1870s and later. These were huge affairs with important political and military leaders present. Nearly every political figure was addressed as "General" or "Colonel." Local people were very interested in baseball and organized teams after the Civil War. The *Mt. Vernon Free Press* of September 6, 1867, had stories about the local baseball games and the following ad: "This exciting and healthy game is all the rage now. Varnell has a large number of Chadwick's Treaties on the game, which tells all about playing it. Buy a copy." And Jefferson County had a major celebration in 1876 for the centennial.

John A. Logan

The first famous visitor of the 1860s was then Civil War General John A. Logan. Before the Civil War Logan was a strong, southern-oriented Democrat. His father, Dr. John Logan, profited from slave catching and trading. For a time he made most of his money that way. The younger Logan as a state legislator made anti-black speeches and persuaded the General Assembly to pass a law prohibiting black immigration into Illinois.[75] In his first speech after being elected to the U. S. Congress in 1858 Logan defended the Fugitive Slave Act, saying: "We are willing to perform that dirty work (catching fugitive slaves)." After this speech Republicans began calling him "dirty work" Logan.[76]

When Lincoln was elected president in 1860 and the South began to secede to form the Confederate States of America, many in Jefferson County and southern Illinois supported the rebels. Given his background, most thought John A. Logan would support the South as well. Mt. Vernon resident, Edward V. Satterfield, claimed to have seen Logan draw a knife and threaten to cut down the United States flag in McLeansboro in 1861. (Satterfield had been a friend of John A. Logan in the 1850s when both were strong Democrats and Satterfield was associated with the Democratic newspaper, the *Mt. Vernon Star*. One report said they "fiddled" together at many a country dance.[77] As Logan came to support Lincoln and the Republicans, their friendship ended.)[78] But Logan joined the Union army, which bitterly disappointed the southern sympathizers. So when he returned to southern Illinois during the Civil War and expressed his opinions in fiery speeches, Logan stirred up a hornets' nest.

Logan may have been in Jefferson County in August of 1863 after participating in the Battle of Vicksburg. He stopped and spoke in Cairo and then rode the Illinois Central to Carbondale. He gave speeches in Carbondale on July 30 and DuQuoin on July 31. His three hour speech in Carbondale forcefully condemned southern sympathizers and peace factions in the North and argued that the Union must be preserved. Although shouted down by some in the large crowd, most of the people cheered wildly for the home-town hero. He repeated the same speech throughout Illinois and his Chicago address was spread widely by the *Chicago Tribune*. President Lincoln was pleased with General Logan's ability to sway opinions in his home area and extended his leave from the army through August. By late August he was back in southern Illinois, spoke at Salem on August 18 to a crowd of three thousand to five thousand, and was scheduled to speak at Nashville before cancelling because of illness.[79]

Sketch of John A. Logan

The Lincoln Administration had been hearing of the Confederate support in Jefferson County from several sources. Illinois Governor Richard Yates was corresponding with the administration and Republicans in Mt. Vernon. One letter to Yates from Mt. Vernon dated June 7, 1861, warns: "We have quite a number in this county who openly oppose the government… we hear it almost every day from some source, some one asking their friends to leave Jefferson County for fear of the secessionists here in the free state of Illinois." The letter goes on to ask for armed intervention to destroy the secession paper and arrest the principals.[80] Government officials were also hearing, no doubt, from General Grant about secessionist activities in Jefferson County. It was reported to General Grant in September of 1861 that a man named Cash had left Jefferson County for Texas with horses and family and was carrying sixty or seventy letters of support for secession from people in Jefferson and Williamson Counties.[81] On February 23, 1862, U.S. Marshal D. L. Phillips sent a report to the Lincoln Administration listing possibly disloyal persons in Jefferson County. The report was based in part on information from a spy who had infiltrated the Knights of the Golden Circle in Mt. Vernon. Among those listed were William Dodds, Dr. Duff Green, and James M. Pace. Phillips recommended that Dr. Green be arrested, and four days later the War Department ordered that Dr. Green should be seized and taken to Fort Lafayette, New York.[82]

JEFFERSON COUNTY COURT   1840

Sketch of Jeff. Co. Courthouse 1840-1870

General Logan returned to southern Illinois in the fall of 1864 after commanding the Army of the Tennessee at the Battle of Atlanta. This time he most definitely was in Jefferson County. President Lincoln was concerned about the activities of the Knights of the Golden Circle, who burned homes and barns and threatened those who supported the Union. He wired a message to General Sherman stating Logan's presence in Illinois was important for the nation. Lincoln was running for re-election against former Union General George McClellan, and his chances did not look good. On September 20, 1864, Logan was granted a thirty-day leave of absence. Although technically still a Democrat, Logan spoke for Lincoln and the Republicans throughout Illinois. On October 1 he spoke to a rabid crowd in Carbondale. He spoke in Springfield, Belleville (October 10), Centralia (October 12), DuQuoin, Clinton (October 15), Grayville (October 18), Phillipstown (October 19), Alton (October 20), and Benton (October 24) where his own sister heckled him. His tour was having such a great effect that his leave was extended until after the election. The Knights of the Golden Circle threatened to kill Logan.[83]

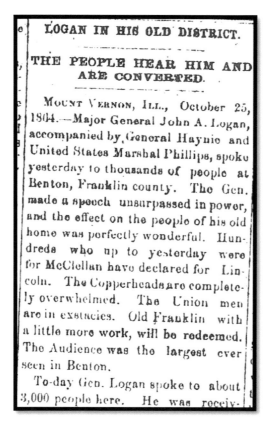

Logan Tour Article

When Logan came to Mt. Vernon on October 25, 1864, during this explosive time, a serious incident took place. Accounts differ as to the details, but the essential facts remain the same. When Logan arrived in Mt. Vernon, the atmosphere was quite tense. The *Mt. Vernon Star*, published rent-free in a room at the Jefferson County Courthouse, had been attacking Lincoln and the Republicans since the beginning of the war. The editor once wrote: "Democrats arouse and protect yourselves; prepare not with the ballot box, but with the cartridge box."[84] Meanwhile, John A. Wall returned from the war as a wounded veteran and started the *Unconditional Unionist* to attack the Democrats and support the Union cause. One night three copperheads attempted to kill Wall in the streets of Mt. Vernon.

John A. Logan and Dr. Green

John A. Logan met Dr. Duff Green, a former friend and fire-eating southern Democrat, as he spoke to a crowd of three thousand either in the streets or at a barbeque. The two men exchanged harsh words. Later at a Union meeting in the Jefferson County Courthouse Logan said the editor of the *Mt. Vernon Star* was "a traitor and a liar." He also referred to "a pill peddler," who once had been his friend but now was a rebel. Next according to a local correspondent, General Logan "… pitched into our local coppers in his own peculiar style."

At this point Dr. Green strode down the center aisle of the courtroom and interrupted the speech by demanding that Logan retract what he had said. Logan replied, "What I did say was any man that indorses the

Chicago platform (Democrats) is a sympathizer with traitors, and I say it yet, whether you like it or not." Green yelled, "I say any man who indorses the Lincoln platform is an enemy of his country." Logan shouted back, "I say you are a d__d liar," grabbed a heavy water pitcher, and hurled it at Dr. Green. The doctor dodged behind a column and drew a revolver. (Both Dr. Green and his eighteen-year-old son were armed, but General Logan was not.) Logan seized another pitcher and started toward Dr. Green. One of the "widow women," dressed in black and on the front row as usual in Republican rallies, jumped up to grab the general's arm. (There was a "colony" of war widows who lived together at the Commercial Hotel at 11th and Main.) David L. Phillips, one of Logan's colleagues, also intervened. The general turned to the woman who held his arm and said: "That's all madam. That's all," and put the pitcher down. Others escorted Dr. Green and his son out of the meeting.

Later the woman (Mrs. Elizabeth Boswell Welch, widow of Edwin Welch who died in the Civil War, and grandmother of longtime *Mt. Vernon Register-News* editor, Edwin Rackaway) said: "I don't know how I had the nerve to do it, but I felt that if the general threw that pitcher, a riot might have broken out and someone might have been killed. I know what men are."[85] She may have been right. A friend and colleague, Senator Shelby Cullom, said of Logan: "I believe he would not have hesitated for a moment to kill any one who would have questioned his honesty. He was a man of intense feeling, intense friendships, and I might also add that he was a man of the most intense hatreds."[86] John A. Wall in his *History of Jefferson County* mentioned this incident and said: "In this court room took place the noted altercation between our former fellow citizen Dr. Green and General John A. Logan, during the War for the Union."

After the encounter Logan continued his speech and attacked what he called "peace-sneaks," and "home rebels," whom he labeled traitors. During the last hour he had the audience laughing, crying, stamping, and shouting. One old timer said he had never seen anything like it, not even at the old camp meetings.[87] This must have been an exceptionally busy day in Mt. Vernon. On the evening of the same day as the Logan visit there was a "Grand Soiree," a dance with a string band and refreshments at Varnell's Hall.[88]

At McLeansboro on October 26 Logan encountered even more trouble. This time he was armed and ready. In a speech before a crowd of about ten thousand people Logan was heckled and threatened by nearly one thousand copperheads. Logan drew his revolver and said: "If I hear any more heckling from those windows it shall be put into action, and if any more copperheads care to have it tested upon them, let them step forward." The crowd quieted and Logan finished his speech in a heavy rain. But later he did fire at someone who yelled "Harrah for Jefferson Davis." These two campaign stops must have been difficult on the general because at his next appearance on October 27 in Fairfield with Governor Yates and General Haynie he was reported to be "unwell" and spoke only fifteen minutes.[89]

The results of the 1864 election gave the Republicans a tremendous victory and Logan was given much credit. In his five week tour he had spoken to over fifty thousand people. Lincoln won Logan's old district 11,714 to 10,926 when he had received only about five thousand votes four years earlier. Even in the Democratic stronghold of Jefferson County Lincoln received about two hundred more votes in 1864 than 1860. In Jefferson County Lincoln received 649 votes in 1864 and 459 in 1860 but lost to Democrats McClellan (1,487 votes) in 1864 and Douglas (1,852 votes) in 1860. The Republican candidate for governor, Richard Oglesby, won a majority in southern Illinois. Egypt had gone Republican for the first time in its history.

Because of this success and because of his poor relationship with his army superior, General Sherman, Logan considered leaving the military and seeking a political position. By the time he came to Mt. Vernon in October he was convinced by Isham N. Haynie, who was campaigning with him, to make a bid for the United States Senate seat. Haynie then contacted Mt. Vernon resident John A. Wall, who was the editor of the *Unconditional Unionist* and an acquaintance of Haynie (Both had attended the Mt. Vernon Academy although at different times.), and arranged for him to write an editorial endorsing Logan. They spread the "Logan for senator" slogan by sending a copy of the editorial to every newspaper in the state. They also sent copies to every member of the legislature. Poor communication and Logan's ambivalence doomed the campaign. Logan sent a letter to Mt. Vernon, thinking Haynie was there with Wall. He was not. By the time Haynie received the message it was too late to make arrangements for Logan to speak in Chicago and

Governor Yates became the Illinois senator. Later Haynie wrote: "There is no question but that the senatorship was within his grasp if he had been able to be present during the contest."[90]

Robert G. Ingersoll

Robert G. Ingersoll came back to Mt. Vernon in June of 1867 and June of 1868. He was appointed attorney general of Illinois in 1867 by his good friend, Governor Richard J. Oglesby, which may explain his visits to town during his term (1867–1869). He also may have been in Jefferson County as part of a brief campaign for the Republican nomination for governor of Illinois. But what is not so easily explained is his change of heart about Mt. Vernon. In a letter to his brother from Mt. Vernon dated June 6, 1867, he wrote:

> This noon I arrived at this ancient and decaying town. I feel that I am again in heathen lands. A vision rises before me—I see shapeless felt hats, surmounting heads covered with long lank "yaller" hair—the hair falling down upon a shirt open in the front showing a breast covered with dirty frowsy moss—and there are knit suspenders holding up jean breeches, and below the breeches I see brogans with the toes of the wearers thrust through the upper leather. I see dogs "follering—I see women in sun bonnets, and home spun dresses,—I see sore eyes, and long, flabby breasts, hanging down upon leathery bellies—the bellies supported by dirty legs and the legs sustained by spraddling feet. I hear people say "I have saw", and "I've hearn", and "I seed". They talk about "his'n", and "her'n", and "your'n". I see meeting houses without windows, graveyards without fences—dooryards without grass—without vines, without flowers. I see people without education, without thought—without ambition who seem to be waiting for death. I see young women without beauty and without youth, the youngest are as old as the oldest. I see young men without an aspiration and old men without a hope. A little while ago I saw the house where I used to live. May God spare me a second sight.[91]

The people of Mt. Vernon didn't know about this attack until these private letters were published in 1951 by Ingersoll's daughter. He was even invited back to Mt. Vernon to speak at the Fourth of July celebration in 1876. In a reply to Ingersoll in 1952 Edwin Rackaway wrote in part: "Conditions were far from ideal in those distant days, but we doubt that they were nearly as bad as the colonel tried to paint them in his 'vision.' If Satan, or whoever has the soul of Old Bob in custody, would permit him once more to visit this 'ancient and decaying town' he might be surprised at what he saw."[92] Ingersoll returned again in the 1860s as shown by a letter to his brother, Ebon Clark Ingersoll, dated June 7, 1868, in which he states: "I just returned from Mt. Vernon and glad enough to get home."[93]

John M. Palmer

The next visitor to Mt. Vernon was John M. Palmer, who in 1868 was a Republican candidate for governor of Illinois. Palmer was one of the founders of the Illinois Republican Party and helped his friend, Abe Lincoln, get the Republican nomination for president in 1860. He served as a major general in the Union Army and led his forces at the Battle of Chickamauga and in Sherman's March to the Sea. In 1868 he resigned from the army and was elected governor of Illinois. He served from 1869 to 1873. He was also elected to the United States Senate and served from 1890 to 1896. The *Mt. Vernon Register* reported that in 1868, "he was received in this city with tumultuous enthusiasm by thousands of people, and conveyed in a carriage through the principal streets which were lined with people ready to do him honor…"[94]

Supreme Court Visitors

The Supreme Court continued to draw famous visitors to Mt. Vernon in the 1860s. Sidney Breese, of course, continued to be a judge on the high court and was in Mt. Vernon throughout this period. His presence is further confirmed by a letter mailed in Mt. Vernon on September 11, 1863, from Breese to Abraham Lincoln. In the letter Breese notes that he has been in Mt. Vernon for "some days" doing legal work and came across part of Lincoln's inaugural address. He wrote that in his opinion, "a more beautiful idea, more beautifully expressed, cannot be found in any writer, ancient or modern." He signed it, "I am your friend as ever, Sidney Breese."[95] In November, 1866, and June, 1867, John A. McClernand had cases at the Supreme Court.[96] Robert Ingersoll was at the Supreme Court on June 6, 1867, and June 6, 1868.[97]

Robert Waterman

One last notable visitor of the 1860s was Robert Waterman in December of 1869. He helped form the Illinois Republican Party in 1854 and was one of two Illinois delegates to the first National Republican Convention in 1856. (The other delegate was Abraham Lincoln.) He moved to California in the 1870s and made a fortune in gold and silver mining. He was lieutenant governor of California in 1886, and governor from 1887 to 1891. The *Mt. Vernon Register*, using the *Mt. Vernon Free Press* of 1868–69, reported "… in September, 1869, while Henry Waterman, late Governor of California, embarked in business in this city in December of the same year, having come here from Will County." (Henry was Waterman's brother, but Robert was the one who became governor. So, the newspaper must have used the wrong first name.)[98]

The Secret Service

In 1870 Mt. Vernon was the headquarters of a band of counterfeiters. The leader of the gang was a Dr. Charles T. Laur, the owner of a drug store in East St. Louis, who was formerly a Mt. Vernon resident. They flooded Jefferson County and southern Illinois with the bogus money. It was so bad that S. D. Ham of the First National Bank in Mt. Vernon wrote a letter to the Treasury Department stating: "There is more counterfeit money in circulation in Mt. Vernon than genuine money." In those days the Secret Service was in charge of stopping counterfeiting rather than guarding the president. (This changed in 1894 when agents were assigned to guard Grover Cleveland.) As a result in 1870 Patrick D. Tyrrell, the chief of the Chicago district office of the Secret Service, was dispatched to Mt. Vernon.

When Mr. Tyrrell arrived in town, he couldn't believe it was really that bad and told Mr. Ham so. Ham basically told him that "it was no exaggeration," and that he should check it out for himself. Tyrrell went to a local store, purchased a small item, and received $2.50 in counterfeit money for change. Now convinced of the problem, he went to Mayor Varnell and asked for a trustworthy local man who could infiltrate the gang. The mayor suggested a James Stansbury who agreed to the plan. Tyrrell pretended to be Stansbury's rich uncle from the west and the two men were taken into the gang. After they had enough evidence to convict each member of the gang, a big raiding party of federal agents from St. Louis along with Jefferson County officers captured all of the counterfeiters.

Two gang leaders, Dr. Laur and a John Fairchilds, were released on bond and escaped. The search for Fairchilds went on for years with many instances where he was surrounded but made daring escapes. Finally, in June of 1878 he was found at his home near Roaches. (Roaches was founded in 1870 and named after a David Roach who owned a store there. It was located in Casner Township just north of the L. & N. Railroad tracks near Woodlawn.)[99] Fairchilds refused to surrender, "shot it out" with the posse, and was killed. Dr. J. H. Watson of Woodlawn, well-known local physician, was called upon to perform the autopsy. The search for Dr. Laur also went on for years. He was captured in 1882 on a train in the South, brought back to Illinois for trial, and sent to jail.[100]

In the same time period the Secret Service was involved in another sensational case. In 1876 they learned that a gang of counterfeiters from Chicago was planning to steal the body of Abraham Lincoln. The gang hoped to force the governor of Illinois to release their best engraver of counterfeit plates from prison. Patrick D. Tyrrell, the same Secret Service agent who came to Mt. Vernon, was sent to Springfield to break up the plot. When the would-be grave robbers arrived in the dead of night at Oak Ridge Cemetery, Tyrrell and his agents were waiting for them. After a comedy of errors including an agent accidentally firing his weapon, the grave robbers escaped but without Lincoln's body. They were captured by Agent Tyrrell a few days later in a Chicago saloon.[101]

Jeff. Co. Courthouse 1873

Dewitt Cregier

One of the first notable people to visit Mt. Vernon in the 1870s was Dewitt C. Cregier. He came to town on June 7, 1871, as grand master of the Masons in Illinois. The Jefferson County Courthouse had burned in 1870 and the Masons were in charge of the ceremony laying the cornerstone of the new building. This new courthouse was destroyed by the 1888 tornado and the cornerstone was opened in September, 1889, revealing many old documents and newspapers from the 1870s.[102] Cregier went on to become the mayor of Chicago from 1889 to 1891. He also invented and patented a combination drinking fountain, fire hydrant and water basin for animals that was used all over Chicago.

Oglesby, Beveridge, and Raum

The next event to bring notables to Jefferson County was a big political gathering as part of the state and national elections in 1872. On October 14, 1872, Governor Richard Oglesby (running for governor), General John Beveridge (running for lieutenant governor), and General Raum (running for U.S. Congress), came to Mt. Vernon. Oglesby was governor of Illinois from 1865 to 1869. Previous to that he had served in the Mexican-American War and was a major general in the Civil War. Later he served as a United States senator from 1873 to 1878 and in 1884 was elected Illinois governor for a third time. Oglesby was one of the most popular figures in Illinois history. One contemporary said of him: "His honesty, his patriotism, his earnest eloquence, the uniqueness of his character, made him beloved by the people of his state; and wherever he went, to the day of his death, Uncle Dick Oglesby, as he was called, was enthusiastically and affectionately received."[103] In 1872 he had agreed to run for governor. But if successful he was to resign, turn the office over to Lieutenant Governor Beveridge, and be appointed to the United States Senate. (In those days U.S. senators were appointed by the state, not elected by the voters.) As a result of this scheme, John L. Beveridge, himself a former member of the U.S. House and a former brigadier general in the Civil War, became governor in 1873.

The newspaper called this Oglesby-Beveridge Republican rally the "largest in Jefferson County this year." The procession was nearly a half mile long with colorful banners. The crowd gathered at the fairgrounds, located in East Mt. Vernon from 1860 to 1906, and according to the reporter, "listened to the words of truth and eloquence as they dropped from the lips of the next governor of Illinois, the gallant General Richard J. Oglesby, whose fame is world-wide and whose honesty of purpose is not questioned by anybody, of any political suade, unless it be by a few leading Liberal Republicans in Illinois, who seeing that they are soon to enter their political graves, never to be resurrected, are tearing their flesh, crying corruption, and cursing the god that gave them birth." Talk about unbiased reporting! But passions were high between the regular Republicans who favored Grant and the Liberal Republicans/Democrats who favored Horace Greeley and an end to the corruption in government. Further raising emotions was "waving the bloody shirt" or blaming the Democrats for the Civil War dead and wounded, which was a favorite Republican campaign tactic.

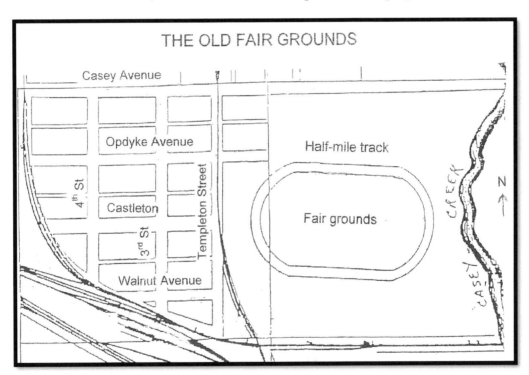

Map of Fairgrounds East Mt. Vernon

After spending the night at L.A. Smith's, the three visitors were escorted to the "new brick building of Messrs. Stratton and Johnson," southeast of the public square at Ninth and Broadway, where General Beveridge spoke to three or four hundred people and the Bavarian Brass Band from Belleville played. It was a very successful day for the Republicans—if you can believe the reporting.[104]

Supreme Court Visitors

The Supreme Court drew even more well-known attorneys to Mt. Vernon in the 1870s. In June, 1873, and November, 1879, former United States Senator Lyman Trumbull argued cases at the Mt. Vernon division of the Supreme Court.[105] Former Illinois Governor John M. Palmer was in town for court sessions in June, 1873, June, 1875, and June, 1876.[106] He and former lieutenant governor and minister to Spain, Gustave Koerner, spoke at the court in June, 1876, upon the death of William H. Underwood.[107] Koerner had cases in Mt. Vernon throughout this period, as did Silas Bryan, father of William Jennings Bryan. Former U.S. Congressman Samuel S. Marshall represented a client at the court in June, 1879.[108]

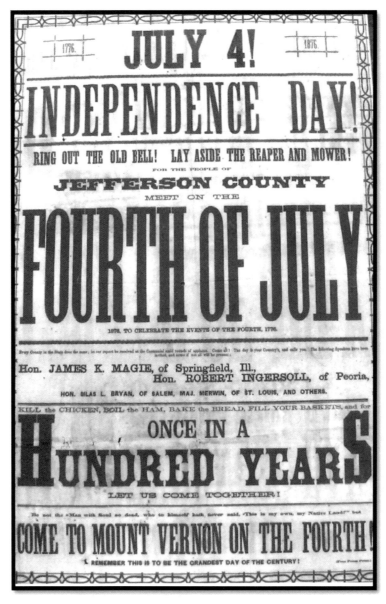

Poster of July 4, 1876

Centennial Visitors

Several important people came to Mt. Vernon in 1876. The July 4th Centennial celebration was intended to be a special occasion. According to a large poster, which survives from that year, "The following speakers have been invited, and some if not all will be present: Hon. James K. Magie of Springfield, Illinois, Hon. Robert Ingersoll of Peoria, Hon. Silas L. Bryan of Salem, Maj. Merwin of St. Louis, and others."[109] Robert Ingersoll most likely did not come. Other records show he gave an address at the July 4th celebration in Peoria. No local newspaper exists for that time. So one can only assume that the other speakers were in town. James Magie was an editor of the *Macomb Journal* and the *Canton Register*. Later on July 19, 1885, he gave testimony in the famous Haymarket Square Affair where nine Chicago policemen were killed, supposedly by an anarchist bomb. In 1886 he testified for the prosecution in *Illinois v. August Spies*. Spies was one of the accused radicals in the same incident.

Thomas A. Hendricks

Thomas A. Hendricks (1819–1885) was another famous visitor in 1876. When he came to Mt. Vernon, he was governor of Indiana and a candidate for vice president of the United States on the Democratic ticket with Samuel Tilden. (Hendricks was nominated for vice president in July of 1876 at the Democratic National Convention in St. Louis, Missouri. A sixteen-year-old William Jennings Bryan paid his own way to attend the convention.)[110] Hendricks had a long political career including membership in the U.S. House in 1850 and the U.S. Senate in 1862, which led him to be considered a potential presidential candidate from 1868 until his death. He was elected vice president of the United States in 1884 on the Grover Cleveland ticket and died in office.

Vice presidential nominee Hendricks' visit was announced with the usual hyperbole in those days as "a Barbeque and Mass Meeting on a most mammoth scale." The newspaper article stated that "about twenty-five fat cattle and twice that number of sheep and hogs will be slaughtered for the occasion." It also promised that in addition to Hendricks, Governor Palmer, General John A. McClernand, Gustave A. Koerner, and many others would speak. However, on the appointed day Palmer, McClernand, and Koerner were not present. Still it must have been a memorable event because observers were talking about it forty to fifty years later. In an article about Hendricks's career *Mt. Vernon Register-News* editor J. Frank Bogan wrote: "Hendricks was much better known to the people of the country (than Cleveland), was very popular, was a man of proved natural and acquired ability, was governor of Indiana, and opponents of Cleveland often declared the ticket was a case of the tail wagging the dog. In other words the Vice Presidential candidate was a much bigger man than the head of the ticket. Mr. Hendricks once visited Mt. Vernon and spoke here to thousands of people in 1876."[111]

Hendricks Tour Article

41

The *Mt. Vernon News* article of October 21, 1876, gave this description of the previous day's activities. By early morning the citizens of Mt. Vernon heard "the rattle of wagons, the sound of soul-stirring music, and the shouts of the people, as delegation after delegation came in, carrying flags and banners," until the town held ten thousand men, women, and children. At about 9:00 a.m. the Mt. Vernon and Salem Brass Bands led a parade over a mile long to the L. & N. depot to greet Governor Hendricks. Taking off his hat to acknowledge the shouts of support from the crowd, the governor was taken by a "fine and luxurious" carriage to the residence of Dr. W. D. Green (located on Broadway between 7th and 8th Streets).

DR. W. DUFF GREEN,
Builder and Owne. of Armory.

Dr. W. Duff Green

Dr. Green came to Jefferson County in 1846. His medical practice prospered, and he soon bought the Stinson Anderson farm, giving him ownership of all the property in Mt. Vernon east of Eighth Street. Part of this land contained springs, which he called Green Lawn Springs, located where the "old" football field at Mt. Vernon Township High School is today. Dr. Green promoted these springs as having healing capabilities. In October of 1859 he had seventy acres laid out into blocks and lots as Green's Addition to the City of Mt. Vernon. However, he retained blocks fifteen and sixteen, which included the springs, and block twelve where he intended to build his home. During the Civil War he built a large, two-story, brick residence, which he called Green Lawn Place. The home became a social center as Dr. Green and his family (wife, Corinne, and eventually ten children) frequently gave lavish parties. He also became active in civic affairs as president of the Mt. Vernon Railroad Company, which brought the first railroad to the city in 1869–70, and in Democratic Party politics. As a delegate to the Democratic National Convention in 1876, he helped nominate Samuel Tilden and Thomas Hendricks for president and vice president respectively. So it clearly was due to Dr. Green's influence that Hendricks came to Mt. Vernon in 1876.

Sketch of Green Lawn Place

After delivering Hendricks to the Green estate, the crowd rushed to find seats at Casey's Grove where stands had been erected. The speaker's rostrum was decorated with evergreens, flags, and mottoes and was supplied with sofas and chairs. After a period of time Hendricks was escorted to the grove by the Tilden and Hendricks Guards of Centralia and the Mt. Vernon Brass Band. His two-hour-plus speech, which was cheered wildly, was a general review of the "short-comings" of the Republican Party, not surprising in a heated political campaign. Other Democratic speakers followed later with specific attacks on Republican John A. Logan as the "humbug of all humbugs." According to the article, to say that they thoroughly "skinned" Logan would be "putting it mild indeed."

But the festivities were not over yet. After the barbeque at about 7:00 p.m. rockets were shot from the dome of the Jefferson County Courthouse; guns were fired; hundreds of torches were lit; dozens of Chinese lanterns were hung from trees; and ropes were stretched across the streets. Then a torchlight parade began with bands and with at least eight hundred boys dressed in "Tilden and Hendricks caps and capes" and carrying torches. More political speeches and band music both inside and outside the courthouse followed. Then the crowd marched to Dr. Green's home to "serenade" Governor Hendricks. He came out and spoke again to thank the people for their support. Next the crowd moved to the residence of Colonel Tom Casey (son of Zadok Casey) where other Democratic candidates were staying. Casey's home, built in 1867, is now the Hughey Funeral Home. It was about 11:00 in the evening when the events came to a conclusion. Even taking into account the obvious bias of the newspaper, these activities must have made up one of the largest events of the era and might have merited the reporter's description as "the Grandest Rally Ever Witnessed in Egypt!"[112]

All of this campaigning was for naught as Rutherford B. Hayes defeated the Tilden/Hendricks ticket in a highly controversial election. This was one of those elections where the winning candidate actually lost the popular vote. There were three southern states with electoral votes in dispute. A commission was appointed to decide the matter. They voted along party lines to award all of the electoral votes to Hayes, making him the winner. Democrats shouted "corrupt bargain," claiming that Republicans had promised to end Reconstruction and remove all federal troops from the South in order to receive the three southern states' votes. But after threatening civil war over the election the Democrats gave up and Hayes was inaugurated president in 1877. John A. Logan, who was attacked in many of the speeches, lost his Senate seat but won Senator Oglesby's seat in 1879.

Jesse and Frank James

The last visitors of 1876, Jesse James and Frank James, were and are extremely famous, but very elusive— as any outlaws would be. As a result it is difficult if not impossible to find documentary evidence of their possible visits. One story says that Jesse James at an earlier date paid a visit to a friend in Spring Garden, Jefferson County, Illinois. He had given up his gun in one of his attempts to "go straight." After a fight over a card game James went back to his friend's house, grabbed a gun, returned and shot the man. Fleeing out of Jefferson County, he threw the gun into a creek that became known as "Gun Creek."

The 1876 visit was reported by Ed B. Moss in an address to the Jefferson County Historical Society in 1961. According to Mr. Moss: "Jesse James came through Jefferson County in 1876 on his way home to Missouri after his gang was shot up in an unsuccessful attempt to hold up the bank at Northfield, Minnesota. The bad man patronized a local livery stable." The visit can't be proven, but it does have a ring of truth to it. Jesse James did try to rob the bank in Northfield on September 6, 1876. His gang was shot up badly. Jesse and his brother, Frank, were separated from the others and escaped into Iowa. Rather than going directly south to their home in Missouri where the "law" would be waiting for them, they came into Illinois and traveled south. And it makes sense that they would come through Jefferson County where they may have had friends.

Jesse and Frank may have been in Jefferson County at another time. According to a family story from the Horse Creek area of Wayne/Jefferson County, Jesse and Frank came to the home of George and Sarah Garrison in a buggy. They asked for help for a friend who had been shot in the leg. On another occasion part of the Younger Gang (often associated with the James Brothers) came to the Garrison home.[113]

According to another local story, Frank James came to Jefferson County long after his outlaw days. After Jesse's death in 1882 Frank gave up, went through several trials, and by 1885 became a free man. He lived in St. Louis most of the time where he worked as a theater guard. He also gave tours of the family farm and in 1903 started the James-Younger Wild West Show. He died in 1915.

Susan B. Anthony

One of the most famous and important women in the United States, Susan B. Anthony (1820–1906), was scheduled to be in Mt. Vernon in February of 1877. Before the Civil War Anthony worked in the temperance and abolition movements. After the war she and other women such as Elizabeth Cady Stanton began the movement for woman suffrage. In 1866 Anthony helped found the American Equal Rights Association. In 1868 she and Stanton founded the National Woman Suffrage Association. In 1872 Anthony attempted to vote in the presidential election; she was arrested, tried, and found guilty of breaking New York law. In the late Nineteenth Century she traveled the nation speaking for women's rights, particularly woman suffrage, and became one of the best-known women of her time. She is recognized today as one of the most important women in U.S. history.

Anthony was in Illinois from February to May of 1877 for a series of fifty lectures for the Slayton Lyceum Agency of Chicago. The *Mt. Vernon News* reported that: "Miss Susan B. Anthony will deliver her celebrated lecture entitled 'Women and the 16th Amendment,' in Mt. Vernon February next." The United States had given black men the right to vote with the Fifteenth Amendment. It was forty-three years after her scheduled visit to Mt. Vernon and fourteen years after her death when the U.S. passed the Nineteenth Amendment giving women the right to vote.[114]

Barnum's Circus

In 1877 P.T. Barnum's "Greatest Show on Earth" Circus made a swing through southern Illinois. Although it didn't stop in Mt. Vernon, there is no doubt the circus traveled through Jefferson County. The itinerary included shows at Washington, Missouri, on September 27, Nashville, Illinois, on September 28, and Evansville, Indiana, on September 29. This route at this pace would require them to travel by train through Jefferson County on the way from Nashville to Evansville. The circus began to travel by railroad in 1872 and could make trips of one hundred miles per night. Barnum, himself, traveled with the circus as late as 1872. But as he grew older, he increasingly stayed home in Bridgeport, Connecticut, where he was elected mayor in 1875. Whenever possible he would be present with the circus in large cities. So he probably was not with his circus as it came through Jefferson County in September of 1877. Barnum's Circus merged with Bailey's Great London Circus in 1880 to form Barnum and Bailey's Greatest Show on Earth. Barnum died in 1891.[115]

Political Visitors—Cullom, Palmer, and Oglesby

One of the most outstanding events in Mt. Vernon history was a soldiers' reunion held in Casey's pasture (probably now the south side of Broadway west of Casey Middle School) on August 14th and 15th of 1878. Among those who attended were Governor Shelby M. Cullom, ex-Governor John M. Palmer, Senator Richard Oglesby, and Civil War Generals John A. Logan, James Shields, William Tecumseh Sherman,[116] Alexander M. McCook, and James H. Wilson.[117] Some have called it "Mt. Vernon's Biggest Day."[118]

A NOTABLE REUNION OF MANY YEARS AGO

First Gathering of Its Kind Held in This Section of Illinois After Close of the Civil War.

Back in 1878 there was held a reunion in Mt. Vernon the like of which has never been held since in this part of the world. It was the first big reunion in the state, so it is said, that was held after the close of the civil war.

Thousands gathered here at that time and thousands experienced one of the most complete soakings they had ever had as the rain fell in torrents and there were not houses enough in the vicinity of Casey's grove to offer shelter for but very few people.

Among the notables there were Gen. J. A. Logan, Senator Shelby M. Cullom and Gen. W. T. Sherman.

The following letter was received by J. W. Baugh from Gen. Sherman in answer to the invitation extended to him:

Hdqtrs Army of United States, Washington, D. C., June 30, 1878.
J. W. Baugh.
Late Adjutant 40th Illinois, Mt. Vernon, Ill.

My dear Sir:—Your letter of June 15 inviting me in most pleasing terms to unite with you at a soldiers' reunion at Mt. Vernon, Ill., Aug. 14 and 15th of August next, was received some days ago but laid aside that I might answer positively.

I now feel contsrained to decline your hearty invitation and to substitute for my actual presence this letter.

Sherman Article

45

Shelby Cullom (1829–1914) held many local, state, and national offices in a political career that lasted from 1855 to 1913. He was a Republican member of the U.S. House from 1865 to 1871. He was governor of Illinois from 1877 to 1883. He was elected to the U.S. Senate in 1882, 1888, 1894, 1900, and 1906. Clearly he was an important figure in Illinois during this period.

John M. Palmer was governor of Illinois from 1869 to 1873. During the Civil War he was a major general of volunteers and had an important part in the Battles of Stones River, Chickamauga, Chattanouga, and Atlanta. In 1891 he was elected to the U.S. Senate and served one term.

Senator Richard Oglesby was a major general in the Civil War. He was severely wounded at the Battle of Corinth in 1862 but returned to the war in 1863 and 1864. He served in the U.S. Senate from 1873 to 1878. In 1884 he became the first man in Illinois history to be elected governor three times.

Military Visitors—Logan, Shields, McCook, and Wilson

General Logan (1826–1886), of course, was a huge political and military figure in Illinois and the nation. He was a member of the U.S. House from 1867 to 1871 and the U.S. Senate from 1871 to 1877. At the time he came to Mt. Vernon he was running for the U.S. Senate again. He was elected and served from 1879 until his death in 1886. While in the House he joined the "Radical Republicans" and was one of the managers of the impeachment of President Andrew Johnson. But most important to the soldiers who came to town, he was a wounded Civil War veteran, a founder of the Grand Army of the Republic (the organization that fought for veterans' welfare), and one of the creators of Memorial Day as a national holiday. He was an extremely popular war hero who parlayed that enthusiasm into a national political career, culminating in his nomination for vice president of the United States in 1884. Many thought he would have been a better candidate for president than James G. Blaine, the Republican candidate that year. Shelby Cullom said that Logan, "had an ambition to become president and I believe he would have realized his ambition had he lived."[119] He was so popular in Jefferson County that even as late as 1909 his bed was used as an attraction in the Johnson Furniture Store in Mt. Vernon. [120]

General Shields (1810–1879) is not so well known today as Logan or Sherman. But he was a well-known figure in 1878. By that time he had already been Illinois auditor, and a member of the Illinois legislature and the Illinois Supreme Court. He almost fought a duel with Abraham Lincoln on September 22, 1842. He and Lincoln actually traveled to Missouri for the duel but were talked out of the fight by their seconds. He also was elected to a United States Senate seat from Illinois in 1849 and Minnesota in 1858. In 1879 he was elected to the U.S. Senate from Missouri, making him the only person in U.S. history to serve in the Senate from three different states. In addition he was a brigadier general in the Mexican War (wounded at the Battle of Cerro Gordo), and a brigadier general in the Civil War (wounded at the Battle of Kernstown). So the people of Mt. Vernon certainly knew him in 1878.

General McCook came from an Ohio family called the "Fighting McCooks" because his father, seven brothers, and five first cousins fought in the Civil War. He fought in the First Battle of Bull Run, commanded a division in Tennessee in 1862, and led the I Corps in Kentucky in the same year. His forces were defeated in the Battles of Perryville, Stones River, and Chickamauga. He was court-martialed but not convicted and ended the war as commander of the district of Eastern Arkansas. From 1875 to 1880 he was the aide-de-camp to general-in-chief of the U.S. Army, General Sherman. So it's not surprising that he was in Mt. Vernon with Sherman in 1878.

General Wilson was born in Shawneetown and attended McKendree College before graduating from the U.S. Military Academy in 1860. In 1862 he was topographic engineer and aide-de-camp to General George McClellan and participated in the Battle of Antietam. He was transferred to the West and served under Grant at Vicksburg and Sherman at Chattanooga. In 1864 he served as division commander of cavalry under General Philip Sheridan and chief of cavalry for General Sherman in Mississippi. His soldiers captured Confederate President Jefferson Davis in 1865. After the war he became a railroad engineer and executive. He re-joined the army for service in the Spanish-American War in 1898 and the Boxer Rebellion in China in 1901.

Sketch of William T. Sherman

William Tecumseh Sherman

But the star of the reunion had to be William Tecumseh Sherman. Other than U.S. Grant he had to be the most famous Union general of the Civil War. Known for his "War is Hell" comment, Sherman with many Illinois soldiers (40th Illinois with many from Jefferson County) burned Atlanta and "marched to the sea," breaking the back of the Confederacy. However, Sherman did not like politics and was a reluctant speaker. When he was asked to run for president in 1871, he made his position perfectly clear with this famous statement: "I have never been and never will be a candidate for President; …If nominated by either party, I should peremptorily decline; and even if unanimously elected, I should decline to serve."[121] So when J. W. Baugh asked him to attend the reunion in Mt. Vernon, he wrote that he felt "constrained to decline your hearty invitation…." He also wrote: "I do honestly think the soldiers of 1861–5, especially the members of the brave 40th Illinois, Col. Hicks commanding, should meet as often as possible to commemorate the Battle of Shiloh, in which it took so honorable and memorable a part."[122] He must have changed his mind because Mr. Baugh later stated that General Sherman was a visitor at the reunion and enjoyed it immensely.

Sherman may have changed his mind for several reasons. It was apparent that he really wanted to come because he wrote that he put the invitation aside so that he "might answer positively." He also may have been worried that the soldiers were being overshadowed by those who didn't serve. In his letter he wrote: "When the war of arms ceased, the war of words began; and then is the real danger that the men who stayed at home can beat us at the latter game." In addition he had a long-lasting feud with another attendee, General John A. Logan, and may have wanted to deny him some of the attention. During the war General Sherman had selected General Howard rather than Logan to replace General McPherson. After the war while Logan was a congressman he introduced bills lowering Sherman's pay from eighteen thousand dollars to twelve thousand dollars and reducing his staff from six to three. Sherman wrote to his brother in 1874: "But this reduction of my staff looks personal, invidious and mean." In his memoirs published in 1875 Sherman gave Logan an unfavorable review and wrote privately to his brother, "Logan did not make the March to the Sea at all, but was in Illinois making speeches."[123]

On a personal level Sherman may have wanted to attend the reunion to change his gloomy mood resulting from the disappointment of having his son join the priesthood. Sherman's wife was a devout Catholic and Sherman was not. He wrote to a friend on May 27, 1878, "… but I do oppose most vehemently his purpose to abandon — to desert me now, and to enlist in a Church which claims his soul, his mind and his person. I can hardly endure the thought. I cannot turn against him, but I do against that Church, which has poisoned his young mind, wound its tentacles around his heart and weaned him from his Father." Sherman's son sailed for England on June 5, 1878, to join a Jesuit monastery. Sherman didn't speak or write to his son for two years. He wrote: "I feel as though his life was lost, and am simply amazed he doesn't see it as I do."[124] Sherman probably received the invitation to come to Mt. Vernon about three weeks later.

THE GREAT REUNION.

Mt. Vernon Alive with Soldiers.

Speeches by Gov. Cullom, Gen. Logan and Others.

THE YELLOW FEVER.

MT. VERNON, ILL., Aug. 14.—Owing to the admirable excursion arrangements of the Southeastern Railway Company, and to a suddenly developed excess of patriotic feeling, Mt. Vernon has to-day within her limits more strangers than the town has ever seen at any one time since Douglas and Lincoln were stumping Illinois in 1858.

Mt. Vernon Reunion Article

By late July of 1878 Sherman and many of the others must have agreed to be at the reunion and stories began to appear in area newspapers. For example, the *Decatur Republican* of August 3 reported that General Sherman has "promised positively" to be in Mt. Vernon, that almost all railroads in southern Illinois would sell tickets at reduced rates, and that Mt. Vernon had the "most ample hotel accommodations of any city in the south end of the state." Word soon spread across the Midwest that Sherman would be at Mt. Vernon. Many ex-soldiers must have thought this might be the last chance they would have to see their old general. Reunion organizers probably had no idea that so many people would come to the celebration.

Officials in Mt. Vernon made many preparations. Speakers' stands had been built and decorated with flags, emblems, pictures and mottoes. One hundred tents were pitched and a large number of refreshment stands were built and placed around Casey's Grove. Arrangements were made to open up various churches, halls, and homes to accommodate the visitors. But the town was still overwhelmed. One account stated that fifteen thousand attended the first day and thirty thousand the second. It was reported that it was so crowded you couldn't get through the streets, and that it looked like Sherman's whole army had reassembled in Mt. Vernon. Old timers spoke of that time as "the day Sherman was here." They claimed there was never anything like it before or after. It may have been one of the largest crowds ever in Mt. Vernon!

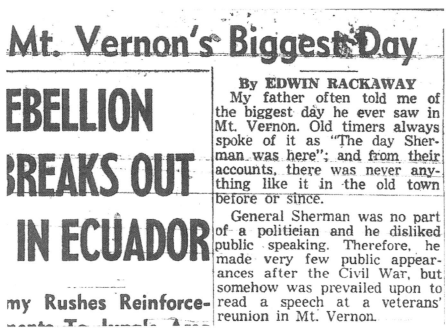

Mt. Vernon's Biggest Day Article

Mt. Vernon's Biggest Day

On the first day a large parade through the main streets of the city began at 10 o'clock. It consisted of four brass bands, the Governor's Guards, the 11th Regiment of General Pavey, and carriages with Governor Cullom, General Logan, and other notables. A large number of civilians followed on foot and horseback. Col. T. S. Casey gave a welcoming address that was followed by Governor Cullom's remarks. The governor spoke about the past military successes of the United States. The greatest applause came when he spoke about General Grant. At this point they took a two-hour break for lunch. General Sherman and his staff, and Senator Oglesby arrived on the noon train. They were greeted with booming cannon and were escorted by the Governor's Guard and part of the 11th Illinois National Guard to an informal reception at the Commercial Hotel/Johnson House, southwest corner of 11th and Main. This building, which was completed in 1854, was one of the largest in the area and had a banquet room and dance hall on the second floor. General Logan must have felt right at home since the hotel had a "Logan room" named after him because of his frequent visits.

Johnson House/Commercial Hotel

After dinner General Shields and then General Logan addressed the crowd. Shields, a veteran of the Mexican War, spoke of that war as well as the War of 1812 and the Indian Wars. He said he dreamed of the annexation of Mexico and hoped to live long enough to see it happen. (He died the next year in 1879.) General Logan spoke next. Logan was in a difficult situation. He had a long-running feud with General Sherman who was at the reunion, and although he wasn't saying so publicly, the word was out that he was aiming for the U.S. Senate seat of his old friend and rival Dick Oglesby who also was in the crowd. The jealousy between Logan and Oglesby had become so strong that Governor Cullom wrote that on one occasion, "Governor Oglesby sat silent and glowering when the audience applauded General Logan, and General Logan occupied the same attitude when the audience cheered Governor Oglesby."[125] Logan began by saying he would not make a political speech. General Sherman must have been amused. Sherman surely remembered another reunion twelve years earlier in Salem, Illinois, where he, Logan, and Oglesby spoke. On that occasion Logan and Oglesby had "waved the bloody shirt" as they gave very political speeches. Sherman telegraphed General Grant from Salem: "Attended here a large celebration but Logan and Oglesby spoke more politics than I think the national occasion warranted. I do not wish to be compromised by their speeches."[126]

Apparently Logan gave a great but rain-shortened speech. He received tremendous applause as he gave rousing praise to the common Civil War soldier and ended that section of the speech with this line: "… by the eternal God who reigns above, this government shall be one government, and the nation one people." He even praised General Sherman by saying that he and Grant had saved the Union and deserved much of the credit. According to the reporter Logan had the crowd so enthralled that they wouldn't let him stop even when the rain came. Finally the rain became so heavy that Logan had to stop. The first day ended with an evening reception by Governor Cullom at Stratton's Hall.[127]

On the second day an even larger crowd came to Casey's Grove. After opening ceremonies veterans of the Black Hawk, Florida, Mexican, and Civil Wars marched by the reviewing stand and shook hands with General Sherman and the others. Thirty-four regiments from Illinois, ten from Ohio, nine from Indiana, seven from Missouri, two from Iowa, and one each from Wisconsin, Tennessee, West Virginia, Kentucky, New York, and Virginia were represented. At this point Col. Casey introduced General Sherman. He was not a great speaker, but it didn't matter. *Mt. Vernon Register-News* Editor Edwin Rackaway's father was an eye-witness to this event and told his son about this special day. "My father often told me of the biggest day he ever saw in Mt. Vernon," Rackaway wrote. He further stated that, "When Sherman made his appearance, he was not greeted with cheers, but with a great savage roar. Bewhiskered old veterans cried like babies at the sight of Sherman." According to Rackaway, "the devotion of Sherman's men to their general bordered on the fanatical." The crowd enthusiastically applauded throughout Sherman's short speech. When he sat down, the silver cornet band struck up "Yankee Doodle."

Following Sherman's speech Senator Oglesby brought a lighter note with an address filled with jokes and witty remarks that was well received. After dinner General Sherman, Governor Cullom and others left on the 2:10 train. In the late afternoon General Logan again addressed the crowd. By 9:00 p.m. it was over. Certainly it was one of the most remarkable events in Mt. Vernon history.[128]

Edwin Rackaway

Frances E. Willard

Frances E. Willard (1839-1898) was another visitor in the 1870s. She was one of the founders of the Women's Christian Temperance Union (WCTU), which was the most important national organization working for temperance and women's rights in the Nineteenth Century. She was elected secretary of the WCTU in 1874 and traveled to small towns and cities organizing local chapters. That would account for her coming to Mt. Vernon. In 1879 she was elected president of the WCTU and broadened its goals to include women's rights, education reforms, and labor reforms. At that point she began another multiple-year tour of thousands of cities and towns to promote her goals.

Mt. Vernon's temperance movement began in the 1830s with Zadok Casey and Rev. John Johnson heading the organization. In the 1840s and 1850s a second temperance movement—The Sons of Temperance and the Order of Good Templars was led by Judge Scates, H. T. Pace, James Kirby, and others. Divisions in the organization and the Civil War ended these movements until the new temperance reformers started the local WCTU in the 1870s.

In the winter of 1878–79 local temperance supporters brought Frances Willard to Mt. Vernon to help the movement. Willard had just lost her brother, Oliver, in March of 1878. But she and others spoke in town and brought enthusiasm to a high point. Then in May of 1879 she came back to Mt. Vernon to organize a local chapter of the WCTU. This was done by her assistant, Mrs. Anderson, on May 22, 1879, along with many local women. Many Mt. Vernonites wore blue ribbons symbolizing their support for the anti-drinking crusade, and Mt. Vernon was voted dry for about ten years.[129]

Shelby Cullom

Shelby Cullom (1829–1914), the governor of Illinois from 1877 to 1883, was in Jefferson County in 1878 before his August visit to the soldiers' reunion. This was reported in a letter from Louis Davison to the *Mt. Vernon Register-News* in October of 1920. Davison, who was a Mt. Vernon journalist in the 1870s, told the following story. In 1876 he was offered control of the *Mt. Vernon Free Press* by R.A.D. Wilbanks, who was then the clerk of the Southern Grand Division of the Supreme Court (now the Appellate Court). Wilbanks had been elected as a Democrat but by 1874 had joined the Greenback Party and wanted a local newspaper to support that party. The *Free Press* with Davison as editor did support the Greenbackers, and they elected a number of local and state officials.

By 1878 Wilbanks wanted to return to the Democratic Party but was bitterly opposed by some in the party who considered him a traitor. Davison wrote: "I desired to support Mr. Wilbanks, but my paper espousing the Greenback Party, I concluded it was not policy to do so." Therefore, he sold the paper to two staunch Democrats.[130] According to Davison, "I went to the Supreme Court house and handed Mr. Wilbanks the notes and money. Chief Justice Sidney Breese and Senator Shelby Cullom were in the office at that time." So Cullom was in town. But there is no information as to why the governor of Illinois was visiting the Supreme Court in Mt. Vernon in 1878.[131]

CHAPTER IV

The 1880s and 1890s

The 1880s and 1890s brought many changes to the United States that were reflected in Jefferson County. The country was about evenly divided between Democrats and Republicans with Jefferson County remaining a mainly Democratic Party stronghold. However, the Republicans were extremely competitive and brought many political leaders to the area to campaign. Also, many "third party" candidates representing farmers and laborers, such as the "greenbackers," the "silverites," and the "populists," came to the county during this time. In foreign policy the U.S. emerged as a world power after the Spanish-American War in 1898, and debated the effects of becoming an imperialist nation. This development also brought local consequences.

Economically the U.S. was being transformed by the twin forces of industrialization, and urbanization. Industrial tycoons such as John D. Rockefeller and Andrew Carnegie became extremely wealthy and famous in this "Gilded Age." Workers were having trouble, and some turned to labor unions. Big strikes in the mines, factories, and railroads brought violence and calls for reform. Many reformers came to the region calling for lower tariffs and using silver as well as gold to back up government-issued paper money. This became a huge issue reaching a high point with the election of 1896.

In the social/cultural area the U.S. saw an end to the "frontier," continued to deal with the "race issue," and developed national sports and entertainment trends. As if to illustrate the end of the frontier, the people of Jefferson County saw "Indians" brought through the county on the way to new homes in Florida. Nationally-known Wild West shows and circuses glorified the Old West and brought exotic animals and acts to the county. Mt. Vernon built an opera house that brought in nationally-known entertainers. Mt. Vernon also built a baseball park that was visited by professional teams. As you would expect, Jefferson County participated in all of the trends that affected the whole country.

Robert G. Ingersoll

In the 1880s a number of well-known people came to Mt. Vernon. Jefferson County's old friend, Bob Ingersoll, came back in November of 1882. He was making a living practicing law and lecturing on political and religious topics around the country. On November 27, 1882, he gave a lecture in Springfield, Illinois, and on November 28, 1882, he was at the Opera House in Evansville, Indiana. Somewhere between these dates, he traveled through Mt. Vernon.[132] Here is the comment from the December 8, 1882, *Mt. Vernon News*: "Bob Ingersoll passed through this city on the train yesterday on his way to Evansville where he delivered one of his famous lectures last evening to a crowded house at one dollar and a half a head. The 'wages of sin is death' it is said, but Bob's wages are about a thousand dollars a day for a couple of hours' work in getting off a lecture to prove that it is not true."

Many years later another writer speculated about Ingersoll's thoughts as he traveled through the town where he once lived and worked. This author wrote, "Curious thoughts peeped out of the crannies of his memory, no doubt, in passing thro' this town, where his father used to live and preach the orthodox faith from a Presbyterian standpoint; and the Old Seminary building (located at 8th and Jordan), where Bob himself used to teach school, in plain view from the car windows, must have opened out a vista that will keep him thinking for a long time."[133]

Political Visitors

On October 10, 1883, Governor Richard Oglesby came to the Jefferson County Fair (located in East Mt. Vernon in those days). He had been in the United States Senate until 1879 and was preparing to run for governor again. The fair with its guaranteed large crowd was a big attraction for all politicians.[134]

The 1884 Mt. Vernon Fair brought a number of political figures to Jefferson County. On October 17, 1884, General F. W. Palmer was the featured speaker. He was a Civil War general, editor of the *Dubuque Times*, and a member of the United States House of Representatives. The ad for the fair states: "As the campaign is nearing a close, and as Gen. Palmer is one of the ablest speakers in the state, the Republicans of Jefferson County should turn out en masse to hear him. Come in wagons; come on horseback; come in clubs; come with your wives and children; come on foot, and let us have a grand, enthusiastic meeting."[135]

On October 21, 1884, Illinois Governor John M. Hamilton came to Mt. Vernon.[136] After a procession through the main streets of the city headed by Governor Hamilton and the Fairfield Band the governor gave a two-hour speech at the fairgrounds. Hamilton was a soldier in the Civil War, was a teacher and attorney, and was a member of the Illinois State Senate in 1876. In 1880 he was elected lieutenant governor, and when the legislature chose Governor Cullom as U.S. senator, he became governor. He served from 1883 to 1885.

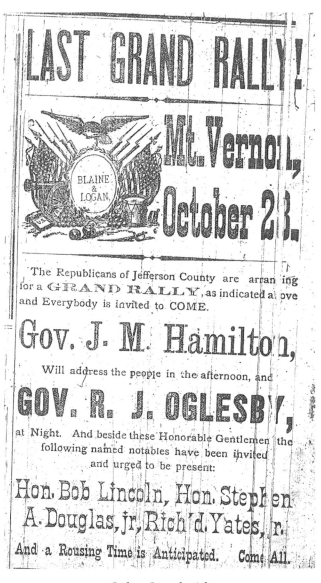

Robert Lincoln Ad

Robert Lincoln and Stephen A. Douglas, Jr.

It was announced on October 15, 1884, that Governor Oglesby, Governor Hamilton, Robert Lincoln, and Stephen A. Douglas would be in Jefferson County on October 28, 1884.[137] If all of these men had actually come, it would have been a special occasion—not so much because of the two governors but because of the two sons of very famous men. Stephen A. Douglas, Jr. was the second son of Stephen A. Douglas, Sr., the U.S. senator and presidential candidate from Illinois who died in 1861. Robert Lincoln was the first son of President Abraham Lincoln and was at the time of his possible visit serving as secretary of war under President Arthur. Many thought he could have been president if he had been ambitious for the office. How strange that Douglas could have been in the county with the three Republicans since his father debated against Republican Lincoln in 1858 and ran against him for president in 1860. The October 29 *Mt. Vernon Register* confirmed the October 21 visit of Governor Hamilton, but no other local newspapers exist to determine whether Oglesby, Hamilton, Lincoln, and Douglas were in Mt. Vernon on October 28, 1884.

The Orphan Trains

The Orphan Trains

Mt. Vernon had some very special visitors on March 26, 1885. They were not famous individually so far as is known. But as a group they were part of a famous historical movement—the "orphan trains." From 1854 to 1929 various eastern orphan societies sent over 150,000 children to the West in hopes that they would find good homes. In some cases it worked very well; two of the children grew up to be the governors of South Dakota and Alaska. And in other cases it didn't work out at all; one orphan train child named Charley Miller shot two boys in Wyoming.[138] One of the organizations bringing children west was the New York Juvenile Asylum. They brought fifteen children, mostly boys, to Mt. Vernon at the Commercial Hotel (located at the southwest corner of 11th and Main) for one day only. Those families interested in providing "kind treatment and fair advantages" could take the children on trial for several weeks. If all parties were satisfied, the children would be "indentured" until they came of age. No follow-up articles indicated if any of the children were taken in by families in Mt. Vernon.[139]

Apaches and Other Indians

In the 1880s the U.S. began moving Western Indians to new homes in Florida. One group came through Mt. Vernon in June of 1884. The June 7th, 1884, *Mt. Vernon Register* reported that "Four car loads of Indian prisoners en route to Florida stopped here for an hour." About September 15, 1886, a group of Apache Indians, one of the most famous and fierce tribes of the West, were reluctant visitors in Mt. Vernon. At 2:30 p.m. on a Friday on an L. & N. special train about 460 Warm Springs and Chiricahua Apache prisoners of war guarded by three companies of United States troops arrived in town. They were being taken to Florida as part of a government plan to pacify the Arizona/New Mexico area.

The Apaches had been fighting U.S. and Mexican troops and raiding civilian ranches and farms for years. Some Apache leaders such as Geronimo, Natchez, Mangus, Chihuahua, and Ulzana became well known not only for their courage but also for their vicious attacks in 1885 and 1886. First General Crook and then General Miles used as many as five thousand U.S. troops to try to capture them. On April 7, 1886, Geronimo's wives and family were sent to Fort Marion, Florida. This was done in hopes that it would cause Geronimo to surrender. It worked. His final surrender was on September 8, 1886. The United States government then decided to send all of the Apaches on the reservation as well as Geronimo and his band to Florida. Geronimo, Natchez, and their men were sent to Florida by a southern route on a special train of three cars. The Apaches on the reservation were sent to Florida via Kansas City, St. Louis, and Atlanta.[140] This was the group that came through Mt. Vernon.

THE INDIAN PRISONERS

Pass Through Mount Vernon on their Way South.

Last Friday, at 2:30 p. m., the L. & N. special train, containing about 460 Warm Spring and Chihuahua Indians, prisoners of war, in charge of three companies of United States troops en route for Florida, arrived in this city. It was known that they would be transferred at this point to the Louisville & Nashville Southern Division coaches, and a crowd of about 2,000 pale faces flocked to the depot. The public school was dismissed and nearly 700 scholars and teachers viewed the curiosities during their transfer. The Indians were good humored and well behaved, with a few exceptions, and not a few strings of beads were sold by the Indian girls to persons in this city. One old white-haired woman was quite a curiosity. The only time the Indians deigned to smile was when they re-

Apache Article

When the train stopped in Mt. Vernon to transfer the Indians and troops to L. & N. Southern Division coaches, a "crowd of about 2,000 palefaces flocked to the depot." According to the *Mt. Vernon Weekly Register*, "The public school was dismissed and nearly 700 scholars and teachers viewed the curiosities during their transfer." The Indians were described as "good humored and well behaved with a few exceptions." They sold strings of beads to people in the crowd.[141] Although Geronimo and Natchez were not on the train, the *St. Louis Globe-Democrat* reported, "… a number of hardly less famous braves are in this band, and will, no doubt, draw a crowd."[142] They certainly did just that in Mt. Vernon. The articles do not name the other famous braves in the group that came through Mt. Vernon. They could have been Chiefs Loco and Nana of the Warm Springs Apaches, Mangus (son of Mangus Colorado), Ulzana (famous for the movie "Ulzana's Raid"), or Chatto (the Apache scout who helped persuade Geronimo to surrender).

R. W. Townshend

An article in the *Mt. Vernon Register* from October 27, 1886, tells of a speech at the courthouse by Congressman R. W. Townshend. It tells of a sad scene where only a few, unenthusiastic people showed up, leaving the gallery as play room for a half dozen youths. The writer contrasts this scene with an earlier visit on September 29, 1884, when Townshend also spoke at the courthouse. He wrote that, "On that evening he was met at the hotel and escorted to the Court House by a large number of admiring political friends, carrying with them a fine silk banner, upon which was inscribed 'Townshend Guards'." The reporter explained that the crowd filled the court room "both floor and gallery," and that the audience was so enthusiastic the "very joists and rafters" of the courthouse trembled. The article doesn't tell why there was such a big difference in reception. Perhaps it was an attempt to say that Townshend had so disappointed the people that the other candidate should be elected.[143]

Sketch of Jeff. Co. Courthouse 1871–1888

Belva Lockwood

Sometime before July 13, 1887, noted feminist Belva Lockwood came to Mt. Vernon. In 1880 she became the first female attorney to argue a case before the United States Supreme Court. In 1884 she became the second woman (after Victoria Woodhull) to run for president of the United States. She ran again in 1888 as the candidate of the National Equal Rights Party. She was also an active member of the National American Woman Suffrage Association. The article in the *Mt. Vernon Weekly Register,* which mentioned that she had appeared in Jefferson County, was about Mrs. Lockwood being sued for debt in her home town, Washington, D.C. The article made the editorial comment that "Belva should pay her debts." The article did not give an exact date but stated she "will be remembered as having once lectured in this city." It had to be before the July 13, 1887, date of the newspaper. It could have been in 1884 when she ran for president. Or, it could have been a lecture about women's rights anytime during the 1880–1886 years. During that time she had a contract with the Slayton Lyceum of Chicago, which provided speakers for local community groups.[144]

The Fourth Annual Veterans' Reunion

The Fourth Annual Reunion of Southern Illinois Veterans was held in Mt. Vernon over three days starting the week before September 21, 1887. The event was held at the fairgrounds and brought approximately fifteen thousand people, a huge crowd for a town of about four thousand. Downtown businesses and many residences were decorated with welcome signs while large streamers hung at each corner of the square. The entrance to the fairgrounds had large arches with a life-size oil painting of George Washington and a sign that read: "Come in boys, and get some bacon and beans." On the grounds were over two hundred veterans' tents, fifty family tents, and the "headquarters of the Ladies Relief Corps of the Coleman Post of this city...." In spite of rain on the second day the veterans stayed up late giving short speeches, singing, and talking about old times. An "old fashioned campfire" at the speakers' stand and "the latest improved gasoline lamps" made it "as light as day" for the old soldiers.[145]

The reunion brought many important people as speakers. United States Senator Charles B. Farwell was part of the celebration. He was a former member of the U.S. House of Representatives who was elected to the Senate to fill the vacancy caused by the death of John A. Logan in 1886. Ex-Governor John M. Hamilton was also in town. He was Illinois governor from 1883 to 1885. Like so many of the speakers, he praised the soldiers and in particular defended soldiers' reunions against charges of "waving the bloody shirt." He said: "There came no cry of protestation 'you are doing wrong,' when Jeff Davis planted the corner stone at Montgomery, Alabama." State senator and future Illinois governor, Joseph W. Fifer, was another important speaker. He served as governor from 1889 to1893. He seconded the previous speakers' praise of the recently departed John A. Logan, but said, "We stand too near to him as yet to properly estimate or measure his virtues." In addition to these public figures in attendance were Illinois Secretary of State Henry Dement,[146] Illinois Attorney General George Hunt, U.S. Representative Jehu Baker, and Illinois Speaker of the House W. F. Calhoun. So it must have been quite a grand affair.

The Mt. Vernon Cyclone

On February 19, 1888, one of the worst events in Mt. Vernon history occurred when a cyclone (or tornado) devastated the city. It traveled from southwest to northeast right through the heart of Mt. Vernon—killing over thirty people, injuring hundreds, and destroying about three hundred homes and four hundred buildings (including the Jefferson County Courthouse).[147] It was such a huge blow to the city that people talked about it at almost every social gathering for the next thirty years. Each person in turn would tell his or her own personal experience. It was considered impolite to interrupt, even if you had heard the same stories many times before.

Stories about the cyclone in Mt. Vernon were even published in the *New York Times*. The first story reported that the cyclone struck about five o'clock and "swept away houses like cardboard...." The second story described Mt. Vernon as a "beautiful little city of 4,000 inhabitants. Its streets were broad, illuminated by electricity, and were lined with shade trees. Its residences were trim, homelike, and many of them artistically constructed. Its business blocks were of substantial brick and stone, and its Court House was the pride of the County." The article then went on to describe the scene of destruction after the tornado struck: "Today Mt. Vernon is a waste, where death and ruin stalk unchallenged. Two thirds of the town have been blotted out completely. Its broad streets are filled with shattered brick and shivered timbers."

The *New York Times* article further quotes a J. W. Wallace of the Southern Express Company who saw the tornado firsthand. He said: "I turned and looked toward the southwest, and saw a fearful black cloud coming up. It was shaped like a large funnel or inverted cone, and could be plainly seen revolving around an imaginary axis, while at the same time it had a bounding motion, up and down, through the air. As it approached it grew denser, and the blackness was appalling. As the cloud would dip down and rise again, it would carry trees upward into the air and throw them to the ground with mighty force a hundred yards away. The sight at this juncture was one which would make the bravest pale with fear. Parts of roofs, trees, boards, bricks...and all kinds of debris were flying through the air at a fearful rate.... Women and children were carried along at the mercy of the savage wind, and their screams for help were heard above the noise of the storm."[148]

Southeast Corner of the Square

Clara Barton

On March 5, 1888, one of the best-known people of the time, Clara Barton, arrived in Mt. Vernon to help. She was invited to the town by the local relief committee, Illinois Governor Oglesby, and Congressman R. W. Townshend. However, according to Morris Emmerson of the relief committee, it "required not only an appeal from U.S. senators and congressmen, but the president (Cleveland), himself, to finally induce her to visit the scene." At this time she was founder and president of the American Red Cross, but gained fame first in the 1860s during the Civil War as the "angel of the battlefield" for organizing female nurses to tend to the wounded soldiers. According to the *Mt. Vernon Register*, "Miss Barton is known, well known, by many of the principal rulers of the world, and while many of us had read of her, still we never knew her as now. Now she is our friend."[149]

The sixty-six year old Barton arrived in Mt. Vernon at three in the morning and walked through the streets with a lantern to appraise the damage. She helped organize the relief work, used the Supreme Court building (now the Appellate Court) as a temporary hospital, helped gather homeless children to be taught in vacant rooms around town, and probably most important of all issued a call for help to the entire country. An appeal had already been sent but, according to Barton, had failed because of "unfortunate press representation." Morris Emmerson of the relief committee said: "She handled the telegraph instruments in the L. & N. railroad office herself, sending out the message calling for help." Her telegram over the press-service wires stated: "The pitiless snow is falling on the heads of people who are without homes, without food or clothing and without money."[150]

On March 6, 1888, Barton wrote a letter to a friend in which she stated: "I scarcely know what to tell you of the place, for there isn't much left to tell about. I have never seen more complete destruction. Nothing lived a second in the track of the storm; the wonder is that any persons escaped alive. There is one space of 60 acres—as large as Boston Common—which was entirely covered with small cottages of workingmen, mainly railroad employees, on which not a corner of a house is left upright; it is as flat as a potato patch." She confessed that she felt incompetent to take care of the situation. She wrote: "I am almost frightened to see what reliance they place upon me. I surely cannot do as much for them as they think I can." She said Chicago ought to raise the money needed to help by itself but was unlikely to do so. She further wrote: "There is a danger that this little suffering town will be forgotten, and I don't know if I can keep it alive...." However, she ended on a positive note by saying: "I shall try, with my pen...."[151]

She used her pen to write a personal note to Robert G. Ingersoll on March 7, 1888, asking for his help. She wrote later that she wanted him to know "how warmly and hopefully he is turned to, by his old friends." She said that she told him many people in Mt. Vernon suggested: "If Col. Ingersoll could only give one of his masterly lectures for our benefit." Apparently unknown to her, he had already sent a check for fifty dollars on March 2 with a note that read: "I enclose you a check for a small amount, hoping that it may relieve the immediate wants of some sufferer. I remember the old town with pleasure, and although many of my friends have long ago fallen asleep, my sympathies are with you."[152] Her pen was a tremendous success, and by the end of her two week stay in Mt. Vernon she handed over ninety thousand dollars to the relief committee.

The late 1880s was an eventful time for Clara Barton. In 1887 she had gone to Central Texas to help people suffering from a severe drought. Then she came to help Mt. Vernon residents in March of 1888. There were many everyday matters for her to deal with. About this time she wrote to her niece, Mamie, "Then just think what a washing there was on hand; had never had time to have a full wash done since our return from Mt. Vernon ... and all ironed yesterday, and clothes put away this very minute, and I ... am just dropped down ..." Shortly after leaving Jefferson County she learned of a personal tragedy. On March 15, 1888, her brother, David Barton, died possibly by his own hand. Barton wrote: "I have no words! It is all so dreadful, so shocking, so pitiful. To what misery he must have been driven."[153] In August of 1888 she visited Jacksonville, Florida, to help yellow fever victims. Finally on

May 31, 1889, in what became the most celebrated effort in the early history of the Red Cross, she arrived in Pennsylvania to tend to the needs of the victims of the famous Johnstown Flood.

Congressmen Marshall and Mills

Also in March of 1888, former United States Congressman Samuel S. Marshall (1821–1890) came to Mt. Vernon. Marshall, an attorney from McLeansboro, Illinois, was a member of the state legislature in the 1840s and a circuit court judge in the 1850s and 1860s. He was a member of the U.S. House of Representatives from 1855 to 1859 and from 1865 to 1875. He was the Democratic Party candidate for speaker of the U.S. House in 1867, and if he had not been defeated for re-election in 1874, may have been chosen speaker in 1875. Marshall was in Mt. Vernon as chairman of the Democratic State Supreme Court convention. The convention lasted three days, and was held in the Presbyterian Church at 14th and Main since the Appellate Court was still being used for the tornado victims.[154]

A very important figure, Congressman Roger Q. Mills, came to Mt. Vernon on October 10, 1888, as part of the presidential campaign between Democrat Grover Cleveland and Republican Benjamin Harrison. Mills, a Democrat and former confederate from Texas, was a United States congressman from 1873 to 1892 and a U.S. senator from 1892 to 1898. He led the fight for the Mills bill, which would have lowered tariffs on certain items. Republicans opposed this vehemently and the tariff became the main issue in the presidential race in 1888.

Mills arrived by train from St. Louis and was escorted down Main Street to the fairgrounds by the Independent Silver Band, 151 wagons and buggies, and seventy-five men on horseback. The fairgrounds gate keeper reported over six hundred wagons and buggies entered altogether and the crowd was estimated at five thousand. There were decorations around the square, glee clubs singing, and fireworks "probably never equaled in this city before." But the *Mt. Vernon Register*, a Republican newspaper, couldn't resist making some negative comments such as: "...fireworks do not convert voters.", "There was about as much hurrahing on the streets for Harrison as for Cleveland.", "One man ... could not refrain from hurrahing for Jeff Davis.", "He (Mills) falsified the Republican position at the outset....", and "The rally was a success in every particular save that it failed in having a good speaker."[155]

The Ringling Brothers Circus

In 1889 the circus came to Mt. Vernon—August 7 to be exact.[156] It was not the first time a circus came to Jefferson County; they had been coming at least since the 1840s. But this one was the Ringling Brothers and Van Amburgh Circus, which meant the famous Ringling brothers were in town. They didn't just own the circus but actually traveled with it and performed different duties. There were five brothers—Albert, Alfred, Charles, John, and Otto. One brother was the business manager; one was the production supervisor. Al Ringling was the ringmaster from 1884 to 1909 and 1911 to 1915. John Ringling was in charge of publicity and was the advance man who traveled ahead to the towns the circus was to visit. He put up posters, placed ads in the local papers, did interviews with local newspaper editors, and checked out the streets and locations the circus would use. By the mid-1920s John was the only surviving brother; he became the sole owner of the circus, moved its winter quarters to Sarasota, Florida, and became one of the richest men in the world.

Ringling Bros. and Van Amburgh's

UNITED MONSTER CIRCUS,

MUSEUM AND MENAGERIE,

Roman Hippodrome and Universal World's Exposition

WILL EXHIBIT AT

Mt. Vernon, Wednesday, August 7th.

A SOLID FACT! A SUBSTANTIAL REALITY! A GREAT SHOW!

A Grand Triple Circus Given by Three Distinct Companies of Autocratic Champions.

A Complete and Comprehensive Double Menagerie of Wild Beasts.

A COLOSSAL CARAVAN.

Mammoth Moral Museum of Living Wonders.

250 LORDLY THOROUGHBRED HORSES. 250

Imposing Assemblage of Royal Japanese Performers.

A Ponderous Herd of Performing Elephants,

Including Babylon, the Largest Elephant in the World; Fanny, the only American born Elephant; Jewel, the wonderful Umbrella-eared Elephant, the only one of this remarkable species in captivity; Spot, Lilliputian Clown, Elephant.

Ringling Brothers Circus Ad

Many circuses had a bad reputation in the late Nineteenth Century as pickpockets "worked" the crowds, and rigged games of chance separated the local "suckers" from their money. Although he may not have said it, P. T. Barnum was reported to have said, "There is a sucker born every minute." It was so bad that many circuses had to change their names before going back to a town that had been cheated the previous season. But the Ringling Brothers ran a clean circus. They discouraged pickpockets, banned rigged games, and charged fair prices. In 1889 admission was fifty cents for adults and twenty-five cents for children. As a result the Ringling Brothers Circus was welcomed back to Mt. Vernon many times—1889, 1893, 1912, etc.

Supreme Court Visitors

In the 1880s the Supreme Court was still being held in Mt. Vernon from time to time, and well-known attorneys were drawn to town as a result. Gustavus Koerner continued to have cases at the court in the eighties.[157] Lyman Trumbull and Walter B. Scates were at the court on November 15, 1883, to file a case about the Mt. Vernon Railroad.[158] John M. Palmer may have been at the Supreme Court on June 13, 1885.[159] John Breese Hay, a member of the United States House of Representatives from 1869 to 1873, was at the court on a number of occasions in the eighties.[160]

John M. Palmer

The first notable visitor of the 1890s was ex-Governor John M. Palmer. He had been in Jefferson County in 1868 running for governor as a Republican. Now he was in the county for his United States Senate campaign running as a Democrat. He switched political parties throughout his career. He started as a Democrat, became a Republican, and then joined the Liberal Republicans. Next he became a Democrat again and finally allied with the Gold Democrats. He won the Senate seat in 1890, but rather than run for re-election he decided to run for president on the Gold Democratic ticket in 1896.

When Palmer came to Mt. Vernon in August of 1890, the local newspaper reported that the Democrats promised thousands would come in carriages and wagons, on horseback, and by special trains. They had secured the fairgrounds and hired the "best band in Southern Illinois" for the event. But when they found out that crowds would not be large, they moved the meeting to the Opera House, which could seat eight hundred. Later they decided this building also would be too big for the small group. Therefore, they "hastily arranged" a platform on the north side of the courthouse. They estimated the crowd at no more than five hundred. The newspaper reported that Palmer gave his "stereotyped speech for the campaign, varying very little to suit the locality." They suggested the small turnout resulted from Palmer starting his campaign too early and foolishly basing it on lowering the United States tariff. Despite this possibly poor political event, Palmer went on to win the race and became one of Illinois' U.S. senators from 1890 to1896.[161]

Frank W. Gunsalus

On February 26, 1891, Dr. Frank W. Gunsalus (1856–1921) came to Mt. Vernon as part of the lyceum lecture program. Gunsalus was a minister of the Plymouth Congregational Church in Chicago and one of the great orators of the period. He was part of the social gospel movement of the time and urged his church members to support public education for all people. He particularly wanted the wealthy men of Chicago such as George Pullman, Marshall Field, and Philip Armour to take responsibility for helping the poor. In 1890 with Philip Armour in the congregation Gunsalus gave his famous "Million Dollar Sermon." The theme of the sermon was that if he had a million dollars, he would start a school to help children prepare for work in the new industrial age. After the talk Philip Armour offered money to start a trade school, and the Armour Institute of Technology (now called the Illinois Institute of Technology) was established in 1893.

Myers Music Hall

Dr. Gunsalus gave his lecture at the Music Hall, probably Myers Music Hall at 122 N. 10th St. in Mt. Vernon. There is no record of the subject of the speech. But his favorite lecture titles included: "A Chapter in the History of Liberty", "The Later Eloquence of Puritanism", "Rembrandt as an Interpreter of the Gospel", and "The Next Step in Education." Since it was during this period when Gunsalus was about to be named president of the Armour Institute, it seems likely that his subject was education. Others on the lyceum program for the year 1891 were Dr. Joseph Cook, an Anglican missionary to the Cheyenne Indians in 1868–1869, and Roswell G. Horr, a journalist and member of Congress.[162]

John P. St. John

The next person of note to come to Jefferson County was ex-Governor John P. St. John of Kansas. When Governor St. John was in the Kansas State Senate, he helped create the Kansas Freedmen's Relief Association to help blacks who came to Kansas in the Great Exodus of 1879. He was very active in the temperance movement and helped pass a prohibition amendment to the Kansas Constitution. He served as governor from 1879 to 1883, and then he ran for president on the Prohibition Party ticket in 1884.

He came to Mt. Vernon on June 11, 1891, to speak on the prohibition issue. He spoke at the courthouse and according to the *Mt. Vernon Register*: "The Court room was crowded, every seat was filled, the aisles and entrances were packed with suffocating humanity and many were unable to gain admittance." He attacked both Democrats and Republicans, and President Harrison in particular—asserting that only the Prohibition Party could bring an end to the evil of liquor.[163]

Jeff. Co. Courthouse

Jehu Baker

July 4th, 1891, brought important speakers for the celebration. Jehu Baker (1822–1903) was a United States representative from Belleville, Illinois. Baker was first in Jefferson County on October 20, 1858, campaigning for Congress. He was also in the county in September of 1887 as a featured speaker at the Fourth Annual Reunion of Southern Illinois Veterans. At that time the reporter described him as follows: "Mr. Baker is possessed of a great big brain, well developed and trained in deep thought and learning." In addition to his time in Congress, he was U.S. minister to Venezuela from 1878 to 1885. Another featured speaker was Chauncey S. Conger, a judge and member of the state legislature from Carmi, Illinois. Conger's brother, Everton, was in command of the troops that captured and killed John Wilkes Booth after the assassination of President Lincoln in 1865.

Ten thousand people came to the celebration that was held at the fairgrounds on a hot, dusty Saturday. The Independent Silver Band played; a choir sang "America." And Judge Conger gave the morning address, which was described as "very pleasing." The afternoon address by Representative Baker was also "received with great enthusiasm," but the reporter noted that he "constantly referred to some notes that had been jotted down during the hour of adjournment...." The reporter also wrote that just as the crowd expected Baker to "launch out upon something new, the gentleman sat down." Maybe his big brain failed him on this occasion![164]

James B. Weaver

Another presidential candidate was in Mt. Vernon on October 12, 1892. He was James B. Weaver (1833–1912), the Populist Party candidate for president. Weaver was a former Civil War general and

Republican member of the U.S. House of Representatives from Iowa. He became upset with the Republican Party during the Grant Administration, feeling that it was controlled by big business interests. He joined the Greenback Party—which advocated a silver-and-gold-based currency, an eight-hour work day, and a graduated income tax. He was elected to the U.S. House of Representatives as a Greenbacker in 1878 and ran for president of the United States on the Greenback ticket in 1880. After the Greenback Party merged with the Democrats, he helped found the Populist (People's) Party in 1891. In 1892 he ran for president as the Populist Party candidate and had one of the best outcomes of any third-party candidate in United States history, receiving over a million popular votes and winning four states with 22 electoral votes.

The *Mt. Vernon Register* of October 19, 1892, described the political event under the headline "the People's Party Day." Some three thousand to five thousand people were in town to see General Weaver. In addition the Spring Garden Band, the Independent Silver Band, and a drum corps from Marion County were part of the event. Weaver told about his campaign tour from its start in Denver until it reached Mt. Vernon. He predicted success for the Populists that he said would bring the "greatest political revolution ever witnessed." He claimed that God and the people were on his side. The *Register* article disagreed, stating that the farmers were doing well as shown by their fine clothes and carriages. Still, the article reported that "his remarks were well received with great enthusiasm, and he was given a grand reception at the close by almost every man, woman, and child in the audience marching by the stand and shaking hands with he and Mrs. Weaver."[165]

Coxey's Army

On June 12, 1894, part of Coxey's Army moved through Mt. Vernon. The Panic of 1893 had hit the country; it was the worst economic depression the United States had faced up to that time. Millions were affected by the crisis with farmers losing their land and workers losing their jobs. A populist named Jacob Coxey organized the first important "march on Washington" in our history. His purpose was to pressure the U.S. government to create jobs for the unemployed by starting huge road building and other public works projects. The government at that time was very much influenced by business interests and supported the high protective tariff, the gold standard, and a laissez-faire economic philosophy. As a result Coxey didn't really have a chance for success. He was arrested and his movement died. But it certainly caused a big uproar.

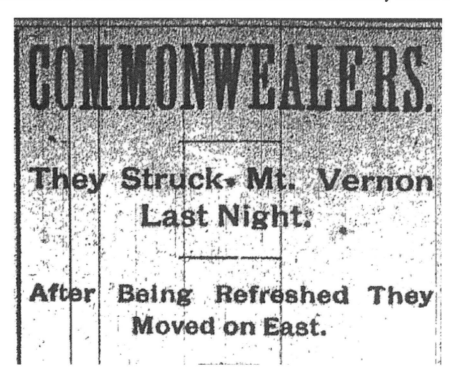

Commonwealers Article

The men who came to Mt. Vernon were mostly from California. They were called "Commonwealers" after their official name, "Commonweal in Christ." The name "Coxey's Army" (taken from their main leader Jacob Coxey) stuck, and that is the name used in most history books. There were one hundred fifty men, and they rode the Air Line (later known as the Southern Railway with depot located on east Main Street)

Air Line Depot

freight train from Dix to Mt. Vernon. A telegram had warned of their arrival and hundreds of people came to the depot to watch. When the train arrived, the men climbed down from the top of the box cars and formed a line to march into Mt. Vernon. However, the newspaper reported that "Policemen England and Jordan were on the scene with a large number of sworn deputies and at once informed the commander that they would not be permitted to come down town." They were allowed to camp at the fairgrounds as long as they made themselves "scarce" the next morning. After an informal meeting of the mayor, city council, sheriff, police chief, and state's attorney at Ed McClure's store it was decided to provide them with food and coffee "rather than let the army scatter over town on a begging tour." Clearly the arrival of one hundred fifty unemployed men in the form of an "army" worried local officials, but the newspaper reported that most of "these men were very polite and gentlemanly."[166]

The next morning Coxey's Army moved on to McLeansboro where they were also feared by the townspeople. They armed themselves, closed down the businesses, and "some people began putting up barricades and laying in supplies against the possibility of a long siege." But the army just camped overnight in a field on the outskirts of town. The next day they rubbed soap on the rails of the L. & N. When the train came to a halt, the men jumped on board and continued their journey to Washington D.C.[167]

Clark E. Carr

October of 1894 brought many important figures to Mt. Vernon. On October 5, 1894, Clark E. Carr, ex-minister to Denmark was in town. Carr had a varied career. He was an aide to Governor Yates during the Civil War and accompanied him and Senator Kellogg of Louisiana to California in 1869 on the new transcontinental railroad. Descending the Rockies into Salt Lake City, Carr was persuaded to sit on the "cow catcher" to see the view. But contrary to his expectations the train traveled at "breakneck" speed, and the young Carr feared for his life. Later he learned that Governor Yates, under the influence of alcohol, had bribed the engineer to go much faster than normal. Clark survived the trip in spite of Governor Yates's jokes and went on to become a lawyer, editor, and ambassador. Carl Sandburg, who was at one time his newspaper boy in Galesburg, Illinois, called him "the most roly-poly fat man in town." President Benjamin Harrison appointed him ambassador to Denmark, a position he held from 1889 to 1893.[168]

Franklin MacVeagh

On October 16, 1894, Franklin MacVeagh, the Democratic nominee for the U.S. Senate, campaigned in Mt. Vernon. He had made millions as a grocer, lawyer, and banker. At a later date (1909) he was named secretary of the treasury by President William Howard Taft. As treasury secretary he made a number of reforms and incidentally was involved in the creation of the buffalo nickel.

MacVeagh's Mt. Vernon campaign event was held at the Opera House (now 124 North Tenth Street). Although the Mt. Vernon Band played and MacVeagh was a scholarly man, he evidently was not much of a speaker. The *Mt. Vernon Register*, although obviously biased against Democrats, said the campaign "played a one-act comedy, with $$$Franklin MacVeagh, the Democratic nominee for U.S. Senator, as the star...." (The dollar signs were apparently to remind the readers of his wealth and were repeated throughout the article.) As usual in those days the tariff was a big issue. When MacVeagh asserted that the Democrats' lower tariff helped raise wages for the working man, he was interrupted by "someone in the audience" who wanted to know how wages in the Mt. Vernon car shops compared with those paid two years ago. Similarly, when MacVeagh said the lower tariff helped lower prices for the consumer, he was interrupted by a "commercial traveler in the audience" who demanded to know three common articles that had become cheaper. These questions from the audience may have been placed there by the opposing party. Political tricks have been going on for a long time. So the event in Mt. Vernon was apparently not a success, and MacVeagh was defeated in the election.[169]

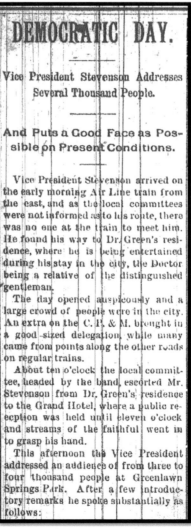

Stevenson Article

Adlai E. Stevenson

A very high ranking person with a very well-known name came to town on October 23-24, 1894. Adlai E. Stevenson (1835–1914), who was then serving as vice president of the United States in the Grover Cleveland administration, made a campaign swing through Mt. Vernon. Stevenson, an attorney, served as assistant postmaster general in the first Cleveland administration in 1885. In 1892 the Democrats nominated Stevenson, a free silver advocate and former "greenbacker" to balance the ticket with the gold standard supporter, Cleveland. He served as vice president from 1893 to 1897, and unknown to him, could have become president in 1893 when President Cleveland was secretly operated on to remove cancer of the mouth. Cleveland feared that the possibility of Stevenson becoming president would cause gold to be hoarded, shake the financial markets, and make the depression worse. Thankfully the surgery was successful and the few who knew of it kept it a secret for the next twenty-five years. Stevenson's son, Lewis, was Illinois secretary of state (1914–17); his grandson, Adlai Stevenson II, was Illinois governor (1948–52) and Democratic presidential candidate in 1952 and 1956; his great grandson, Adlai Stevenson III, was U.S. senator from Illinois (1970–1981).

The vice president arrived in Mt. Vernon without fanfare on the Air Line train (5th and Main) from the east and found his way to Dr. Green's residence. (This is the same Dr. Green who almost came to blows with John A. Logan in 1864.) Dr. Duff Green was one of the most important and influential citizens of Mt. Vernon until his death in 1904. In 1890 he was chairman of a group that helped bring the car shops to Mt. Vernon. This business became the most important industry in town, employing thousands of people. And with two sons who were elected state's attorney for Jefferson County and members of the state legislature he remained active politically. After his home, Green Lawn Place, was damaged in the 1888 tornado he had it re-built at the same location (715 Broadway) and in the same lavish manner.

Dr. Green's family, somewhat insulated with servants catering to their needs, followed intellectual pursuits such as reading literature and poetry. But the town had begun to grow up around Green Lawn Place as Broadway was extended east to the edge of Mt. Vernon. Dr. Green, himself, built and owned the "old" Armory across the street from his home. Shortly after his death the "new" Mt. Vernon High School and the Carnegie Library were built on what was his property. Since Dr. Green was such a prominent man, as well as a relative and fellow Democrat, it isn't surprising that he had enough influence to bring Vice President Stevenson to Mt. Vernon.[170]

Dr. Duff Green

By the next day the word had gone out, schools were closed, and large crowds made their way to town. The band escorted Stevenson from Dr. Green's house to the Grand Hotel (east side of North 10th St. at 110-116) where a public reception was held and "streams of the faithful went in to grasp his hand." In the afternoon Vice President Stevenson addressed a crowd of about five thousand people at Green Lawn Springs Park (near the current high school gymnasium at 6th and Jordan Streets).

In his address he criticized the Republicans for their hard money, high tariff policies—which he said caused the economic depression of 1893. He said: "The enforced idleness which has brought sorrow to so many hearts and hearthstones, was the direct result of what a Republican Congress had done...." He also said the Republicans had been in power for over twenty-five years and their legislation had brought "financial disaster, monopoly, combinations and trusts...." In addition he criticized the Republican "Billion Dollar Congress" and said the Democrats had lowered the high McKinley Tariff and cut expenditures by twenty-eight million dollars. He defended the income tax provision in the new tariff law passed by the Democrats by saying it was only the wealthy who would have to pay. He stated: "Individual incomes of less than four thousand dollars are wholly exempt from the tax. Savings banks and building and loan associations are exempt from the tax."(The U.S. Supreme Court ruled the income tax unconstitutional in 1895. The first permanent income tax was passed in 1913.)

This probably was the first visit ever to Mt. Vernon by a sitting vice president of the United States. Stevenson made a half-hearted attempt to secure the Democratic Party nomination for president in 1896 (which, of course, went to William Jennings Bryan). As part of this weak effort for the nomination in 1895 he sent copies of his speeches to Democratic Party leaders. The Democrats nominated Stevenson for vice president again in 1900, this time running on the William Jennings Bryan ticket. They lost, and Stevenson retired except for an unsuccessful run for Illinois governor in 1908.[171]

Political Visitors—Mason and Cullom

On the same date as Vice President Stevenson's visit, October 23, 1894, Congressman William E. Mason came to Mt. Vernon. Most likely this was political gamesmanship. Republican Mason was in town to counter Democrat Stevenson. Mason was a member of the U.S. House of Representatives from 1887–1891, the U.S. Senate from 1897 to 1903, and the U.S. House again from 1917 to 1921. Under the headline "Billy Mason" the *Mt. Vernon Register* of October 24, 1894, reported that the former congressman was escorted from the train to the Mahaffy House (305 S. 9th St.) by the Enfield Band and a "committee of five hundred." At the hotel he addressed the "assembled thousands for a few moments and made several very happy hits, among them being that he had no apology to offer to any one for being here...." (This may have been a reference to Democratic criticism of his coming at the same time as the vice president.) According to the article, the crowd greeted his remark by going "wild with enthusiasm and cheer after cheer rent the air." Later Mr. Mason spoke to twelve hundred to fifteen hundred people "packed like sardines" in Brumbaugh's Hall.[172]

The next important visitor in October of 1894 was U.S. Senator Shelby M. Cullom. Cullom (1829–1914) was one of the most important political figures in Illinois in the late Nineteenth and early Twentieth Centuries. A Republican, he held many local and state positions until 1865 when he was first elected to the U.S. House of Representatives. He was governor of Illinois from 1877–1883 and served in the U.S. Senate from 1883 to 1913. When Senator Cullom came to Mt. Vernon on October 31, 1894, he was campaigning for re-election against the previously mentioned Democrat, Franklin MacVeagh. In an article headlined "Our Day" the *Mt. Vernon Register* gushed: "Today has witnessed the grandest, most inspiring, and largest outpouring of the Republicans ever known in Jefferson County."

Thousands came to Mt. Vernon by train and horseback and "amid the booming of cannon" formed in a line to march to the Air Line depot. When Senator Cullom arrived, they formed a procession with twenty-four horsemen dressed in black and wearing black silk hats, twenty-four young horsemen wearing dark overcoats and white pants, hundreds of additional horsemen four abreast, Senator Cullom's carriage drawn by four large gray horses with plumes, other carriages with speakers and the reception committee, and of course, the band. They marched down Main Street to Fourteenth Street, south to Broadway, east on Broadway, and south on Ninth Street to the Mahaffy House where a reception was held. This successful event was a sharp contrast with MacVeagh's reception of October 16th.[173]

Mahaffy House

William Jennings Bryan

In the spring of 1896 William Jennings Bryan came to Mt. Vernon to speak for the free silver cause. At this point he was just an ex-congressman from Nebraska, well known in Jefferson County because of his roots in Salem but not famous in the country as a whole. No one would have predicted that his Cross of Gold speech at the Democratic Convention in the summer would catapult him to the nomination for president of the United States. On March 16, 1896, Bryan arrived in town on the Air Line train from Centralia and registered at the Grand Hotel, 110-116 N. Tenth Street. On March 18, 1896, the *Mt. Vernon Register* reported that he had "addressed an immense throng of people at the court house last night on the subject of Bimetallism." He apparently made a very favorable impression.[174]

Grand Hotel

William Jennings Bryan was probably in Mt. Vernon many times as a boy. He grew up in Salem, Illinois, only twenty miles away. He told a crowd at the Nashville, Illinois, Chautauqua in 1921 that he had been there many times with his father who was a circuit court judge. His brother, Charles Bryan, while visiting Mt. Vernon said that he had been to Mt. Vernon many times as a boy with his father. The elder Bryan was also an attorney who had many cases at the Supreme Court in Mt. Vernon during the 1860s and 1870s as the boys were growing up. Therefore, it seems likely that both boys came to Mt. Vernon many times as they grew up in Salem.[175]

Sam P. Jones

On July 4, 1896, famous evangelist Reverend Sam P. Jones (1847–1906) came to Jefferson County. Jones, one of the most celebrated evangelists of the late Nineteenth Century, was from a family full of Methodist ministers. He, however, decided to become a lawyer and was admitted to the bar in 1868. In spite of a successful marriage, he drank so heavily that he lost his practice, and by 1872 he was driving freight wagons for a living. His father's death-bed plea to stop drinking led him to become a Christian and to become a minister. He was very good at this new profession and soon was preaching to crowds numbering in the thousands. He spoke to state legislatures, religious organizations, and even President Theodore Roosevelt. Known for his wit and strong story-telling, he is considered an important influence on Will Rogers. He is famous for the quote: "The road to hell is paved with good intentions."

Reverend Jones came to the Bonnie Holiness campground for the July 4th celebration. The July 1, 1896, *Mt. Vernon Weekly Register* stated: "No one can afford to miss this meeting. Not one dollar to hear Sam Jones in an overpacked house, but twenty-five cents to hear Rev. Sam Jones, Rev. C. W. Ruth and Prof. J. H. Brownlee under the magnificent tabernacle which will resemble one of our great national convention auditoriums, and enjoy the whole day with your friends from the four quarters of Egypt. Ample accommodations for fully 10,000 people to eat, drink and be merry." On July 8, the *Mt. Vernon Register* reported that three to four thousand people attended and heard Rev. Jones give his famous lecture on "Character and Characters." He reportedly kept the audience "in an almost constant roar of laughter," but also made some very serious points.[176]

Shelby Cullom

Senator Shelby Cullom was back in Mt. Vernon as part of the McKinley for President Campaign on September 9, 1896. This time he was joined by Illinois Secretary of State James A. Rose as well as many regional Republican speakers. Rose, from Pope County, Illinois, served as secretary of state from 1896 to 1904. McKinley and the Republicans, of course, favored the protective tariff (McKinley authored the high tariff bill in Congress.) and the gold standard for currency. These stands were also strongly favored by the big businessmen of the country. As a result, McKinley's campaign coffers filled to overflowing with over 3.4 million dollars—a figure never before seen in the nation's history. McKinley's campaign was thus able to outspend Bryan's by about twelve to one. Mark Hanna, who headed McKinley's campaign, reportedly said: "There are two things that are important in politics. The first is money, and I can't remember what the second one is."[177]

Fueling this funding was fear of the brash young "Silver Tongued Orator," William Jennings Bryan, who was nominated by the Democrats. Bryan spoke for "free coinage of silver" and the lower tariff. Bryan was known as a great orator and had won the Democratic nomination with his famous "Cross of Gold" speech at the convention. In those days before primaries, conventions actually picked rather than ratified candidates. Although most often controlled by political heavyweights, sometimes tired delegates could be swayed by a great speech. And the thirty-six-year-old Bryan was a great speaker. McKinley was not a great speaker, so the shrewd Mark Hanna decided to run a "front porch" campaign where McKinley stayed home in Ohio and allowed surrogates in each state to speak for him. Senator Cullom and Secretary of State Rose being in Mt. Vernon was part of that strategy.

L. & N. Depot

Under the heading "Sound Money Men" the *Mt. Vernon Register* described another huge political rally. The article stated that twenty thousand people came to hear Senator Cullom. This crowd, according to the writer, was not just a partisan group, but a "spontaneous outpouring of the people," including farmers and workingmen turning to the Republican Party as the only hope to "redeem them from the bondage of hard times...." The L. & N. train arrived from St. Louis at 11:00 a.m. and was greeted by the Young Ladies McKinley club and the band playing "Yankee Doodle." The parade to the fairgrounds was described as "one of the largest ever seen in this city." In the front were three to four hundred horsemen, followed by gaily dressed glee clubs, uniformed footmen and citizens in vehicles...." The article stated that as the parade passed Porter and Bond's corner (southwest corner of 10th and Broadway), it contained nine hundred and ninety-one persons by actual count. The evening program headed by Secretary of State Rose was also well attended with a crowd estimated at ten to fifteen thousand. This meeting must have been downtown because the article reports that the crowd was so large that two additional stands were erected further up the street where other speakers delivered the message. So, it was quite a day for Mt. Vernon and the Republicans.[178]

William Jennings Bryan

The Democrats had their day on September 16, 1896, when their presidential candidate, William Jennings Bryan (1860–1925) came to Mt. Vernon. Bryan was one of the most famous political figures ever produced in southern Illinois. Deeply religious, Bryan graduated from Illinois College in Jacksonville, Illinois, became an attorney, and after moving to Nebraska was elected to the U.S. House of Representatives in 1890 and 1892. He was the Democratic candidate for president in 1896, 1900, and 1908. He was U.S. secretary of state from 1913 to 1915 under President Woodrow Wilson. He became one of the most celebrated Chautauqua speakers ever—speaking for the Bible, and against liquor and Darwinism. In 1925 he was part of the prosecution in the famous Scopes Trial, which successfully defended the Tennessee law prohibiting the teaching of evolution in the public schools. Among other nicknames he was known as the "Great Commoner" for his faith in the goodness of the common people.

Bryan Campaign Rally

But when Bryan came to Mt. Vernon in 1896, he was a political phenomenon crusading for the "free coinage of silver" and against the banks, railroads, industrialists, and eastern money interests. His strategy was to use the railroad system to take his case directly to the American people. He changed political campaigning of that era by giving five hundred speeches in twenty-seven states. The Democratic festivities actually began the day before Bryan's arrival with speeches and a torchlight procession of eight hundred and forty-three people—"the largest that has taken place in this city during the present campaign." Several stands (Although the photo is labeled northwest corner, it is probably the southwest corner of the square.) were erected at the corner of Broadway and 10th Street, and according to the *Mt. Vernon Register* various speakers "harangued" the people on the idea of free silver. Bryan arrived in town from St. Louis on the L. & N. Railroad and then continued on to McLeansboro, Carmi, Evansville, and Kentucky. The *Mt. Vernon Register* reported a crowd of at least ten thousand with campaign clubs and "unorganized footmen" forming a procession in front of the Bryan club headquarters at the corner of 9th and Jordan Streets. They marched north to Whitacre Brothers Corner, then west on Main Street to the L. & N. depot.

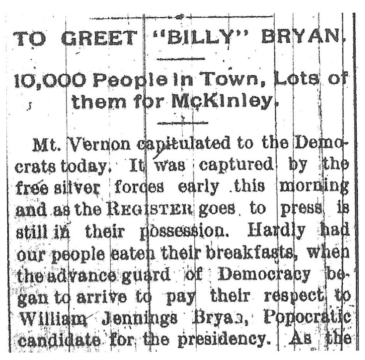

Bryan Article 1896

Bryan arrived about 9:00 a.m. and was escorted to a platform erected near the west entrance to the Supreme Court. The *Mt. Vernon Register* reported that "Mr. Bryan in his speech at the Supreme Court house this morning reiterated one of his favorite 'arguments' in the following phrase: 'We believe that the U.S. is a great enough nation to establish and maintain its own financial policy without waiting for the aid or consent of any other nation on earth.'" Although calling this sentence "meaningless" and criticizing Bryan's speech as "full of political platitudes and campaign sophistry," the reporter had to admit that "The personal appearance of Mr. Bryan is greatly in his favor as an orator... ," and his "is a well cultivated voice and he knows how to utilize all its resources of range, richness, and flexibility." So Bryan's speech was apparently well received, and his train left at 9:45 a.m.

However, the *Mt. Vernon Register* had this to say in its headline: "10,000 People in Town, Lots of Them for McKinley." They referred to Bryan as the "Popocratic" candidate for president, an effort to associate him with the perceived radicals of the Populist Party who had also nominated Bryan for president. They made a retraction of a previous assertion that Bryan was received poorly (was "given a frost") at various stops on the way to Mt. Vernon. They wrote: "The *Register* has no desire to belittle Mr. Bryan's candidacy nor to misrepresent the enthusiasm of his party followers...."[179]

Political Demonstrations and Visitors

After Bryan's departure the Democrats continued their campaign with various speakers at Green Lawn Springs from 1:30 to 5:00 p.m. Among those who spoke was Walter Thomas Mills who was described as a four-feet-six-inch man with a leonine head and magnetic eyes. In 1901 he helped found the Socialist Party of America, and in 1912 after moving to New Zealand he helped start the United Labour Party of New Zealand.[180]

Bryan Campaign Ribbon

Still more Republican political demonstrations took place on September 22 and 23, 1896, again with large crowds and parades featuring the Tanner Bicycle Club, the Albion Drum Corps, and the Mt. Vernon Car Shops Club. Like industries elsewhere in the U.S., the Car Shops owner and management were very pro-McKinley and anti-Bryan. And like other businesses they were accused of telling their employees that if they voted for Bryan, they would be fired. The *Mt. Vernon Register* published a letter from some Car Shops' employees who denied that they were threatened. Other organizations in the parades were the Mt. Vernon Coal Miners' Sound Money Club, the Mt. Vernon McKinley Club, the Mt. Vernon Military Band, the Ladies' McKinley Club in carriages, the Young Men's Mounted McKinley Club, the Junior McKinley Club and several glee club wagons "gaily and handsomely decorated." The main address was given by Republican Congressman Roswell G. Horr at the fairgrounds. At this time he was associate editor of the *New York Tribune*. Prior to that, he was a member of the U.S. House of Representatives from 1879 to 1885.[181]

Mt. Vernon Military Band

The Republicans rallied again on September 29 and 30, 1896, in similar fashion to the earlier demonstrations. The parade from the Air Line depot included bands from Nashville, Salem, Centralia, Albion, and Mt. Vernon, various McKinley and "Sound Money" Clubs from southern Illinois, and the Young Ladies' Billy Mason Drill Corps. This time a cannon was fired at the corner of 9th and Jordan. This was probably the cannon made at the Car Shops for the McKinley campaign.[182] The parade down Main Street led to the fairgrounds where the main speaker was the Republican governor of Kentucky, William O. Bradley. His election was quite a coup for the Republicans since Kentucky was part of the "Solid South" for the Democrats. Bradley was the first Republican ever elected governor of Kentucky (serving from 1895 to 1899), and went on to win election to the U.S. Senate in 1908.[183]

STREET SCENE IN MT. VERNON DURING A POLITICAL PARADE.

Political Parade

John P. Altgeld

The Democrats had one last chance to influence the voters before the 1896 presidential election when Illinois Governor John Peter Altgeld came to Mt. Vernon. Altgeld was elected governor of Illinois in 1892, the first Democrat to win the office since the 1850s. He was also the first foreign-born person and the first Chicago resident to win the governorship. (He toured the entire state that year and may have come to Mt. Vernon. However, there is no proof of any visit except to DuQuoin and Pinckneyville.) He immediately appointed women to important offices and persuaded the legislature to pass strong child-labor laws, workplace-safety laws, and increased funding for public education. Nearly all the public universities in Illinois have a castle-like building constructed in the 1890s and named after Altgeld. He also famously pardoned the radicals convicted after the Haymarket Riot, and tried to stop President Cleveland from sending federal troops to Chicago to quell rioting associated with the Pullman Strike in 1894. The Progressives (liberals of that era) loved him. If he hadn't been foreign born, he might have been nominated for president of the United States. But the conservatives of the time hated him, accusing him of overspending, and encouraging radical unions, socialists, and anarchists. One of the conservative newspapers of the era, the *Chicago Tribune,* called him John "Pardon" Altgeld to remind people that he pardoned the anarchists.

According to the *Mt. Vernon Register* of October 7, 1896, Governor Altgeld was to be in town "next Tuesday." The visit was confirmed by later articles as being October 12. No stories tell of the substance of his speech. However, the stop in Mt. Vernon was between his two most important speeches of the campaign. The topic of his first speech on September 19 was free coinage of silver. The title of his second major speech was "The Chicago Riots— Government by Injunction—Federal Interference." This lecture was given in New York on October 17, just five days after his visit to Mt. Vernon. Since he was campaigning for his own re-election and the election of fellow Democrat, William Jennings Bryan, Altgeld most likely spoke for free silver and Bryan, and defended himself against charges of corruption and supporting radicals.

The local papers were ready to pounce. The *Mt. Vernon Register* quoted a number of allegations against him (mostly accusing him of personally profiting from state office such as: "that the governor borrowed from $50,000 to $60,000 of state funds… without paying any interest.") and the *Register* also quoted the *Mt. Vernon Daily News* of June 30, 1893, "It took 17,000 words for Governor Altgeld to justify his pardon of the Anarchists in his opinion, but evidently it would take many times that number to condone the matter with patriotic citizens of Illinois." On Election Day he was defeated by Republican, John R. Tanner, although he ran ahead of fellow Democrat, Bryan, by ten thousand votes.[184]

The Election of 1896

The presidential election of 1896 was probably the most hotly contested election in Jefferson County history. Edwin Rackaway wrote of his memories of the campaign in 1952. As a boy he personally marched in torchlight parades along with hundreds of grown-up men. He described "anvil firing" where powder was set off by a blow to an anvil. According to Rackaway, "it made one hell of a racket," and at the car shops one blast "blew out about half the windows in an L. & N. train that was standing at the old water tank." "The startled passengers thought they had been bombed," he wrote. He also remembered wearing a McKinley badge at the old East Side School, 5th and Harrison, and defending it from the other schoolboys with "fist and claw." The children for Bryan chanted: "Hurray for Bryan, He's the Man. If I can't vote, My Daddy can!"[185]

East Side School

Another story of the 1896 campaign shows the depth of feelings even among families. James and Mallie Warren and their two sons, Clyde (about four), and Hill (about two) attended a Bryan rally. James was a Democrat and bought a Bryan cap for Clyde. Mallie, a strong Republican, bought a McKinley cap for Hill. After a time Hill needed to be carried. James refused to carry him with the McKinley cap on; Mallie refused to take it off unless Clyde took the Bryan cap off. Neither would give in, so Mrs. Warren carried the baby the whole day.[186]

The newspapers of the times were full of reports of rowdyism and fisticuffs over the election. There were fights on the square and at the Air Line depot. One man was arrested for hitting a man in the head with a brick as he marched in a political parade.[187] Emotions were very high. After the campaign ended the *Mt. Vernon Register* reported that Bryan and the Democrats had won Jefferson County by a "substantial majority," (eight hundred votes according to *Wall's History of Jefferson County)* but McKinley won a huge victory nationwide. At least some people in Jefferson County still had a sense of humor about the result. At the Republican "ratification rally" Democrats Jacob O. Chance, Luther Bond, and Curran Williams had to ride "jacks" as a result of bets they made on the election. Another Bryan man, Otto Boudinot, had to ride a cow as a result of losing his wager with City Marshal Watson.[188]

Henry Watterson

The December 16, 1896, *Mt. Vernon Register* announced that well-known journalist Henry Watterson (1840–1921) was to be in town on January 9, 1897. During the Civil War he fought for the Confederacy with famous General Nathan Bedford Forrest. After the war he became the editor of the *Louisville Courier-Journal* and in 1872 was a leader of the Liberal Republican movement. In 1876 he was elected to the U.S. Congress as a Democrat. But his greatest fame came as an editor who wrote controversial editorials read across the nation. In 1918 he won the Pulitzer Prize for editorials supporting U.S. entry into World War I.[189]

Sousa and Ingersoll

In early 1897 two very famous visitors traveled through Jefferson County by train on the way to Evansville. John Philip Sousa (1854–1932) and his band came to Mt. Vernon on January 24, 1897. Sousa was famous as a composer and conductor of American military march music and was known as "The March King." Among many other tunes he wrote "The Stars and Stripes Forever" (1896) just a year before he came to town. Sousa was the conductor of the U.S. Marine Band from 1880 to 1892. At that point he organized his own band and toured the United States and Europe. The *Daily Register* reported: "Professor Sousa and his famous band of musicians passed through here on a special train on the L. & N. today en route from Belleville to Evansville." On April 16, 1897, Robert G. Ingersoll wrote a letter to his daughter from St. Louis stating, "We are just starting for Evansville." He arrived in Evansville on the same date for an evening lecture. Therefore, he must have passed through Mt. Vernon on the L. & N. on the same date.[190]

The "Millionaire Tramp"

In May of 1897 one of the most colorful characters in Mt.Vernon history appeared. He was James M. Berry, nationally known as "The Millionaire Tramp." He made quite an impression around the town and the May 26, 1897, *Mt. Vernon Register* wrote a story about his bizarre behavior. He was in town a week earlier and went to one of the local banks with a check for fifteen thousand dollars. A friend told the press that he had been a hobo for thirty years when he learned that his parents had died, leaving him an inheritance so large he didn't know what to do with it. Apparently he had been in Jefferson County several years earlier picking fruit for a few dollars, and liked the county and Mt. Vernon so much that he decided to come back and spend his money. He began doing just that right away. He bought a twenty-five hundred dollar horse and decorated it elaborately with wreaths of roses and other bright-colored flowers; he purchased a fancy buggy from R. L. Strattan & Company. He dressed himself with checked trousers, brown-cutaway coat with buttonhole flower, a bow-neck tie, bright yellow shoes, kid gloves, and a brown derby hat.

If Berry's appearance wasn't enough to gain attention, he also began to literally "throw his money away." He toured the town buying drinks for one and all, and upon emerging from any of the taverns would throw handfuls of coins and dollars to the crowd. Edwin Rackaway, a youngster in the 1890s, remembered the scene: "Presently Berry and his retinue emerged from the saloon and he stood up in the back seat of the very stylish two horse livery rig… (and) with a silly grin on his red, foolish, drunken face he thrust his hand into his pocket and pulled forth a fist full of small coins. With a wild yell he tossed the coins among the assembled youth of Mt. Vernon and as the mad scramble began, shouted to the driver to lash the horses and head for the next refreshment stand. It was a thrilling spectacle and one which I shall never forget."[191]

Many were happy to see Berry spend his money in Mt. Vernon and liven up the town. Plus he was a national celebrity and Mt. Vernon shared his fame. But his drunkenness brought him trouble. He was arrested in Mt. Vernon on May 26, 1897, for disorderly conduct. On June 14, 1897, he was arrested in Salem and brought back to Mt. Vernon on a complaint of wife abandonment by Mrs. Sadie Berry. (He married a Miss Sadie Miller at Woodlawn at some point while in Jefferson County.) On June 26, 1897, he left his wife and friends and traveled elsewhere. On July 7, 1897, he was arrested in St. Louis for brandishing a pearl-handled revolver and threatening to shoot whoever "bothered his horse." He was back in Mt. Vernon on August 11, 1897, with a wad of cash and four checks of five thousand dollars each. His notoriety brought tramps from everywhere, threatening to make Mt. Vernon the hobo capital of the United States. Dr. Andy Hall, Mt. Vernon Mayor from 1897 to 1898, ordered local police not to tolerate him but instead throw him in jail whenever possible, and Berry soon left town for good. He died a pauper at the age of fifty-eight in Paducah, Kentucky, January 17, 1899.[192]

The Cincinnati Redlegs

On September 28, 1897, the Cincinnati Redlegs Baseball team of the National League visited Mt. Vernon.[193] One of their key players was first baseman Jake Beckley who was inducted into the Hall of Fame in 1971. Nicknamed "Eagle Eye," Beckley compiled a .308 career batting average while playing for the Pittsburgh Pirates (1888–1896), New York Giants (1896–1897), Cincinnati Redlegs (1897–1903), and St.

Louis Cardinals (1904–1907). The Redlegs were in town to play the local Mt. Vernon team and apparently drew a large crowd with eighty people coming from Mt. Vernon, Indiana, on a special train. The game was probably played at Merchants Baseball Park near 6th and Casey. Cincinnati defeated Mt. Vernon fifteen to six, but "There was wild excitement in the first inning when Dahlrymple of the Mt. Vernon team poled a home run." The Redlegs finished fourth in the league in 1897 with a record of 76 and 56.

PICTURE OF MT. VERNON'S BASEBALL TEAM - 1897

BOTTOM ROW - SEATED - LEFT TO RIGHT: 1. GRIFFEN; 2. GERALD.
SECOND ROW - SEATED - LEFT TO RIGHT: 1. JOHN WILBANKS; 2. KANE; 3. FRITZ WLECKE; 4. LYNCH.
TOP ROW - STANDING - LEFT TO RIGHT: 1. BELT; 2. CALLAHAN; 3. DALYRIMPLE; 4. WORKS.

Mt. Vernon Baseball Team 1897

Evelyn Baldwin

Also in 1897 the polar explorer, Evelyn B. Baldwin, came to town as part of the lyceum lecture series of that year. Baldwin (1862–1933) was a high school principal from Kansas whose boyhood interest in the North Pole led him to a life of adventure. His first expedition was in 1893 with Admiral Peary. His second expedition was with Walter Wellman. In 1900 he made still another attempt to reach the North Pole. The *International Herald Tribune* in 1900 reported: "It is to be an international race to the North Pole. On two sides of the globe preparations are now being made for a dash further north. Evelyn B. Baldwin, an explorer, and William Ziegler, a New York millionaire, are fitting up an expedition which, they say, will reach the Pole if it is within the range of human possibility." None of these attempts was successful until Admiral Peary reached the Pole in 1909. Baldwin spoke in Mt. Vernon at the Opera House (10th and Harrison) on November 17, 1897.[194] As he lectured throughout the country, Mr. Baldwin brought with him dogs, furs and other things of interest from the arctic region.

John Mitchell

On July 9, 1898, John Mitchell (1870–1919) of the United Mine Workers gave an address at the Courthouse at 8:00 in the evening.[195] Mitchell was from an Irish coal mining family. He worked in the mines most of his life and joined the Knights of Labor in 1885. In 1890 he was a founding member of the United Mine Workers of America. He worked with famous union organizers like Mother Jones and was elected president of the United Mine Workers in September of 1898. As a vice president of the American

Federation of Labor, he worked with Samuel Gompers, one of the most important labor leaders in U.S. history. In the early 1900s Mitchell led a mine-workers strike, which was settled when President Theodore Roosevelt brought the two sides to the negotiating table. The result of the strike was an eight-hour workday and a minimum wage.

There is no article telling about his speech in Mt. Vernon. But coal miners lived and worked in difficult conditions, and the union was organizing and recruiting heavily in Illinois. The miners' contract favored the employer. If they went on strike, they could be fired and forced to forfeit all pay due to them. They could be thrown out of their company-owned homes. And there was no unemployment insurance. After the coal owners announced a twenty percent reduction in pay on May 1, 1897, the UMW called for a strike. (The Mt. Vernon miners went on strike March 1, 1897, according to the March 1, 1897, *Daily Register* because of a "reduction in the price paid by the company.")[196] The successful strike gave the union a boost and membership nationwide rose from eleven thousand in 1897 to twenty-five thousand in 1898 to fifty-four thousand in 1899. Illinois, led by John Mitchell, made the greatest gain in membership of all the states.[197]

The Mt. Vernon Coal Mine

The Mt. Vernon Coal Mine

The Mt. Vernon Coal Mine was opened in 1894 and the miners faced many of the same problems as those elsewhere. Many of the miners lived in company-owned homes called "Happy Row" between 10th and Shawnee Streets, and they were paid in "scrip" (tokens that could only be used in local stores) rather than real money. This tied the miners to the company and gave the mine owners more control over the workers. Mine records show that many workers were in debt to the company for wage advances and never earned enough to overcome the deficit.[198] And of course the work was very dirty and dangerous. On November 5, 1895, a miner named Frank Bowman was killed in an accident at the Mt. Vernon Coal Mine.

In addition to the general conditions, events in Williamson County may have caused Mitchell's visit to Mt. Vernon. On March 31, 1898, the miners at the St. Louis and Big Muddy mine near Carterville went on strike. On May 20, 1898, the mine owner, Mr. Brush, brought in 178 black miners to take the place of the striking white miners. For a time strikers with shotguns faced off against armed company guards. The miners backed down and went back to work, but resentment toward the owner and the black replacement workers remained high.[199] John

Mitchell's speech in Jefferson County came about a month after the end of the Carterville strike. So Mitchell and the UMW must have recognized the opportunity to organize the local miners.

The next year, 1899, brought strikes to the coal mines in Mt. Vernon and Carterville. The Mt. Vernon strike began about March of 1899 and was settled on June 13, 1899.[200] But the Carterville strike, which began on May 15, 1899, was a much more difficult one. Again Mr. Brush, the owner, brought in black miners to replace the whites on strike. Striking miners fired at an Illinois Central train bringing the black miners and their families to Carterville, and a woman was killed. Black and white miners clashed again later and five black men were killed. The governor ordered Company F of Mt. Vernon and Company C of Carbondale, both with veterans of the Spanish-American War, into the town and the strike was defeated.[201]

John P. Altgeld

In October of 1898 John Peter Altgeld came through Mt. Vernon twice. At this time he was ex-Governor Altgeld and was campaigning for local and state Democrats. On October 19, 1898, he passed through on the L. & N. on the way to McLeansboro to give a speech. Then on October 25 and 26, 1898, he was back again. He wasn't actually scheduled to be in town but stopped for the night when his train failed to make connections for his trip to speak in Pinckneyville. He was to take the W. C. & W. Railroad, originally called the Chester and Tamaroa Road, but before leaving he spoke briefly at the depot (306 S. 10th) to a small crowd of about two hundred.[202] Apparently most of his talk was about the gold/silver issue. The *Mt. Vernon Register* story brought up the old allegations of over spending and poor management, and stated: "Just around the corner of the depot was a pile of stone window sill shipped here by Altgeld's former superintendent of the stone department, upon which even the freight has not yet been paid."

The newspaper also speculated on the governor's future. The article stated: "The ex-Governor, who is a political corpse, is also a perfect picture of a physical corpse. He is pale and haggard and his face indicates that he is in pain and distress."[203] The *Mt. Vernon Register* was right in its judgment of Altgeld's political and physical health. Politically, he fell fast and suffered a humiliating defeat in a run for mayor of Chicago in 1899. (He agreed to run for mayor as an independent in December of 1898, just two months after leaving Mt. Vernon.) Physically, he was in poor condition. Never very healthy since a brush with death in the Civil War, the governor suffered a nervous breakdown while in office and could barely walk by the end of his administration. He died at age fifty-four, four years after his second visit to Mt. Vernon.

W. C. & W. Depot

William Jennings Bryan

On November 3, 1898, William Jennings Bryan passed through Mt. Vernon on the L. & N. Railroad.[204] He was now Colonel Bryan and was en route to Nebraska for a two-week furlough from the army raised to fight in the Spanish-American War. The army was stationed in Tampa, Florida. He supported the war as a way to bring justice to the people of Cuba and volunteered for the Nebraska militia. Like many volunteers he spent the war (which was only about three months long) in Florida and never saw combat. Others like Teddy Roosevelt and the Rough Riders had to fight their way onto the troop-transport ships in order to reach Cuba for the war. About December 10, 1898, Bryan's war horse came through Mt. Vernon on the Air Line freight train. Possibly Bryan was preparing to return to Florida. But on that same date Spain accepted the Treaty of Paris that ended the war. On December 21, 1898, Bryan arrived in Salem for a few days of rest. After the war Bryan opposed the policy of taking control of Spanish colonies and ran for president on an anti-imperialism, free silver platform.[205]

"Coin" Harvey

William H. "Coin" Harvey (1851–1936) came to town in 1899. Harvey was a teacher, lawyer and author who became famous for his book, *Coin's Financial School* (1894). The book, which promoted "free silver," became a sensation and sold almost a million copies in the 1890s. It helped promote populism, the Populist Party, and William Jennings Bryan's 1896 campaign for president of the United States. Historian Richard Hofstadter said of Harvey: "He was the Tom Paine of the free silver movement, and *Coin's Financial School* was to the silver men of 1896 what "Common Sense" had been to the revolutionaries of 1776." The U.S. had suffered through a depression in 1893 and farmers and working people were looking for someone to blame. Harvey provided that by blaming the Jewish bankers of England and New York, the rich industrialists, and the "gold bugs." He suggested they were a conspiracy to take over the United States and steal the fruits of the working people's labor by restricting silver, which he called "the metal of the people" and the "dollar of our daddies."

Coin Harvey Article

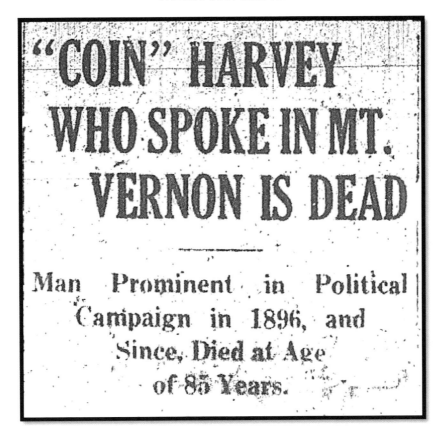

Coin Harvey Article

When Coin Harvey came to Mt. Vernon on February 28, 1899, the "free silver" issue was still important, but was overshadowed by a new issue—imperialism. Bryan's defeat in 1896 was a setback for populism and "free silver." The U.S. victory over Spain in 1898 brought colonies to our country and we debated the issue of imperialism. Mr. Harvey had a new book, *Coin on Money, Trusts, and Imperialism* (1899), which focused on imperialism. The *Mt. Vernon Register* of March 1, 1899, reported: "The Circuit Court Room was crowded last night to its utmost capacity to hear an address by W. H. (Coin) Harvey on 'How to Bring Prosperity'."[206]

Lawrence Y. Sherman

July 4, 1899, brought a crowd estimated at ten thousand and a future United States senator to Mt. Vernon. Lawrence Yates Sherman was serving as Illinois speaker of the house in 1899 and was in town as a featured speaker for the Fourth of July celebration. He was elected lieutenant governor in 1904 and served as U.S. senator from 1913 to 1921. Trains brought people from all over southern Illinois. A parade featuring the Carmi Military Band, speakers' carriages, the United Mine Workers of America, the Albion Drum Corps, and the Mt. Vernon Lodge American Federation of Labor formed on the square and headed to the fairgrounds. Although rain stopped some of the sports activities, the balloon ascension was successfully held. An "aeronaut" named Professor Jones took his balloon up about a half mile and then parachuted to the ground "near the iron bridge, a mile east of town."[207]

The Veterans' Reunion of 1899

The annual Veteran's Reunion was held in Mt. Vernon August 16–23, 1899. In addition to the aging Civil War veterans, the veterans of the Spanish-American War (1898) were in attendance. As a result there was a mixture of themes, symbols, and speeches to show support to both groups. The tent city on the fairgrounds was named Camp McPherson after a civil war general, and the veterans sang "Marching

Through Georgia." You could get a cream soda from the "Dewey fountain" (named after Admiral Dewey, hero of the Spanish-American War) and one of the midway attractions was the "starved Cuban woman" who supposedly represented the Cuban people mistreated by the Spaniards. (The "Yellow Press" whipped up enthusiasm for entering the war by reporting on Spanish atrocities both real and imagined.) The midway also included: a steam swing, a shooting gallery, a horse with an eighteen-foot mane, a lady snake charmer who "perambulates about the country in a wagon, and who exhibited on the square recently," an Egyptian fortune teller, a minstrel show of "colored home talent," and a "museum" where for a nickel you could see "Little Willie Miller, the demon child who has hoofs for feet, claws on his hands and horns on his head...." The *Mt. Vernon Register* also reported that the reunion drew the biggest collection of "thugs and crooks" ever seen in Mt. Vernon.

To this reunion came the previously mentioned L. Y. Sherman and the governor of Illinois, John R. Tanner. Tanner, who was also in Jefferson County for the September, 1898, reunion, served in the Civil War and held various elected offices in Clay County, Illinois. He went on to serve in the Illinois senate and as state treasurer from 1886 to 1889. Then in 1896 he was elected governor of Illinois. The *Mt. Vernon Register* reported that "when he arrived, accompanied by Co. F and several thousand people, these with the thousands already assembled gave the governor a reception that is seldom met with in a lifetime." But Governor Tanner couldn't enjoy the greeting since he was not feeling well. He told the crowd that he had just come from a sick bed and was in no condition to speak. However, he did speak briefly about the Civil War ("No one would believe the hardships, the hairbreadth escapes I might tell of..."), patriotism ("... we must also have patriotism, for without patriotism, no nation, and no government can stand."), and the Spanish-American War ("... the soldiers of the Spanish war have brought to us increased responsibilities and duties. We warred with Spain for humanity and not for conquest.").[208] The governor probably should have taken his physician's advice to stay home and rest. After a difficult, unsuccessful race for a U.S. Senate seat in 1900, he died in May of 1901, less than two years after his visit to the county.

CHAPTER V

The Progressive Era 1900–1919

The years from 1900 to 1919 are known as the Progressive Era in the history books. The Progressives were a diverse group but generally supported government ownership of railroads and utilities, the income tax, the primary system, and direct election of U. S. senators. Some supported suffrage for women. Fueled by books and newspaper articles by journalists dubbed "muckrakers," the Progressive cause became so popular that in the presidential election of 1912 all three main contenders—William Howard Taft, Theodore Roosevelt, and Woodrow Wilson—claimed to be "progressives." The industrial tycoons and their political-boss allies had become the enemy. Another older reform, prohibition, was also popular and was promoted mainly by ministers and evangelists who toured the country.

In the area of entertainment Wild West shows, circuses, minstrel shows, and burlesque shows were popular. Even smaller towns had an "opera house" for live stage shows. The "Chautauqua movement" with lecturers and music held outdoors spread to the Midwest and was extremely popular. A new form of entertainment, the nickelodeon, led to silent films and local movie houses. Sports was dominated by baseball with small towns supporting their own amateur team, and cities supporting professional teams. In addition to traditional horse racing, automobile racing and even airplane exhibitions became attractions at county fairs. All of these developments can be seen in Jefferson County during this period.

Political Visitors—Madden, Yates, Cullom, Reeves, and Deneen

The first important visitor of the Twentieth Century was Martin B. Madden of Chicago. He gave a speech at the Jefferson County Courthouse on January 26, 1900. Madden, who had a long history in Chicago business and politics, was interested in running for Congress. He was elected to the United States House of Representatives in 1904, and served from 1905 until his death in 1928.[209]

On April 26, 1900, Richard Yates (1860–1936) spoke at the courthouse. Yates had been in Mt. Vernon on October 8, 1892, also for a speech at the courthouse. At that time the son of former Governor Richard Yates, Sr. was a thirty-two-year-old, up-and-coming politician. This time he was in town campaigning for the Republican nomination for governor of Illinois. On October 28 he returned to Jefferson County to campaign for himself and for the McKinley/Roosevelt ticket. Yates was elected and served from 1901 to 1905. As governor he vetoed legislation legalizing horseracing in Illinois. He sent the state militia to stop violence and protect black citizens in Saline County after a race riot there in June of 1902. He failed to get his party's nomination in 1904 and ran unsuccessfully for governor in 1908 and 1912. He would return to Mt. Vernon many times.[210]

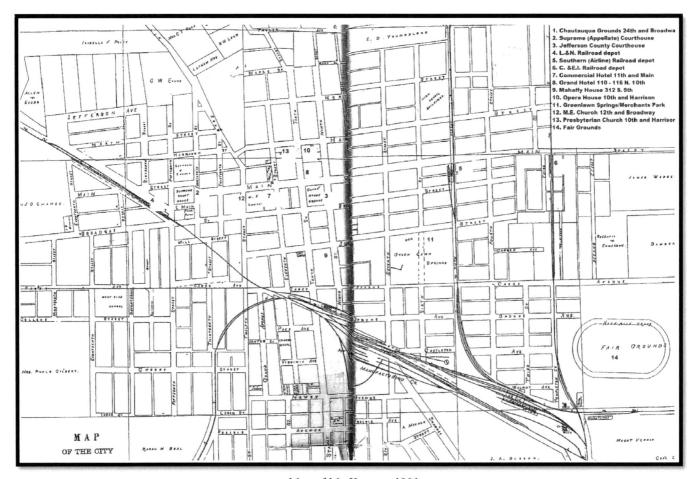

1. Chautauqua Grounds 24th and Broadwa
2. Supreme (Appellate) Courthouse
3. Jefferson County Courthouse
4. L.&N. Railroad depot
5. Southern (Airline) Railroad depot
6. C. &E.I. Railroad depot
7. Commercial Hotel 11th and Main
8. Grand Hotel 110 - 116 N. 10th
9. Mahaffy House 312 S. 9th
10. Opera House 10th and Harrison
11. Greenlawn Springs/Merchants Park
12. M.E. Church 12th and Broadway
13. Presbyterian Church 10th and Harrisor
14. Fair Grounds

Map of Mt. Vernon, 1901

The annual reunion of soldiers and sailors was held at the fairgrounds in Mt. Vernon on September 12–14, 1900, with the usual patriotic songs, speeches, and music. Tents with evening campfires were set up, and the Mt. Vernon Military Band provided music. According to the report, veterans attended in "larger numbers than at any other previous reunion in the district's history." The best-known speakers were Senator Shelby M. Cullom and Congressman Walter Reeves who visited on the 13th.[211]

Republican candidate for governor, Charles S. Deneen was another important visitor of the Twentieth Century. Mr. Deneen was a member of the Illinois House of Representatives in 1892. In 1904 he was elected governor of Illinois and served two terms from 1905 to 1913. In 1925 he was appointed U.S. senator from Illinois and served until 1931. His first visit to Mt. Vernon on October 28, 1903, was only a "stop over" to change trains from the C. & E. I. to the Southern for a speech in Fairfield.[212] He returned to town, as promised, on September 13, 1904, for a rousing reception in his campaign for governor. He was met at the L. & N. depot and, led by "Anderson's Band," marched to the courthouse where the somewhat hoarse-voiced candidate spoke for about an hour. He stated that the Republicans were as much against the trusts (big business combinations) as the Democrats and defended the Republican high tariff as not being "the mother of all trusts" as the Democrats charged. A large part of his speech was a discussion of a new primary election law, which he promised to work for if elected.[213] He was elected and the primary election law was eventually passed in 1912, becoming the first in the nation.

P. G. Lowery's World Famous Colored Band

In between these two Deneen visits was a show at the Grand Opera House by P. G. Lowery's World Famous Colored Band on November 14, 1903. Lowery, a graduate of the New England Conservatory of Music, founded

88

and led many bands and minstrel groups in the late Nineteenth and early Twentieth Centuries. He is credited with being the first African-American to put his own vaudeville act in a circus. He conducted the sideshow band for the Ringling Brothers circus for many years. He was often billed as "the world's greatest solo cornet player." His greatest competition for this title was W. C. Handy who later became known as the "Father of the Blues."[214]

Carrie Nation

Also in between the Deneen visits was the lecture by one of the most famous women of the late Nineteenth and early Twentieth Centuries. Carrie Nation (1846–1911), anti-liquor crusader and hatchet-wielding destroyer of saloons, came to Mt. Vernon on July 29, 1904. Carrie grew up in Kentucky and came to hate liquor as a result of her first marriage to a heavy-drinking, alcoholic husband. She joined the Women's Christian Temperance Union and began by singing hymns and picketing the local saloons. At one point she said she received a divine revelation to smash the saloons. She began by using a rock but soon started using a hatchet. Along with other women singing hymns, she would invade the saloon. And with a Bible in one hand and a hatchet in the other, she would begin to smash liquor bottles. Between 1900 and 1910 she was arrested thirty times for these events. Even though she was in her fifties and early sixties during this time, Mrs. Nation was very active. In the winter of 1903–1904 she took her protest to Washington, D.C. Refused entry to the U.S. Senate chamber, she went to the chamber lobby and shouted until she was arrested for disorderly conduct. In early 1904 she was arrested in Philadelphia and Pittsburgh and dragged through the streets to a patrol wagon.

Sketch of Carrie Nation

When she came to Mt. Vernon, it was part of a lecture tour to pay her court-ordered fines, not to smash saloons. The *Mt. Vernon Register* reported that her appearance at the courthouse brought a curious, overflow crowd and was "the attraction of the season." The *Mt. Vernon Weekly News* of August 3, 1904, explained: "Had the lady been well advertised, no hall in the city would have held the crowd." She must have presented quite an imposing presence at nearly six feet tall and 175 pounds. Her physical appearance was made even more dramatic by a bandaged wound on her forehead that she received from a man attacking her. In July of 1904 in Elizabethtown, Kentucky, while walking to one of her lectures, she stopped to speak out against a saloon that she passed along the way. After her lecture she passed the saloon again and was hit with a chair by a drunken barkeeper. At the time Nation was quoted as saying he, "sent it down with a crash on my head. I came near falling, caught myself, and he lifted the chair the second time, striking me over the back; the blood began to cover my face, and run down from a cut on my forehead." In Mt. Vernon Mrs. Nation explained the wound and said: "It don't worry me, for the Lord helps me and will take care of me; but if I die in the cause I advocate, I will have died well."

Carrie Nation spoke for about an hour in what one article called a "rambling speech." She described herself in this way: "I am not one of those timid, backward sort of women, without any backbone." However, she claimed that she had been "grossly misrepresented" by the big city press as a "wild, uncouth, masculine-like woman…" She attacked local officials for allowing saloons, which she called "murder mills," to do business in the city. She stated that while she had used a hatchet to smash up saloons, she wished that dynamite could be used to blow up every one of them. She attacked women for trying to be fashionable to attract the gaze of vulgar men and not protecting their children. She wore what the newspaper called a "white gown of a clinging, filmy texture," which she said was a better garment for women to wear. She attacked men saying: "A drunkard is no husband… and no woman wants a two legged beer keg to live with; she can't love such an article." She attacked both political parties and said they wouldn't allow women to vote because they would vote to prohibit alcohol. At one point she caused the crowd to gawk when she said: "This is my hatchet." But then she held up her Bible. At the end of her lecture she sold books and "a great number of hatchets at twenty-five cents each."

Reviews of the speech from the local press were generally positive. One article said that while her language was not the best and her address was disconnected, she proved to be a quite interesting speaker. Another said she lacked tact and sound judgment, but had "pluck and indomitable will…" It went on to say that "… if that hatchet was as sharp as her tongue, no wonder she wrought havoc with it."[215]

After leaving Mt. Vernon Carrie Nation continued her work. In August of 1904 she published her autobiography, *The Use and Need of the Life of Carry A. Nation.* In September of the same year she was in Kansas for one of her "hatchetations." She and other women tried to smash Mahan's wholesale liquor house in Wichita. She wrote: "I am coming to do all I can to destroy the works of the devil and if need be to die." She told the women to "Bring your hatchets with you." Guards prevented them from entering the building, so they broke the windows with their hatchets. Mrs. Nation was pushed to the ground seven times and arrested.[216]

Madam Mountford

Another outstanding female lecturer came to Mt. Vernon in 1904. On September 22 Madam Lydia Von Finkelstein Mountford, billed as a "World Famous Lecturer" in the newspaper, came to the Presbyterian Church (located at 14th and Main Streets south of the Appellate Court at that time). She was born and raised in Palestine as an Episcopalian but understood the customs of the local Muslims and Jews. Knowing that there was great public interest in Palestine, she developed a series of lectures and began touring the world. She dressed in native costumes and must have presented a striking figure. One reporter described her as a six-foot-tall, blonde Amazon. She toured India (where she met and married her husband, Charles E. Mountford), England, Australia, New Zealand, and of course the United States. While in Salt Lake City in 1897 she met and became a close friend of the president of the Church of Latter Day Saints

(Mormons), Wilford Woodruff. A rumor developed that she was secretly married to Mr. Woodruff. Her lectures in Mt. Vernon over a three-day period cost fifty cents and were probably on her usual subjects: "Village Life in Palestine", "The Bedouins of the Desert", and "The Life of Jacob."[217]

Political Visitors

A number of politicians visited Jefferson County in October and early November of 1904 campaigning for themselves or others. On October 10 Robert H. Patton, Prohibition Party candidate for governor, came to Mt. Vernon. On October 11 Charles S. Deneen was back in his campaign for governor. On October 20, 1904, Governor Richard Yates was in town campaigning for Deneen. And on November 2 Congressman Vespasian Warner was in Jefferson County for Deneen as well. Warner was a veteran Republican member of the U.S. House of Representatives (1895–1909).

Under the headline "A Rousing Meeting Held" the *Mt. Vernon Register* of October 21, 1904, described an evening meeting at the Grand Opera House where one thousand people packed the hall to hear Governor Richard Yates. The governor was described as being tired and hoarse-voiced due to two earlier meetings at Enfield and McLeansboro. He paid "glowing tribute" to Deneen and the other Republican candidates. This must have been difficult for him since he had wanted the party nomination to run for a second term and failed to get it. Contradicting the headline, the story described a somewhat subdued crowd, but said "… it was not the quiet of indifference, but that of genuine interest…."[218]

William Jennings Bryan

William Jennings Bryan was back in town on February 7, 1905, although very briefly. He was on a special train that passed through and didn't stop. The *Mt. Vernon Register* reported: "A special passed through here yesterday bearing William Jennings Bryan who was en route for some point in Indiana." In early 1905 Bryan was trying to regain control of the Democratic Party after its crushing defeat by Roosevelt and the Republicans in November of 1904. (Bryan was denied the nomination in 1904, which went instead to Alton Parker.) In January of 1905 Bryan met with Theodore Roosevelt and leaders of Congress. Next he was the featured speaker at the inauguration of Joseph W. Folk of Missouri. At that point he probably came through Mt. Vernon on the way to Indiana. Later, in April of 1905 he was in Chicago for a Jefferson Day Dinner.[219]

President Theodore Roosevelt

One of the most famous figures in U.S. history visited Mt. Vernon in 1905. President Theodore Roosevelt (1858–1919) came to town on April 4th, making him the first sitting president to be in Mt. Vernon. (Lincoln was in Mt. Vernon in the 1840s and 1850s but not while he was president in the 1860s.) Roosevelt, who had gained fame as a leader of the Rough Riders in the Spanish-American War (1898), was placed on the Republican ticket as the vice presidential nominee in 1900. When President McKinley was assassinated in 1901, Roosevelt became the youngest president in U.S. history at age 42. He was re-elected in 1904 and served as president from 1901 to 1909.

In April of 1905 Roosevelt was at a high point of popularity in the country. He had won a great victory in his campaign for president in November of 1904, becoming the first Republican to ever win Jefferson County. Then he toured the St. Louis World's Fair with his daughter, Alice. After his inauguration he became involved in diplomacy to try to end the Russo-Japanese War. Frustrated with the stubbornness of both sides, he decided to go ahead with a long-planned hunting trip in Oklahoma and Colorado. The trip would take him through Kentucky (Louisville), Indiana (Huntington, Milltown, Princeton), and Illinois on the way to St. Louis and the West. Between the Louisville speech and the St. Louis speech, the president made three speeches. They were at Milltown and Huntington in Indiana, and Mt. Vernon in Illinois.[220]

G.F.M. Ward

Mt. Vernon Mayor Ward did not learn that his efforts to encourage the president to stop in town had been successful until about noon of April 4th, the day of the president's arrival. He immediately issued a proclamation: "President Roosevelt will arrive at 4:45 and will talk from the train at the East side school house (Franklin School). Let every one, regardless of political affiliation turn out to hear our president." It was a bright spring day, fair and cool with a high temperature of about sixty degrees. The April 5 *Mt. Vernon Register* described the scene under the headline "He Was De-Lighted," referring to one of the president's favorite phrases. News of the president's visit spread "like wildfire" and thousands of people lined both sides of the tracks at Fifth and Main Street, Fifth and Harrison Street, and on the school grounds.

Upon the train's arrival President Roosevelt stepped to the rear of the platform, flashed that famous smile, and "amid cheer after cheer" began to talk. In his brief speech the president, after an opening greeting which included his famous "delighted," began by pointing to the "Grand Army men I see gathered around the flag." He thanked and praised these old Civil War veterans. Then he went on to a favorite theme, the importance of living a vigorous life, and told the parents in the audience "…don't make the mistake of bringing up your children too easy, … or they will know failure in the end." He referred in particular to a little boy being held up by a grandfather so he could see over the crowd. He said: "Begin your teaching while the children are young, like that little boy in your arms." The little boy was Paul Menzer, son of Mr. and Mrs. Frank Menzer, and grandson of L .C. Johnson who was holding him.[221]

Traveling with the president was Postmaster General George Cortelyou and others. In addition to being postmaster general, Cortelyou also served as the first secretary of commerce and labor and secretary of the treasury. The train pulled out before the president finished his speech. Helpless, Roosevelt had no choice but to simply wave his hands and call out "Good luck." After leaving Mt. Vernon the president's train went through Centralia, where he waved to the crowd as the train slowed, but he did not speak. He reached St. Louis at about 8:00 p.m. Not everyone was impressed with the Roosevelt visit. The *Mt. Vernon Weekly*

News of April 5, 1905, placed the story on page four and commented: "Well, we have all seen the president any way, and now we know he looks just like his pictures, teeth and all."

HE WAS DE-LIGHTED

So the President Expressed Himself on Visit Here Yesterday.

GREETED BY THE THOUSANDS

Theodore Roosevelt the First President to Visit and Make Speech in Mt. Vernon.

Mt. Vernon was honored yesterday by a visit from President Roosevelt, president of the greatest country in the world and he is the greatest president.

Not until about noon were the people sure that the president would stop here, but as soon as the fact became known the news spread like wild fire and within an hour nearly every person in the city was talking of the intended visit of the president.

the many things that has made him popular.

The President's Speech.

As soon as the train stopped he started to talk, and talked exactly two minutes.

The president said:

"My fellow citizens: I like to be in the great and beautiful State of Illinois which I know so well and I am delighted to see you. I have but a few moments and I want to speak a few words of greeting.

First, to the Grand Army men I see gathered around the flag—the men who actually did the deed instead of talking about it."

"Next to you young people. It greatly depends upon you whether thirty years hence we are as proud of this country as we are now.

"To you older people, you fathers and mothers, don't make the mistake of bringing up your children too easy. Teach them not to shirk a difficulty, or they will know failure in the end. Begin your teachings while the children are young, like that little boy in your

Roosevelt Article

The president's private car on this trip was the "Rocket." It was probably very similar to the "Elysian," another of his cars. It was described as "… seventy feet of solid mahogany, velvet plush, and

93

sinkingly deep furniture. It had two sleeping chambers with brass bedsteads, two tiled bathrooms, a private kitchen … a dining room, a stateroom with picture windows, and an airy rear platform for whistle-stop speeches."[222]

Even with these luxurious accommodations it took a lot of energy to take these trips. The president always presented himself as a man of vigor, and he was. He was almost hyperactive at times—dictating speeches, reading books and holding conversations all at the same time. His daughter, Alice, once famously said: "My father wants to be the bride at every wedding, and the corpse at every funeral." But his vigorous life had cost him. He caught "yellow fever" while leading the Rough Riders in Cuba and continued to have bouts of fever the remainder of his life. He had one of these episodes on this trip while he was in Colorado.

In addition, his vigorous life left him almost blind in one eye. Just four months before visiting Mt. Vernon, on December 11, 1904, the forty-six-year-old president was in a sparring match in the White House with a young Navy aide. He took a blow to the head that ruptured a blood vessel in his left eye, and his vision immediately began to blur.[223] None of these physical problems was reported to the public at the time. Despite these health problems, the president went on to Colorado for a week-long bear hunt while continuing his negotiations by telegram with the Russians and Japanese over the Russo-Japanese War. Later he helped negotiate the end of the war, and as a result he was awarded the Nobel Peace Prize in 1906.

Lyceum Speakers

During the 1870s, 1880s, 1890s and early 1900s, Mt. Vernon had a lyceum lecture series sponsored by different local organizations such as the Women's Club or the M.E. Church, etc. These talks would be during the winter and wouldn't conflict with the Chautauqua in the summer. As a result many of the same speakers were available for both. One of the most famous and charismatic lecturers, when he was not in elective office, was Robert Love Taylor (1850–1912). Taylor came to Mt. Vernon on October 19, 1905, as part of the lyceum program that year.[224] Mr. Taylor had a long political career as a Democrat in his home state of Tennessee. He was a U.S. representative from 1879 to 1881, governor from 1887 to 1891 (defeating his Republican brother, Alfred Taylor in 1886), and governor again from 1897 to 1899. Later he was a U.S. senator from 1907 to 1912. He was also a newspaper publisher and co-founded the *Johnson City Comet*.

Political Visitors

Also in 1905 (December 5), Eugene W. Chafin came to Mt. Vernon. He was in town to address a Prohibition Party Convention at city hall. Chafin was an attorney from Wisconsin whose entire political career was in the Prohibition Party. He was the Wisconsin Prohibition Party candidate for Congress in 1882 and for governor in 1898. He was the candidate for Illinois attorney-general in 1904. In 1908 and 1912 he was the Prohibition Party candidate for president of the United States.[225]

Governor Richard Yates was back in town March 19, 1906, this time campaigning for the U.S. Senate. Under the headline "Yates Makes Good," the *Mt. Vernon Register* reported that: "Despite a late train, impassable roads, ice and sleet, a rousing meeting is held and the former governor's friends are pleased." The governor's train was due at 3:00 p.m. and he was scheduled to speak at 3:30 at the courthouse. But his train arrived late and he began to speak at 5:00. Because of the bad weather the crowd was expected to be small, but the article stated, "Seldom has the Jefferson County Court House been so crowded and jammed."[226] Unfortunately for Yates he was up against the veteran Shelby Cullom who had been in the U.S. Senate since 1883 and wanted another term. Cullom's campaign sent former Lieutenant Governor W.A. Northcutt to Mt. Vernon on April 17, 1906 to speak for Cullom's candidacy. Northcutt had been lieutenant governor in the Yate's administration (1901–1905). Cullom was re-elected to the U.S. Senate and served his last term from 1907 to 1913.[227]

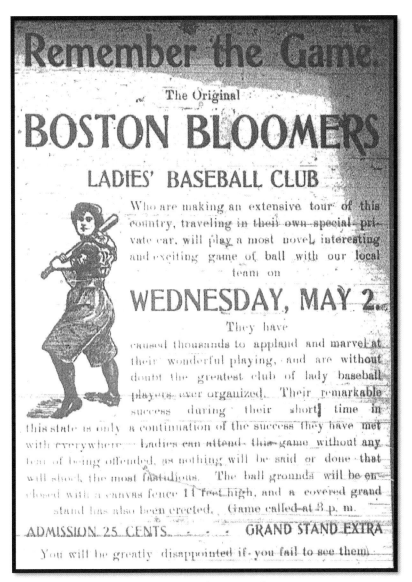

Boston Bloomers Ad

The Boston Bloomers

On May 2, 1906, the Boston Bloomers Ladies Baseball Club came to Mt. Vernon to play "our local team." They were first in town May 23, 1898, at the L. & N. depot. This team was one of a number of women's baseball teams with the same name. There were New York Bloomers, Chicago Bloomers, etc. The name comes from the Nineteenth Century women's rights activist Adelaide Jenks Bloomer, who invented and wore a pants-dress combination that scandalized some people at the time. Starting in the 1880s and continuing into the early Twentieth Century, these "Bloomers" teams toured the country, playing against local men's teams. At that time it was quite a novelty to see women playing baseball, and money could be made. To even the playing field the women's teams carried two men, usually the pitcher and the catcher, called "toppers" because they wore curly wigs over their own hair.[228]

The May 1, 1906, ad for the Bloomers' tour said the Boston Bloomers were "without doubt the greatest club of lady baseball players ever organized." The admission price for the game was twenty-five cents with grand stand extra. The ad also stated: "Ladies can attend this game without any fear of being offended, as nothing will be said or done that will shock the most fastidious." There was no immediate report on the outcome of the game. But the July 11, 1906, *Mt. Vernon Weekly News* stated that the Bloomers had been playing all over southern Illinois and that the "Mt. Vernon boys were the only nine that were gallant enough to allow the young damsels to win a game." The Boston Bloomers came back May 23, 1908, to play the local Mt. Vernon club "on the commons near the L. & N depot."[229]

Chautauqua Speakers

The Chautauqua movement came to Mt. Vernon in 1906 and brought many famous people and organizations to town during the years of its existence. The movement began in the late Nineteenth Century in New York and consisted of outdoor tent meetings on the edge of many small towns. Musical groups, preachers, politicians, and experts presented material to the attendees for a small fee over a seven-to-ten day period in the summer. Mt. Vernon had two Chautauquas in 1906. The first one was the Prohibition Chautauqua (May 27–June 3) organized by the Illinois Prohibition Party and the Women's Christian Temperance Union, and held at Green Lawn Springs (area around 6th and Jordan). It featured Colonel John Sobrieski, Mrs. Florence D. Richards, Frank S. Regan, and Chester L. Ricketts. The second Chautauqua of 1906 was the Mt. Vernon Chautauqua (August 10–19), which was also held at Green Lawn Springs. It was sponsored by local business leaders and became Mt. Vernon's main Chautauqua. It lasted until 1929 while the Prohibition Chautauqua ended after the 1908 season.[230]

Mrs. George Pickett

The 1906 Mt. Vernon Chautauqua had many performers and lecturers, but the most notable was Mrs. George Pickett (1843–1931) or Mrs. General George Pickett as she was billed. Her husband was the famous Confederate Civil War general who led the disastrous "Pickett's Charge" at the Battle of Gettysburg. Mrs. Pickett was much younger than her husband, and when he died in 1875, she was left with a young son and very little income. She turned to writing and speaking as a career, and she became a popular Chautauqua lecturer. She was generally well accepted, even in the North, but once was booed off the stage in New York by a crowd she later called "damn Yankees." Mrs. Pickett's lecture in Mt. Vernon was on Sunday afternoon, August 12, 1906. Known as the "child bride of the Confederacy," she was about 63 years old when she came to Jefferson County. She spoke about slavery, plantation life in the Old South, the Battle of Gettysburg, and of course her husband and "Pickett's Charge." The *Mt. Vernon Register* said: "No woman in America is better endowed for success upon the platform or for attaining the highest results with these subjects."[231]

William Jennings Bryan

On October 17, 1906, William Jennings Bryan made a campaign swing through Jefferson County. He was not running for any office but was speaking for state and federal Democrats. He spoke to a crowd of about seven thousand from a stand erected on the northwest corner of the square. Naturally it was a very partisan event. Here are some of the points and arguments he made. He said that Democrats favored more democracy with direct election of U.S. senators while the Republicans opposed that reform until it became very popular. He stated: "Democrats say prosperity comes up from the bottom. Republicans say it comes from the top." He said that some corporations were paying more in dividends than wages. He said the Republicans supported big business and were not serious about breaking up or regulating the trusts. For example, he recalled that years ago he had supported government ownership of railroads to keep them from cheating the people. He said: "I am glad I said it first."

Bryan also brought up one of his statements from the 1896 campaign that allowed the Republicans to brand him a radical. The statement was: "Burn your cities and leave your farms and the cities will spring up again. But burn your farms and the grass will grow in the crevices of the cities." He implied that he and the Democrats had been right all along. In summary he said that if the voters wanted real reform, they must elect Democrats. The opposition newspaper branded him a "demagogue" and a "calamity howler." It stated: "The speaker had the nerve to claim that the Democratic Party has been vindicated in all the propositions they have stood for in the last ten years. Shades of free silver at 16 to one. Is that corpse still alive?" At the close of an hour and a half address he and his colleagues boarded the special train for Effingham.[232]

Buckham's Drug Store

Pawnee Bill's Wild West Show

On May 15, 1907, Pawnee Bill's Wild West Show came to Mt. Vernon. It first came to Mt. Vernon on October 18, 1898.[233] Its full name was Pawnee Bill's Historic Wild West and Great Far East Ethnological Congress. Pawnee Bill was born Gordon W. Lillie in 1860 in Illinois. He moved to Oklahoma where he lived with and taught the Pawnee Indians. In 1883 he joined Buffalo Bill's Wild West Show, and in 1888 he formed his own show. In 1908 Pawnee Bill merged his show with Buffalo Bill's Wild West Show and toured the world as "The Two Bill's Show." Later he built a well-known tourist attraction in Oklahoma called "Pawnee Bill's Old Town and Trading Post."

When he came to Mt. Vernon in 1907, Pawnee Bill was about forty-seven years old. The *Mt. Vernon Register* said he was "historically famous as cowboy, scout, guide, explorer, plainsman, and soldier." He certainly looked like a plainsman. He dressed in buckskin and wore a sombrero over shoulder-length hair. His wife, May, was a popular act with her expert marksmanship and riding. The ad for the show claimed over one thousand men, women, and horses for the performance, and "Indian Chiefs whose names once made them dreaded, whose battles made them men of history, and whose tepees are still adorned with scalps." A street parade took place daily at 10:00 a.m. and reserved seats were on sale at Buckham's store, northwest corner of 9th and Main. The highlight of the show was "The Great Train Robbery," which employed a locomotive and train of cars. The *Register* reported it was the "sensation of New York City last summer. Nothing like it, it is said, was ever seen under canvas."

Frank Gunsalus and Joseph Folk

The 1907 Mt. Vernon Chautauqua was held at "Casey's Grove" west of the city on the Ashley Road (now about 24th and Broadway). It had many speakers and entertainers, but Frank W. Gunsalus and

Governor Joseph W. Folk were probably the most notable. Gunsalus was in Mt. Vernon in 1891 as a lyceum speaker. By 1907 he was the president of the Armour Institute of Technology, minister of the Central Church, and a major figure in Chicago. As an educator he argued for practical education for the masses, and the Gunsalus Scholastic Academy was named for him. As a pastor he brought important speakers such as Booker T. Washington and President William Howard Taft to his church and was named divinity lecturer at Yale Theological Seminary. He was often called Chicago's "First Citizen" and was a trustee of the Art Institute of Chicago and the Field Museum of Natural History, both of which have buildings named after him. Dr. Gunsalus spoke in Mt. Vernon on July 4th, 1907.[234]

Governor Joseph W. Folk of Missouri was a progressive reformer who crusaded against the special interests of the time. Known as "Holy Joe" he espoused the Missouri Idea that public office is for public good. Along with muckraking journalist Lincoln Steffens he exposed the political corruption in America's cities. He was elected governor of Missouri in 1904 and became one of the country's leading progressive reformers. He spoke at the Mt. Vernon Chautauqua on July 5, 1907.[235]

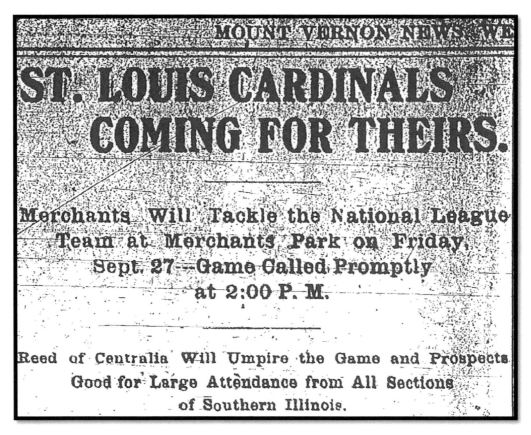

St. Louis Cardinals Article

The St. Louis Cardinals

The St. Louis Cardinals baseball team came to Mt. Vernon on September 27, 1907, via the L. & N. Railroad. Some of the players on the team that year were Harry Arndt, Moose Baxter, Bobby Byrne, and Joe Delahonty. The Cardinals were in town to play the Mt. Vernon Merchants. They played the game at Merchants Park located at about 6th and Casey in those days. The game was first announced with a large headline on September 18th. Then with much home town pride the local newspapers published the line-ups for each team and suggested that regardless of the outcome the Cardinals would know that they had "been in a game." They were clearly expecting a huge crowd. Excursions from neighboring towns were set up; ticket prices for grandstand and bleacher seats were raised; schools were dismissed.

The Cardinals won the game by a score of eight to six with three unearned runs coming as a result of errors by the Merchants' shortstop in the first inning. This so angered the Merchants' management that they publicly released the player, Offa Neal, the next day. They called his errors "inexcusable." However, the "hard feelings" did not last long because Neal, who was the Franklin County Superintendent of Schools, was signed to play shortstop for the Merchants' 1908 season in January of 1908.[236]

Charles Deneen

Illinois Governor Charles S. Deneen came to the King City on December 11, 1907. The governor was escorted from the train depot to the Jefferson County Courthouse where he gave a one hour forty-five minute speech to a standing-room-only crowd. Music was provided by Anderson's Band (probably Robert A. Anderson's Saxophone Band) and the "Deneen male quartet." The governor was preparing to run for office again in 1908. So there is no doubt that this visit was at least partly political. In his speech he touted improvements made in Illinois insane asylums, reformatories, and penitentiaries. He also spoke about convict labor improving the roads and the pure food law improving the quality of food. (The federal Meat Inspection Act and the Pure Food and Drug Act were passed in 1906 after Upton Sinclair's book *The Jungle*, had horrified readers with its description of the Chicago stockyards.) The governor also attacked the legislature for not passing his primary law. The presidential-preference primary law was finally passed in 1912.[237]

Anderson's Band

The Kilties

The Kilties, a well-known touring band from Canada, came to Mt. Vernon on March 13, 1908. (They should not be confused with the Carco Kilties, the local car shops band, which was started in 1919 and disbanded about 1925.) The Kilties was one of Canada's most popular bands of that time (1902–1933). They appeared at the St. Louis World's Fair in 1904 and gave two Royal Command Performances in Britain. From 1908 to 1910 they went around the world, eventually performing in twenty countries. They played in Mt. Vernon at the Grand Opera House at 10th and Harrison Streets. They returned on September 26, 1916, and performed at the King City Fair and the public square.[238]

Political Leaders

With 1908 being an important election year many political leaders came through Mt. Vernon in the first half of the year. Ex-Senator William E. Mason, ex-Governor Richard Yates, Congressman William Lorimer, David Braxton Turney, and Senator A. J. Hopkins made their way to town. Mason had been a U.S. senator from 1897 to 1903. He was in Jefferson County campaigning for the senate seat he lost to Albert Hopkins in 1902. He spoke at 7:30 p.m. at the courthouse on April 23, 1908.[239] Governor Yates came to the county on April 30, 1908, at 8:00 p.m. campaigning for governor again.[240] Daniel Braxton Turney, called "one of the best known men in the state" by the *Register*, visited Mt. Vernon on June 16, 1908. He was the presidential candidate on the United Christian, the Equal Rights, and the American Anti-Mormon tickets and hoped to be the nominee of the Prohibition Party. He did not speak, and "very few people were aware that the distinguished visitor was here." He would be back on July 1, 1911, to open another bid for the White House.

There is no direct information on Congressman Lorimer's reason for being in town. He was a Republican congressman from Chicago and was probably speaking for other candidates when he came to the courthouse on June 10, 1908. About one year later on June 17, 1909, he resigned his seat in the House of Representatives to take a U.S. Senate position. However, on July 13, 1912, the Senate removed him from office for using "corrupt methods" in his election. (He was accused of paying one thousand dollars to an Illinois legislator to buy his vote. In those days the legislature elected senators rather than the voters.)[241]

Senator Albert J. Hopkins (1846–1922) came to Jefferson County on July 13 and again on October 10, 1908, in his campaign for re-election. He was first elected to the U.S. Senate in 1903 after being in the U.S. House of Representatives for many years. In his July visit a reception was held at the Mahaffy House (9th and Jordan), and a meeting was held at the courthouse. The courthouse gathering was chaired by L. L. Emmerson with music provided by the Mt. Vernon Band and a double male quartet from Chicago. Hopkins was unable to speak because of a throat problem, so others spoke for him. They emphasized his support for President Roosevelt and his work on the Panama Canal project. Hopkins provided the *Mt. Vernon Register* with "Thank You" notes from Theodore Roosevelt and Secretary of War Taft for his support of the Panama Canal.[242]

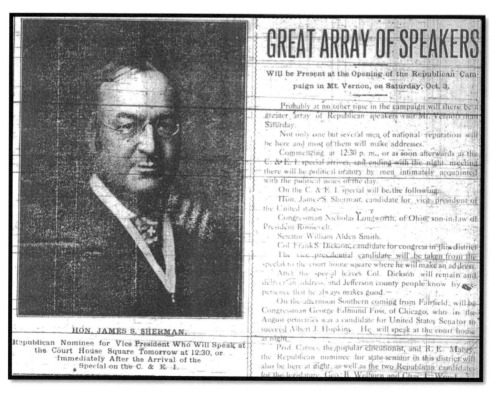

VP Sherman Article

James Sherman, Nickolas Longworth, and Others

On October 3, 1908, Mt. Vernon was visited by a number of very important politicians. The Republican nominee for vice president of the United States, James S. Sherman (1855–1912), was arguably the biggest name among them. Sherman was on the ticket with William Howard Taft who was running against William Jennings Bryan. Nicknamed "Sunny Jim," Sherman was a long-time member of Congress from New York. He and Taft won the election in 1908 and Sherman became the twenty-seventh vice president of the United States.

On the campaign train with Sherman was Nickolas Longworth (1869–1931). Longworth married Alice Roosevelt in 1906; so he was the son-in-law of former President Theodore Roosevelt. A member of the U.S. House of Representatives, Congressman Longworth did not look or act like a typical politician. Described as witty, aristocratic, and debonair, he wore spats and carried a gold-headed cane. But he was very successful. In 1910 he led a revolt against the dictatorial Speaker "Uncle Joe" Cannon. In 1912 he sided with Taft and the conservative Republicans against his own father-in-law, Theodore Roosevelt. This caused serious difficulties at home, and his wife spoke against him in his campaign for office. He became the majority leader of the House in 1923 and the speaker of the House from 1925 to 1931.

The third major figure on the train was William Alden Smith (1859–1932). Smith was a businessman (railroads and steamships), a journalist (the *Grand Rapids Herald*), as well as a U.S. representative and a U.S. senator from Michigan. After the Titanic sank in 1912, he headed the Senate hearings that heard the survivors and issued a report that led to reforms in maritime safety.

C.&E.I. Depot

These three and others came in on a C.& E. I. Railroad special for a 12:30 p.m. rally. At the same time Congressman George Edmund Foss of Chicago arrived on the Southern Railroad for an evening speech. Foss served in Congress from 1895 to1913 and 1915 to1919. He served as chairman of the Committee on Naval Affairs and was billed in the *Mt. Vernon Register* as the "Builder of the Navy." Sherman, Longworth, and Smith arrived at the C.& E. I. depot (3rd and Main) and were met with a booming cannon, the Mt. Vernon Band, and the reception committee. The square was decorated and a special speakers' platform was surrounded by a crowd estimated at five thousand to eight thousand people. Under the heading "Sunny Jim in King City" the *Register* wrote: "The King City gave a rousing welcome to Hon. James S. Sherman,

Republican candidate for vice president, this afternoon." In his speech Mr. Sherman attacked the Democrats for lacking accomplishments and following policies that would cost jobs. He ridiculed the Democrats' slogan, "Shall the people rule," as meaningless. He deflected criticism of Taft's injunctions against labor unions by saying: "The Democratic leader is trying to befog the laboring men of this country by talking about Taft's injunctions." He said that in a sense every man is a laboring man.

The *Mt. Vernon Weekly News*, which strongly favored Bryan and the Democrats, gave a very different account. The headline was: "Whoopee, But What An Early Frost: 'Sonny Jim' and Son-In-Law Nick Came and Went, Leaving a Heap of Mighty Cold Feet In Their Wake." The *Weekly News* estimated the crowd at only twenty-five hundred and claimed the "lack of enthusiasm was painfully evident throughout the day." The *Weekly News* also reprinted a highly partisan *Chicago Journal* article, which said that Sherman and Longworth were hissed and greeted with "How about Brownsville?" at a black church in Chicago. (Theodore Roosevelt had wrongly blamed black soldiers for an attack on Brownsville, Texas.) [243]

St. Louis Browns Ad

The St. Louis Browns

On October 9, 1908, the St. Louis Browns baseball team came to Mt. Vernon. They had two future Hall of Fame players with them that year—Rube Waddell and Bobby Wallace. The ad for the game stated that the "Great Rube Waddell will be here without fail and pitch the game." Waddell was a pitcher who played for the Pittsburgh Pirates (1900–1901), the Chicago Cubs (1901), the Philadelphia Athletics (1902–1907), and the St. Louis Browns (1908–1910). Considered one of the top lefties in history, he had four straight twenty-win seasons. In 1905 he had twenty-seven wins, 287 strikeouts and a 1.48 E.R.A. to lead the league in all categories. According to Connie Mack, "He had more stuff than any pitcher I ever saw." Wallace was a shortstop who played for the St. Louis Cardinals (1899–1901, and 1917–1918), and the St. Louis Browns (1902–1916). Considered one of the greatest fielding shortstops in history, he led the league in assists twice and fielding percentage three times.

The Browns played against the Mt. Vernon Merchants at Merchants Park located at 6th and Casey. Waddell pitched only one inning but played first base the remainder of the game and hit a monster home run. The newspaper reported: "Waddell starred in this inning by lifting the sphere over the fence, and sending it almost up to Skinny Kraft's lunch room near the Southern. Rube played his customary clown stunt, and his play was to appear exhausted as he neared the home plate, and instead of trotting across the plate he made a slide for the coveted station." The Browns won the game by a score of nine to two.[244]

Mt. Vernon Merchants Baseball Team

Ray Chapman

Baseball player Ray Chapman made his first professional appearance in Mt. Vernon in the summer of 1909. He was an up-and-coming star of the Herrin Merchants at that time but made it to the major leagues with the Cleveland Indians in August of 1912. He quickly became their number-one shortstop and led the league in sacrifice hits in 1913, 1917, and 1919. His mark of sixty-seven sacrifice hits remains a major league record to this day. He led the American League in putouts three times, and assists once. He hit .300 in three different seasons and led the league in runs scored and walks in 1917. He was well liked by the fans and his fellow players, and he even became a friend of the notoriously difficult Ty Cobb.

Unfortunately his career and his life came to a tragic end on August 16, 1920, when he was hit by a pitch. He became the first and only player to die from injuries suffered in a major league game. The *Mt. Vernon Register-News* had a front page headline about his death and referred to him as the "famous shortstop" of the Cleveland Indians. According to the details, he was hit by veteran pitcher Carl Mays who was an excellent player but known for "pitching inside." He would sometimes deliberately hit opposing players to intimidate them. But he wasn't just a goon. He could easily be in the Hall of Fame if it were not for this tragic incident. He had a better lifetime won/loss percentage than Hall of Famers like Bob Feller, Cy Young, Tom Seaver, Walter Johnson, Warren Spahn, Bob Gibson, Steve Carlton, and Nolan Ryan. And he probably didn't intend to hit Chapman. He threw a spit ball with a submarine delivery, and Chapman most likely didn't even see the pitch. As a result of this case, the spit ball was banned in the Major Leagues.[245]

Billy Sunday

Famous evangelist, Billy Sunday (1862–1935), came to Mt. Vernon on July 29 and 30, 1909, as the featured speaker at the Chautauqua that year. Mt. Vernon was lucky to have the preacher visit because he only occasionally spoke at Chautauquas before the 1920s. He turned down offers from Chautauqua organizations that would have brought him more money than revivals. Plus he was just at the point of becoming a more nationally-known evangelist. In 1909, the same year he came to Mt. Vernon, Billy Sunday held a revival in Spokane, Washington, which was his first meeting in a city larger than one hundred thousand people.

Sunday started his career as a professional baseball player. He played for eight years for the Chicago, Pittsburgh, and Philadelphia National League teams where he was known for his speed rather than his hitting. In 1891 he quit baseball and became a minister—beginning a career that made him wealthy and famous. By 1914 he had become possibly the most successful evangelist in United States history. He was a strict fundamentalist "fire and brimstone" evangelist who spoke against liberalism, evolution, and especially alcohol. One of his most famous sermons was "Booze, Or Get on the Water Wagon." He was a major force in bringing prohibition to the U.S. in 1919.

Anticipation of the Billy Sunday arrival was great as shown by the news articles prior to July 29–30. On June 19, the *Mt. Vernon Daily News* wrote: "We expect Billy Sunday Day to be the biggest day here for years …." On June 21, they published an ad for the Chautauqua that said: "Rev. W.A. Sunday, the eloquent and beloved Billy Sunday of pulpit and platform, the wonderful evangelist …." On July 18 they stated that he "Is the greatest Chautauqua attraction in the world…," and that "He is a man's man, an athlete in body and a giant in intellect and moral power."

Adding to the excitement was Sunday's agreement to umpire a local baseball game before his lecture. In an article titled "Billy Sunday Will Umpire Game" the *Daily News* stated that Sunday would umpire the game between the Mt. Vernon Merchants and the Kameron White Sox of East St. Louis. Sunday is quoted as saying: "I gave up ball playing and turned down $12,000 a year…." He also said he would never be able to play baseball again due to the sprained ankle he sustained when he jumped from the platform in Springfield to "take a crack at the guy that threw at me." (On February 26, 1909, in Springfield, Illinois, a man named Sherman Potts who was described as a religious fanatic by the Springfield newspapers attacked Sunday with a horsewhip at one of his revival meetings. Sunday fought off the attack but wrenched his ankle.)

On July 29, 1909, Billy Sunday arrived on the L. & N. train and was driven from the depot to the Mahaffy House by a cabman who didn't recognize him. When Sunday asked the cabby, Bill Hall, about catching a train to Chicago, he said: "You don't want to leave; Billy Sunday is umpiring a ball game and lecturing tomorrow." The game must have been exciting as the July 31 article was full of superlatives: "The crowd was the largest of the season and one of the largest in local base ball history.", "The fans witnessed the most spectacular exhibition of base ball ever pulled off here…", and according to Rev. Sunday "It was the greatest game I ever umpired and one of the best I ever saw." The Merchants won by a score of five to four in twelve innings.

Also adding to the excitement of Billy Sunday's visit was his reputation of making physical, athletic moves and having confrontations with hecklers or unbelievers. His would not be a dull, intellectual lecture. He once said: "I don't know no more about theology than a jack rabbit knows about ping pong, but I preach as hard as I can." Apparently the evangelist didn't disappoint. It was a hot, muggy July afternoon, and Sunday removed his coat, rolled up his sleeves, and tore into the evils of society. He vigorously attacked liquor and cigarettes, evolution, and the skeptics and "dreamy eyed philosophers" who undermine faith in the Bible. He often jumped up on the railing and shouted down at the audience. He fell prone on the platform to show how a drunk might commit suicide by throwing himself in front of a train. He caused laughter as he suddenly stopped and gulped down half of a large pitcher of water. The July 31 *Daily Register* titled its story: "Sunday Is Human Cyclone: Great Evangelist Takes Big Audience by Storm and Sweeps All Before Him."[246]

Sunday Article

Chautauqua and Other Visitors

The 1910 Mt. Vernon Chautauqua brought Governor Edward W. Hoch of Kansas as a featured speaker on August 18th. Mr. Hoch was governor from 1905 to 1909. He was also the publisher of the *Marion County Record*. The governor arrived at the L. & N. depot and was met by a reception committee, which took him to a local hotel for rest and lunch. His afternoon speech called "Message From Kansas" drew a large crowd and was well received.[247] Also at the 1910 Chautauqua was U.S. Senator Jonathan P. Dolliver of Iowa. He was a member of the Senate from 1900 to 1910. Dolliver spoke about the progressive reforms of the day, and particularly about doing away with "impure articles" that endanger the lives of Americans. Unfortunately he died on October 15, 1910, less than two months after he left Mt. Vernon.[248]

Although not on the Chautauqua program Raymond Robins was in town on August 25, 1910 to speak on the progressive reforms of initiative and referendum. Robins was a leader of the reform movement in Illinois and spoke at the Jefferson County Courthouse to a large crowd. He said that these reforms were the cure for the legislative corruption in the state. The *Mt. Vernon Daily News* said he was not only a fine speaker but a "fine fellow in general." Robins left petitions for voters to sign if they wanted the reforms to pass into law.[249]

Ellen M. Stone

On May 21, 1911, American missionary Ellen M. Stone came to Mt. Vernon's Methodist Episcopal Church (12th and Main) to speak. She gained world attention in 1901–1902 when she and a companion, Katarina Stefanova Tsilka, were held captive in Turkey. Their captors were Macedonian revolutionaries who demanded twenty-five thousand Turkish lira (about one hundred ten thousand dollars) for their release. The incident received extensive press coverage at the time. Whole chapters of Macedonian and Balkan history books have been devoted to it. A 1958 Yugoslav movie was inspired by it. And in 2003 Pulitzer-prize winning author, Teresa Carpenter, wrote an account of it called *The Miss Stone Affair*.[250]

Suffragettes

In the early 1900s women who campaigned for the right to vote became known in the press and later in history books as suffragettes. The movement began in the late 1800s but became much stronger in the early 1900s. During the Wilson administration women like Alice Paul and Lucy Burns led demonstrations for a constitutional amendment giving women the vote. They used civil disobedience (chaining themselves to doors in public places), hunger strikes when jailed, as well as speeches and parades. They called Woodrow Wilson "Kaiser Wilson" for his opposition to woman suffrage, while at the same time he spoke for "self government for the German people."

On June 15, 1911, two suffragettes, Miss Harriett Grim and Mrs. A.C. King who were touring Illinois in a car, came to Mt. Vernon. They may not have been famous, but their group certainly was. Harriet Grim spoke to a crowd from the bandstand on the southeast corner of the square just after the band concert. She argued that women should have the vote because "Taxation without representation is tyranny." She also said: "Women should have a chance to help make the laws they are compelled to obey." The *Mt. Vernon Register* article was titled "Suffragette Talker Interested A Crowd," and it reported that: "Miss Grim's charming manner makes one forget she is working for a cause that seems somewhat distant in Illinois." It may have seemed distant to the reporter in 1911, but the movement succeeded in 1920 after the passage of the Nineteenth Amendment to the Constitution gave voting rights to the women of the United States.[251]

William Lorimer, Len Small, and William Hale Thompson

On December 30, 1911, Mt. Vernon was visited by three politicians who at some point in their careers would be charged with corrupt practices. Senator William Lorimer (already mentioned for his 1908 visit), Len Small, and William Hale Thompson all spoke "to a good crowd" at the Jefferson County Courthouse. The *Chicago Tribune* published an admission by an Illinois assemblyman named Charles White that he had accepted money from Lorimer for his vote for the U.S. Senate seat.

At the Chicago Senate Hearings on this matter on October 15, 1911, some Mt. Vernon men were called as witnesses. One of the Mt. Vernon men, William C. Blair, was accused of accepting money for his vote for Lorimer at a meeting in Olney, Illinois, and then flashing a roll of one hundred dollar bills amounting to nearly one thousand dollars at a ball game in Centralia. Blair denied everything at first. But in a dramatic development the questioner showed him his name on the hotel register and Blair broke down. The *Mt. Vernon Daily News* reported it this way: "Mr. Blair's face colored perceptibly and his hand trembled so much that he was scarcely able to hold the book. In a trembling voice he admitted that the handwriting was his." At this point Blair admitted all that he previously had denied. The newspaper stated that he had been so intoxicated several days earlier that he was ejected from the witness stand. On this fateful day he appeared "almost a physical wreck when he tottered to the witness chair."[252] (According the *Wall's History of Jefferson County* of 1909 Blair was a "distinguished lawyer and honored official." The people of Mt. Vernon must have felt that in this instance a good man was a victim of corrupt Chicago politics, money, and alcohol.)

The December Lorimer visit to Jefferson County may have been an effort to "firm up" political support for the continuing battle to retain his office. If so, it may not have been successful. The *Mt. Vernon Weekly News* reported that "…there was no apparent rush to climb into the Lorimer bandwagon." The article called him "the blonde boss" and said that the people in attendance heard the "Silvery-tongued senator from Chicago do a sensational oratorical stunt and apply liberal supplies of whitewash to his record in and out of congress." In addition the article said that Lorimer's voice trembled with emotion as he described the fight for his political life. He was removed by the Senate in July of 1912.[253]

The second visitor, Len Small (1862–1936), was a future governor of Illinois. When he visited Jefferson County in 1911, he was not holding a political office. He had been a state senator (1901–1903), and the Illinois treasurer (1905–1907), and would be the treasurer again from 1917 to 1919. He was indicted in the 1920s for running a money-laundering scheme while he was treasurer. He was acquitted by the jury and re-elected for a second term as governor. Later, four members of the jury received state jobs.

The third of the three politicians, William "Big Bill" Thompson (1869–1944), was a future mayor of Chicago (1915–1923 and 1927–1931). He was undoubtedly corrupt but certainly entertaining. He ran a wide open city during the era of Prohibition. Chicago became known as the crime capital of the United States. Al Capone gave Thompson his support in his 1927 campaign for mayor. In return members of the "mob" could count on being released from jail because "the fix was in." Meanwhile, "Big Bill," who was planning on running for president, gathered over a million dollars and picked a very public fight with King George V of England—suggesting that if the King came to Chicago, he would "crack him in the snoot."[254]

Oscar Ameringer

Oscar Ameringer (1870–1943) gave a lecture at the Jefferson County Courthouse on February 9, 1912. He was known as the "Mark Twain of American Socialism" for his socialist beliefs delivered with humor. He started as an organizer for the Knights of Labor in 1886. Soon he was noticed for his colorful and earthy socialist writings. In 1910 he helped elect Victor Berger as the first socialist to serve in the United States Congress. Ameringer became the editor and writer for various newspapers, and in 1918 he ran unsuccessfully for Congress.[255]

Political Visitors

The year 1912 was a particularly important political year, and many notable people passed through Mt. Vernon campaigning for office. Illinois Governor Charles S. Deneen was back in town on February 17 for a speech at the courthouse. On February 23 Edward F. Dunne visited Mt. Vernon seeking the Democratic nomination for governor. On March 26 former Lieutenant Governor Lawrence Y. Sherman was in town campaigning for the U.S. Senate. He was elected and served from 1913 to 1921. On March 27 ex-Governor Richard Yates, Jr. was in Jefferson County for a speech at the courthouse. He was running for governor again but was defeated.[256]

Thomas P. Gore

On April 5, 1912, Senator Thomas P. Gore (1870–1949) was in Mt. Vernon at the Jefferson County Courthouse campaigning for Woodrow Wilson for president of the United States. Gore was known as the "blind senator" because he was totally blind, having lost his sight in childhood. He was elected to the Senate from the new state of Oklahoma in 1907 and served from 1907 to 1921 and from 1931 to 1937. He was distantly related to Senator Al Gore, Sr. and Vice President Al Gore, Jr. But he was the grandfather of the famous author, Gore Vidal. Vidal once said of his grandfather that he was a populist who didn't like people. He quoted him as saying: "If there was any other race than the human race, I'd join it."[257]

Southern Depot

Theodore Roosevelt

Ex-President Theodore Roosevelt came back to Mt. Vernon on April 21, 1912. He was running for the Republican nomination against his old friend William Howard Taft, the current president. On February 21, 1912, Roosevelt told a reporter: "My hat is in the ring, the fight is on and I am stripped to the buff." Roosevelt and Taft had become bitter enemies as T. R. felt that his "progressive" policies were not being followed by Taft. Roosevelt was in Illinois for the primary. He won Jefferson County easily by polling 1,383 votes to 557 for Taft and ninety-six for LaFollette.[258] But Taft controlled the party machinery and eventually locked up most of the GOP delegates for the summer convention. As a result Roosevelt and his followers bolted from the convention, and Roosevelt ran for president on the Progressive "Bull Moose" Party ticket. On October 14, 1912, just about six months after leaving Mt. Vernon, Roosevelt was shot while campaigning in Milwaukee, Wisconsin. The bullet lodged in his chest, but he went on to give a ninety minute speech. He was truly a larger than life figure.

In his visit to Mt. Vernon Roosevelt was only supposed to make a very brief stop with no speech scheduled. But many people came just to see him. The *Mt. Vernon Daily News* put it this way: "… many of Mr. Roosevelt's admirers hope it (the stop) will be long enough to salute the famous Rough Rider, or at least to get a glimpse of his teeth." (Roosevelt was well known for his toothy smile.) The president, traveling from St. Louis on a special train on the Southern Railway, arrived in Mt. Vernon about noon on a Sunday. The Southern depot (5th and Main) was filled with approximately fifteen hundred people. He came to the rear platform of his private car, shook hands with a few people, and told everyone he was "dee-lighted." The *Mt. Vernon Daily Register* said: "Mr. Roosevelt looked fine …. He had his big, broad smile and he fairly beamed on the large crowd that had gathered to greet him."[259] So apparently the crowd did get to see his teeth!

VOLUME 20—NUMBER 219. MT. VERNON, ILLINOIS, MONDAY, AUGUST 19th, 1912

reat Throngs For Bryan Day

at Commner Attracts Hosts of Admirers from this Section of Southern Illinois---The Register Gives Lecture in Full

WILLIAM JENNINGS BRYAN
Who delivered his world-famous lecture at the chautauqua this afternoon.

Bryan Article

William Jennings Bryan at the Chautauqua

In August of 1912 the Mt. Vernon Chautauqua opened at its usual site (24th and Broadway) with William Jennings Bryan as the featured speaker. The early information was that he would arrive on the Southern Railroad and deliver an address called the "Prince of Peace." But instead he went to Salem to visit his cousin, J. E. Bryan, then to Centralia, then to Walnut Hill to visit with his uncle, Z. C. Jennings. Next the Bryan party of about twenty automobiles drove to Mt. Vernon for lunch on August 19 at the R. L. Lacy home at 1106 Oakland Avenue.

After lunch Mr. Bryan drove to the Chautauqua grounds for his 3:00 p.m. lecture, which was called "The Making of a Man." It was a hot, sunny August day in Mt. Vernon. A crowd of at least six thousand, "the greatest crowd that ever poured into the Chautauqua grounds," heard Bryan's lecture about religion, evolution, and the origin of life. It was printed in full in the *Mt. Vernon Daily Register*, and in it Bryan made these points: "Even some older people profess to regard religion as a superstition, pardonable in the ignorant, but unworthy of the educated—a mental state which one can and should outgrow.", "I passed through a period of skepticism when I was in college and I have been glad ever since that I became a member of the church before I left home for college, for it helped me during those trying days.", and "I do not carry the doctrine of evolution as far as some do; I have not yet been able to convince myself that man is a lineal descendant of the lower animals. I do not mean to find fault with you if you want to accept it; all I mean to say is that while you may trace your ancestry back to the monkey if you find pleasure or pride in doing so, you shall not connect me with your family tree without more evidence than has yet been produced." After the speech hundreds of people rushed forward to shake the "Great Commoner's" hand. But according to the *Daily Register*: "… nearly everybody wanted to shake hands with him, (but) the cruelty of the performance in the hot sun kept a large part of the people from doing so." The *Daily Register* called it a "brilliant and able lecture."

William T. Pace

Following the afternoon program, Bryan was entertained with a dinner and reception at the home of Judge and Mrs. William T. Pace at 300 N. 10th Street. Those who attended the dinner were Mr. and Mrs. G. F. M. Ward, Mr. and Mrs. R. F. Buckham, Mr. and Mrs. Louis Bittrolf, Mr. and Mrs. L. L. Emmerson, and T. J. Mathews of Mt. Vernon, and Mr. and Mrs. J. E. Bryan of Salem. At the reception more than two hundred people attended, and "the yard at the Pace home was filled with persons anxious to shake hands with Mr. Bryan." Bryan left on the evening C.& E. I. train for Petersburg, Illinois, where he was scheduled to speak at their Chautauqua on August 20th. However, he would soon be back in Mt. Vernon on a very different mission.[260]

The Ringling Brothers Circus

On September 10, 1912, the people of Mt. Vernon had an additional break from politics when the Ringling brothers and their famous circus came to town. This year the circus featured the story of Joan of Arc, a cast of twelve hundred people, six hundred horses, and one thousand other animals. The artists from around the world included the Ty-Bell Human Butterflies, Caesaro the Human Top, Mijarez the Cuban fire wizard, and the Klarkonian aerialists from England. The circus had grown to huge proportions. The same show filled Madison Square Garden in New York. The article stated that: "When it appears in this city, it will cover fourteen acres of ground." It required an entire train just to transport the stage, costumes and property. Apparently the circus was well attended. The local paper reported, "From all parts of the county and on every train entering the city people are pouring into Mt. Vernon to see the Ringling Brothers Circus." By this time one of the brothers, Otto, had died (1911). But Al Ringling was still the ringmaster; Charles was the business manager; and John was the advance man. Therefore, the Ringling brothers would have been in Mt. Vernon with their circus.[261] (Note that someone has written 1907 on the Ringling Brothers Circus pictures. But the circus actually visited in 1912. The first two pictures seem to show the parade heading west on Broadway at the corner of Tenth and Broadway.)

Ringling Brothers Circus

Hiram W. Johnson

In the fall of 1912 it was back to politics with many famous or well-known political figures coming to Mt. Vernon. Governor Hiram W. Johnson (1866–1945) of California came on September 18th. Johnson was running for vice president of the United States on the Progressive Party ticket with Theodore Roosevelt. As a progressive Republican governor (1911–1917), he helped bring about reforms such as direct election of U.S. senators, initiative, referendum, and recall. After his unsuccessful run for vice president, Johnson was elected to a second term as governor and then was elected to the U.S. Senate from California. As a senator (1917–1945) Johnson was known as a progressive and an isolationist. He pushed for women's suffrage and was the only senator to vote against both the League of Nations and the United Nations. He is often quoted today for his statement that "the first casualty when war comes, is truth." He ran unsuccessfully for the Republican nomination for president of the United States in 1920 and 1924.

The governor arrived on the Bull Moose Special on the C.& E. I. from Benton along with state Senator Frank Funk, the Progressive Party candidate for Illinois governor. The party was taken from the station in four automobiles to the east side of the Jefferson County Courthouse, which had been decorated with huge American flags. A band and large crowd awaited them. Johnson spoke about progressive principles, a fair deal for all human kind, and the importance of initiative, referendum, and recall. After the speeches Governor Johnson shook hands with many people and returned to the station for the ride to his next campaign stop in Fairfield.[262]

Deneen, Dunne, and James Hamilton Lewis

Also in September both political parties had important campaign rallies in Jefferson County. On September 19th Governor Charles Deneen was in Mt. Vernon campaigning for re-election. On September 20th Edward F. Dunne and James Hamilton Lewis were in town for a Democratic rally at the Jefferson County Courthouse. Dunne, the mayor of Chicago from 1905 to 1907, was running for governor of Illinois against incumbent Deneen. He would be elected and serve from 1913 to 1917. Lewis, a former member of the U.S. House of Representatives, was running for the U.S. Senate. He won the contest and served from 1913 to 1919 and from 1931 to 1939. Lewis was a colorful character in appearance. He wore pince-nez glasses, spats, and a wavy-pink toupee. But he was a good speaker and an authority on the U.S. Constitution and foreign affairs. He must have been good at legislative in-fighting as he served as Democratic majority whip. While serving in the 1930s he tried to help the new senator from Missouri, Harry Truman. He sat next to him and said: "Harry, don't start out with an inferiority complex. For the first six months you'll wonder how the hell you got here, and after that you'll wonder how the hell the rest of us got here."[263]

Yates, Bryan, and Dunne

The final political visitors of 1912 came to Jefferson County in October. On October 1, ex-Governor Richard Yates was at an evening rally at the courthouse to speak for the candidacy of Governor Charles Deneen.[264] And on October 28 William Jennings Bryan was back in Mt. Vernon to speak for Woodrow Wilson for president and for other Democrats. With him was Edward F. Dunne, the candidate for Illinois governor, and other officials. They arrived from Salem on a "Flying Special" at the C.& E. I. station (3rd and main) at about 9:00 a.m. and were greeted by a crowd of two thousand people. After lauding Wilson for president, Dunne for governor, M. D. Foster for congressman-at-large, and other Democrats Bryan defended his party against charges that their election would bring a "panic" or depression. According to his assertions, it was the Republicans who had caused all the "panics." He said: "If it be possible that a few men in Wall Street, where Republican laws have enabled them to centralize the wealth of the country, can precipitate a panic, then the Republican Party which freed the slaves has enslaved ninety millions of freemen."

Bryan attacked both Taft and Roosevelt as being creatures of Wall Street and the trusts. About Taft he stated: "Taft has been repudiated by the nation. Roosevelt is responsible for Taft; he patented him and guaranteed him, and then in the hour of failure deserted him. I was not disappointed in Mr. Taft as Col.

112

Roosevelt and others were, who promised so much, for the reason that that I never expected much of him." About Roosevelt he said: "If Col. Roosevelt tells you he can bring about the reforms demanded, tell him he had twice the time and opportunity of Mr. Taft in which to do nothing and he did it, and if he did nothing in seven years, he cannot with good grace ask for another term in which to accomplish the work." And about Republicans in general he stated: "It seems when a Republican gets too bad to remain a Republican he becomes a progressive."

After his speech the train headed south to Benton and other points in the southern Illinois campaign swing. Wilson won the three-way race for the White House (He won Jefferson County by about fourteen hundred votes.), and because of Bryan's help in the campaign, named him secretary of state. Bryan held that job from 1913 to 1915 when he resigned over his disagreement with Wilson's strong diplomatic notes to Germany about U.S. freedom of the seas. Bryan feared this would drag us into World War I.[265]

Charles W. Bryan

William Jennings Bryan's brother, Charles W. Bryan (1867–1945), came to Mt. Vernon on February 13, 1913. At the time Charles Bryan was the business manager of the *Commoner*, a newspaper owned and edited by his brother. He went on to become the mayor of Lincoln, Nebraska, then governor of Nebraska from 1923 to 1925 and from 1931 to 1935. Charles Bryan was also the Democratic vice presidential candidate in 1924. When he came to Jefferson County in 1913, Mr. Bryan was returning from a visit with his brother in Miami, Florida. While in Mt. Vernon Charles Bryan and his wife were the guests of Dr. and Mrs. Letcher Irons at 1036 Maple Street. (Irons was the owner of the W. C. & W. Railroad.) After leaving Mt. Vernon, Mr. and Mrs. Bryan visited relatives in Salem, Illinois, and returned to their home in Lincoln, Nebraska.[266]

Chautauqua Speakers

The 1913 Mt. Vernon Chautauqua was held at the usual place from August 8 to 17. Herbert S. Hadley, the ex-governor of Missouri, was a scheduled speaker for August 13th, which was titled "Hadley Day" on the published program. However, the governor became ill and was replaced by ex-Senator W. E. Mason. Another featured speaker was Bishop Edwin Holt Hughes who was also honored with a "Bishop Hughes Day" title in the program. Hughes was a pastor, then president of DePauw University from 1903 to 1909, and finally a bishop of the Methodist Episcopal Church. He was a major figure in the Methodist Church until his death in 1950.[267]

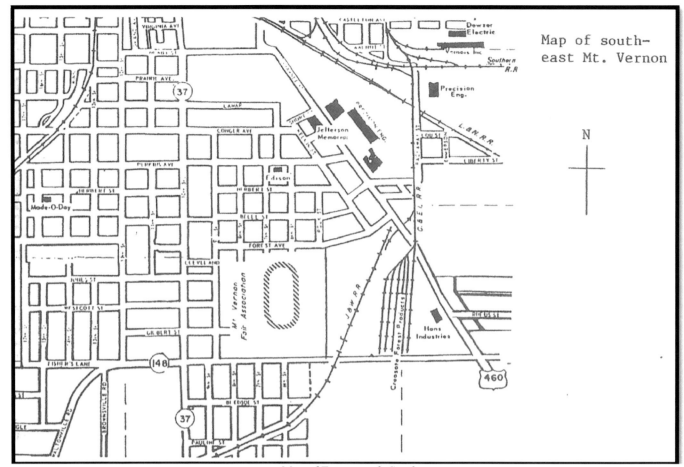

Map of Fairgrounds South

The Benoist Aeroplane Company

Officials of the King City Fair of 1913—which was in south Mt. Vernon by 1906—announced that the Benoist Aeroplane Company would be an attraction. The newspaper reported that this would be "the first visit of aeroplanes to this city…." It had only been ten years since the first successful motorized flight by the Wright Brothers at Kitty Hawk, and seeing airplanes was very exciting for people. The *Mt. Vernon Daily Register* wrote: "A close inspection of the machines will be accorded the public, a favor that is very seldom granted. The privilege of getting a close view of these wonderful air machines is well worth the price of admission to the grounds." Companies like Benoist were the early beginnings of what later became "barnstorming," where groups of daredevil pilots would tour the country using farmers' fields as landing places. Originally the famous "aerialist" Tony Jannus was to be in Mt. Vernon, but due to a conflict with the Centralia Fair, he was replaced with a pilot named Earle Wymark. Wymark's engine failed and he crashed in the "South part" of Mt. Vernon. He was not hurt, but some people received a close-up view of an "aeroplane" without paying admission to the fair.[268]

Raymond Robins

On February 28, 1914, Raymond Robins, the Progressive Party candidate for the U.S. Senate, gave a speech at the courthouse. Robins led an unusual life. He was an attorney, social worker, lecturer, and politician. As a young man he took part in the Alaskan "gold rush" of 1898 where he had a religious rebirth. Next he moved to Chicago where he worked with Jane Addams of Hull House fame. He met and married Margaret Dreier who was president of the National Women's Trade Union League from 1907 to 1922, and both became very involved in the progressive movement. (She gave a speech at the Jefferson County

114

Courthouse on October 15, 1912.) By 1914 Mr. Robins was state chair of the Progressive Party of Illinois and began working with Theodore Roosevelt and other Progressive Party leaders. In 1917 as a member of the American Red Cross he was in Russia during the Bolshevik Revolution where he met Vlademir Lenin and Leon Trotsky. In the 1920s and 1930s his political philosophy shifted drastically as he supported conservative Republicans Calvin Coolidge and Herbert Hoover, and then liberal Democrat Franklin Roosevelt.[269]

Roger Sullivan

Roger Sullivan, the long-time head of the Cook County Democrats and Chicago mayor, invaded the "enemy's stronghold" when he came to Mt. Vernon on May 14, 1914. His political base was Irish-Catholic Chicago, and he was seen as an outsider even by Jefferson County Democrats. However, he was the Democratic candidate for the U.S. Senate and needed to drum up support downstate if he wanted to win. That he had a lot of work to do is indicated by this statement in the *Mt. Vernon Daily Register*: "… visitors began to call to pay their respects to the man from Cook County whom they had been led to believe had real horns, and that he even went so far as to have them manicured every morning." Sullivan made his way from Ashley to Woodlawn where he was met by Mt. Vernon people in automobiles. They paraded through Mt. Vernon honking their horns on the way to the Mahaffy House at 9th and Jordan. There a reception was held where Mr. Sullivan said: "Gentlemen, this is indeed a happy time for me. Delving into the heart of the enemy's country and to find such a warm welcome." He would be back in Jefferson County in the fall for more campaigning.[270]

Cannon Ad

"Uncle Joe" Cannon at the Chautauqua

The famous "Uncle Joe" Cannon (1836–1926) made his one and only appearance at any Chautauqua in Mt. Vernon on August 11, 1914. Cannon is considered the most dominant speaker of the U.S. House of Representatives in history. He was a Republican from Danville, Illinois, who was first elected to the House in 1872. He was the speaker of the House from 1903 to 1911, making him the longest-serving Republican speaker until Dennis Hastert in 2006. He was often described as a farm-belt hick by the eastern newspapers because of his appearance (Nineteenth Century clothes and beard with an ever-present cigar), and manners (rough speech with many curse words). He opposed all progressive ideas and leaders including Democrats like Bryan and Woodrow Wilson, and Republicans like Theodore Roosevelt. He once remarked about Roosevelt that he had "no more use for the Constitution than a tomcat has for a marriage license." After a progressive revolt ousted him from the job as speaker in 1911 he was re-elected to the House and served until 1922. He was certainly one of the most colorful and important political figures to come to Jefferson County.

L. L. Emmerson Home

L. L. Emmerson

There was great anticipation for the Joseph Cannon speech with articles and ads in May, June, and July telling of his visit. Part of the attraction was that his success and position made him one of the most important men of the time, but certainly part of it was his tendency to use profanity in his speeches. People must have thought his appearance wouldn't be dull. August 11 was called "Cannon Day" and brought a record crowd to the Chautauqua grounds. Cannon had lunch at the L. L. Emmerson home at 701 Jordan Street and was given a reception at the Third National Bank at 101-103 South 10th Street where he spoke of famous men he had known from Lincoln and Grant to the present leaders. A few minutes before his speech Speaker Cannon spoke with Edwin Rackaway of the *Mt. Vernon Register* and said: "I am scared to death. I don't know what I can say to entertain that bunch of women and kids. I can make a political speech any time, anywhere, and I have always been able to hold up my end of it in a debate in Congress, but when it comes to entertaining a bunch of women and kids, I am out of my element. I'd rather take a good licking than go through with this." The editor remarked years later that "… the old gentleman was scared, badly scared."

Speaker Cannon was also very concerned about his daughter, Helen, who was touring Europe in August just as World War I began. Part of the headline in the August 26, 1914, *Mt. Vernon News* stated: "Uncle Joe was worrying about daughter when at Chautauqua." Miss Cannon arrived safe in the United States on August 24 and said: "It was my wonderful father that got us through. Long before we had any idea of the seriousness of the situation he was at work over here." The only reason he had come to Mt. Vernon, he said, was to do a favor for his friend, Mt. Vernonite L. L. Emmerson.[271]

Evidently Mr. Cannon was able to pull himself together and gave a ninety-minute speech that was favorably received. Apparently his remarks were spontaneous. Earlier in the day when asked for the subject of his talk, he responded, "Damifino." He spoke about the Constitution, the government, and issues of the day such as woman suffrage. (He was against a Constitutional Amendment, but was willing for each state to decide the matter.) He also told a few "stories for which he is noted." He only "slipped up" once. Toward the end of his address when telling a story about winning a lawsuit for a poor widow who couldn't pay him, he said that he didn't give a blank if he ever got paid. The *Mt. Vernon Register* story said the women in the audience looked at each other and remarked, "There, he's done it." Because of "Uncle Joe's" reputation, the audience took his slip in good humor. As a matter of fact they probably would have been disappointed if he hadn't slipped. Regardless of what the people of Mt. Vernon thought, Joseph Cannon didn't think the speech was worth anything and refused to take any pay. And he never spoke at a Chautauqua again.[272] (Note the wrong date on the picture.)

Chautauqua in Mt. Vernon – Aug 5, 1909

Uncle Joe Cannon   Len Merritt

Dr. Mitchell & Wife, May Willis, Earl Hinman & Wife
Tom Mitchell & Wife, Edna Daniels Mitchell

Uncle Joe Cannon

Frederick Cook

Appearing on August 13, 1914, at the Mt. Vernon Chautauqua was the famous polar explorer, Frederick Cook (1865–1940). Dr. Cook was a surgeon who became interested in the great quest of the late Nineteenth and early Twentieth Centuries to reach the North Pole. He was on Robert Peary's expedition of 1891–92 and in 1903 led an effort to climb Mt. McKinley. In 1909 he claimed that on April 21, 1908, he and two Inuit men were the first to reach the North Pole. Later—in 1909—Robert Peary claimed that his expedition was the first to reach the North Pole in April of 1909 and that Cook was a fraud. At that point a great controversy arose that continues to this day. However, when Cook was unable to provide proof of his success, most of the world began to discredit him and support Peary.

So when Dr. Cook agreed to speak at the Mt. Vernon Chautauqua, the controversy was still ongoing. In a preview article on July 7, 1914, the *Mt. Vernon Register* seemed to support Cook by saying: "People began to wonder how Cook had been able to so perfectly anticipate the description Peary gave of these regions if he had not really been to the Pole." They went on to say, however, that Chautauqua goers should listen to his lecture and decide for themselves as to its truthfulness.[273] Cook spent the rest of his life defending his truthfulness, but attacks from his opponents continued and his reputation never recovered. In 1923 he was convicted of stock fraud and was jailed until 1930.

A Debate on Socialism

Also at the 1914 Mt. Vernon Chautauqua two very well-known men were in town to engage in a debate on socialism. Carl D. Thompson was a Christian Socialist author, lecturer, and politician. He was the Socialist Party's nominee for governor of Wisconsin in 1912. Later he was the head of the Socialist Party's National Lecture Bureau. James A. Bede was a publisher and lecturer. He was elected to the U.S. House of Representatives from Minnesota and served from 1903 to 1909.[274]

Roger Sullivan

As the 1914 calendar moved to September, October, and November, the election campaigns sent many political figures to Jefferson County. The September 23, 1914, *Mt. Vernon Register* had a front page story titled "Hon. Roger C. at Fair Today." It referred to Roger C. Sullivan, mayor and Democratic boss of Chicago, who was back again. In the morning he was met at the C. & E. I. depot by some of the "best known" Democrats of the city and county and escorted to the Mahaffy House for a reception. In the afternoon he visited the King City Fair where he mingled and shook hands with people but did not address the crowd.

However, the absence of some of the most prominent Democrats indicated a split in the party. An article in the August 22, 1914, *Mt. Vernon Daily News* by W. Duff Piercy and reprinted in the October 31, 1914, *Mt. Vernon Register* explains the problem. Sullivan was seen as an old time political boss who didn't believe in the progressive ideas of William Jennings Bryan. As a matter of fact the big city bosses were targets of the progressives who said: "The cure for the ills of democracy, is more democracy." The article asked the question "Shall we follow Bryan or Sullivan?" and answered by stating that the people of this state would not submit to a politician of this type holding such a high office. Mr. Piercy quoted Bryan as saying "Sullivan is the Lorimer of Illinois Democracy." (Lorimer was kicked out of the Senate for bribery.) Piercy also said the only Democrats for Sullivan in southern Illinois had thrown principles to the wind and accepted Sullivan's "golden ducats." As a result, Sullivan lost his bid for the Senate. However, he remained powerful in Chicago until his death. He is even given credit with throwing the Democratic presidential nomination to Ohio Governor James M. Cox in 1920 with his deathbed instructions.[275]

Theodore Roosevelt at the Fair

Theodore Roosevelt came back to Mt. Vernon on September 25, 1914, campaigning for the Progressive Party. After his defeat as the Progressive Party presidential nominee in 1912, the ever active

Roosevelt went on a scientific expedition to the Brazilian jungle in March and April of 1914. While there he suffered from a serious infection and high fever that almost killed him. When he returned to the U.S. on May 19 of 1914, he had lost about fifty pounds. He had continuing health problems for the remainder of his life. On June 11 he left on a trip to Spain to attend his son's wedding. Upon the president's return his doctor recommended total rest "or he will never really be well again," and he advised that Roosevelt "not go into any strenuous campaign this year." Against doctor's orders Roosevelt campaigned for progressives in New York in August and then boarded a train for Illinois in September to campaign for Raymond Robins in his run for a U.S. Senate seat.

First official word that Roosevelt would be in Mt. Vernon came in an article in the *Register* of September 11, 1914, titled "Teddy Coming During Fair." The tentative schedule was for the ex-president to arrive on the C.& E. I. Railroad from Marion, to spend about forty minutes in town, and then to transfer to the Southern Railroad for stops at Centralia and East St. Louis. A follow-up article on the 15th added that Roosevelt would come to the fairgrounds (in south Mt. Vernon) by auto about four o'clock in the afternoon, and that the King City Fair officials would open the gates to the public at that time. Another article on the 24th repeated the above information and added that Raymond Robins, the Progressive Party Senate candidate would also speak.

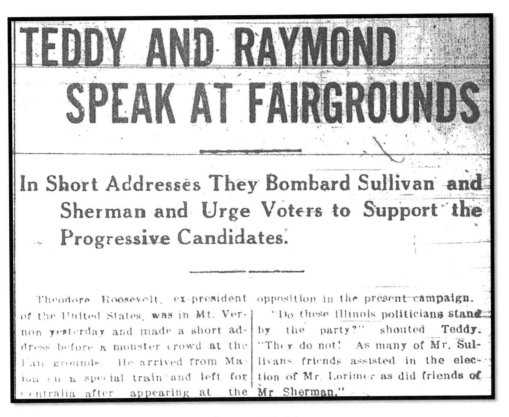

Roosevelt Article

On the 25th of September the Roosevelt train actually came through Mt. Vernon twice. First the party went south on the C. & E. I. tracks through Mt. Vernon on the way to Marion. They picked up Louis G. Pavey, the Progressive Party candidate for state treasurer, and a *Mt. Vernon Daily Register* reporter. Also in the party were the above mentioned Raymond Robins, Medill McCormick, O.K. Davis, Archie Hamill, Ed Carbine, and many Chicago and New York reporters. Second the train returned to Mt. Vernon from Marion, and Roosevelt was driven to the fairgrounds. The weather was perfect and the "monster crowd" was estimated at twelve thousand. The car pulled onto the race track in front of the grandstand, and the crowd was invited to gather around.

After shaking hands and patting a boy on the head Roosevelt spoke for about four minutes. (According to local sources the boy was Wayman Sledge.) He praised the Progressive Party candidates in general and Senate candidate Raymond Robins in particular. And he spoke against Robins' opponents—Democrat Roger Sullivan and Republican Lawrence Sherman. Because it had only been about four months since he returned from his expedition to the Amazon, someone asked him about his health. He replied that he was "worth several dead men yet." The *Mt. Vernon Daily News* reporter wrote: "Reports of his failing health are not borne out by the color of his cheeks. Apparently he is the same vigorous citizen who was want to wield the Big Stick with such famous results."

Robins spoke next for a few minutes. After thanking Roosevelt he also attacked his opponents, called Sullivan a "thick-necked Chicago boss," and said Sherman "has been mixed up with the bipartisan gang at Springfield too long." With that they said their good-byes and the car took them back to their train. Roosevelt was never to return to Mt. Vernon. He died just a little over four years later on January 6, 1919.[276]

Political Visitors—Malone, Sherman, Patterson, Lowden, and Rainey

Many more notable political figures came through Jefferson County in October of 1914. On October 14 Dudley Field Malone came to Mt. Vernon. At this time he was the collector of the port of New York and was in town to deliver an address for Roger Sullivan and the Democratic ticket at the courthouse. In 1912 he was a campaign manager for Woodrow Wilson, and when Wilson was elected, he was appointed assistant secretary of state under William Jennings Bryan.[277] He was probably most well known as one of the defense attorneys in the Scopes "Monkey Trial" in 1925. On October 16 Senator Lawrence Y. Sherman was in Jefferson County campaigning for retention of his Senate seat and spoke at the courthouse. He won and served from 1914 to 1921. On October 17 Malcolm R. Patterson was in the county to speak for the Anti-Saloon League. He was a member of the U.S. House of Representatives from Tennessee from 1901 to 1907 and the governor of Tennessee from 1907 to 1911.[278]

On October 26 Frank O. Lowden was in Mt. Vernon at the courthouse campaigning for the Republican Party. At the time he was a member of the U.S. House of Representatives from Illinois but later would be a governor and presidential candidate. The next day on October 27 Henry T. Rainey came to the Jefferson County Courthouse to speak for the Democrats. He was a fifteen term member of the U.S. House of Representatives from Illinois from 1903 to 1934 and was speaker of the House for the 73rd Congress. One source called him "one of Illinois' most influential national political figures in the first third of the Twentieth Century."[279] When Rainey died in 1934, President Franklin Roosevelt was one of the estimated thirty-five thousand in attendance.[280]

Frank Cannon

On November 24, 1914, Senator Frank J. Cannon came to Mt. Vernon as a lyceum speaker. His father was an apostle in the Church of Jesus Christ of Latter-day Saints (Mormons). Frank Cannon, himself, was a U.S. senator from Utah and later was the editor of several Utah newspapers. By the time he came to Mt. Vernon Cannon had turned against the Mormons and had written an anti-Mormon book. Plus he toured the country speaking against Mormonism and polygamy. He said Mormons were like slaves to the church authorities and had "no more right of judgment than a dead body."[281]

Marie C. Brehm

On April 6, 1915, Marie C. Brehm spoke in Mt. Vernon at the Presbyterian Church (southwest corner of 10th and Harrison). She was a suffragette and an official in the Women's Christian Temperance Union. Later, in 1924, she was the first legally-qualified female candidate to run for vice president of the United States as the Prohibition Party candidate. Her lecture in Mt. Vernon in 1915 was on temperance, one of the many anti-liquor reforms of the era that led to the Eighteenth Amendment in 1919.[282]

Keller Article

Helen Keller and Anne Sullivan

The famous Helen Keller (1880–1968) was at the Mt. Vernon Chautauqua on August 17, 1915. Miss Keller was one of the best-known people ever to come to Jefferson County. By the time she came to Mt. Vernon she was already well known. She was the first deaf/blind person to graduate from college (Radcliffe magna cum laude, 1904), and had written her autobiography, *The Story of My Life* in 1903. The book told the famous story of how Anne Sullivan was able to reach the spoiled little girl and help her overcome her disabilities. Not so well known in 1915 or now was Helen Keller's political activism. She was a believer in women's suffrage, pacifism, and birth control. She founded the Helen Keller International Organization for preventing blindness in 1915. She was a member of the Socialist Party and joined the Industrial Workers of the World (IWW) in 1912. (After leaving Mt. Vernon in August of 1915 she wired President Wilson to plead for his help to stop the execution of the famous IWW member, Joe Hill. Hill was executed by firing squad on November 15, 1915.) In 1920 she helped found the American Civil Liberties Union (ACLU).

However, her address at the Chautauqua was not to be political. Her teacher and companion, Anne Sullivan introduced her by telling her life story.[283] Then Helen Keller gave a lecture titled "Happiness" and answered questions from the audience. One questioner asked if she could distinguish color, and her answer was "Only when I'm blue." Another person asked if she could hear the encores, and she replied "Only through my feet." A third person asked her age. Her smiling answer was "I do not think that is a polite question." (She was thirty-five years old in 1915.) The answers to the first two questions were certainly rehearsed. See the next paragraph on her preparations.

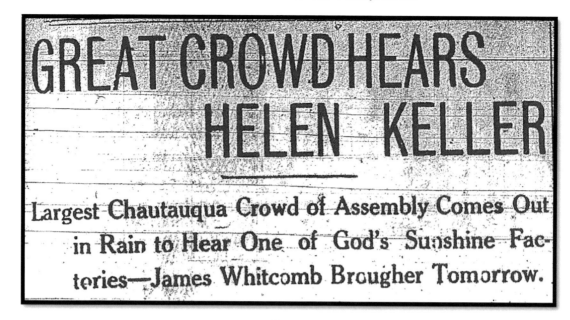

Keller Article

Helen and Anne had prepared for the Chautauqua circuit in many ways. She took voice lessons to make her high-pitched, mechanical voice more understandable. She had both eyes surgically removed and replaced with glass ones. Many people who met her remarked about her beautiful eyes, not realizing they were glass. She and Anne prepared answers for questions she might be asked. For example, if she was asked her idea of unhappiness, she would say "Having nothing to do." If she was asked if she could perceive colors, she would say "Sometimes I feel blue and sometimes I see red." If she was asked if she could tell when the audience cheered, she would say "Only through my feet." She tested herself for the first time on the lecture stage in 1913. She had terrible stage fright and fled the stage in tears. But the audience was enthusiastic, and she needed the three hundred dollar per appearance fee. She went on the Chautauqua lecture circuit full time in 1914. So when she came to Mt. Vernon in August of 1915, she was well prepared.[284]

According to reports, it was raining and very muddy at the west Broadway Chautauqua grounds. But several thousand people waded through the mud to be there that evening. The *Mt. Vernon Register* wrote: "Few attractions would have brought such a crowd under such uninviting conditions, but Miss Keller is such an unusual being that everyone is anxious to see and hear her." The reviews for both Anne Sullivan and Helen Keller were very positive. Speaking of Sullivan the *Register* stated that her work with Keller clearly placed her "among the most wonderful of all teachers," and that the "modern miracle of Helen Keller was due in a large part to her wonderful teacher." Of Helen Keller's presentation and answers the newspaper used words such as witty, clever, intellectual, and interesting. Although the reporter said her voice did not sound "natural," he went on to call her "one of God's Sunshine Factories," and said: "The smiling, cheerful face of Miss Keller made the audience forget her affliction and the hundreds gathered to hear her were entertained and delighted to an unusual degree of satisfaction."[285]

Anne Sullivan's health began to decline about the time she visited Jefferson County, and she died in 1936. Helen Keller carried on with another companion and became even more famous as the years went by. She met every U.S. president from Grover Cleveland to Lyndon Johnson and counted Alexander Graham Bell, Charlie Chaplin and Mark Twain as friends. In 1964 she was awarded the Presidential Medal of Freedom by President Johnson.

Captain Jack Crawford

Also at the 1915 Mt. Vernon Chautauqua was a widely-known, colorful figure. He was Captain Jack Crawford, the "poet scout of the Black Hills." A wounded veteran of the Civil War, Crawford went west as a journalist and became a well-known frontier scout. He replaced Buffalo Bill Cody as chief of scouts for the 5th Cavalry on August 24, 1876. After working for the army he became a post trader, rancher, and miner. Later he traveled the country as an actor and lecturer, and joined Buffalo Bill's Wild West Show. When he came to Jefferson County on August 18, 1915, his talk was called, "The Camp, Field, and Trail." There is no description of him at the Chautauqua. But he usually stepped onto the stage dressed in a buckskin coat and a wide sombrero over shoulder-length hair, and carried a rifle with a six-shooter strapped at his waist. To close his lectures he often illustrated how Wild Bill Hickok defended himself from two outlaws approaching from front and back. He would fire forward and over the shoulder with his gun and exit to thunderous applause. Jack Crawford died in 1917, about two years after appearing in Mt. Vernon.[286]

Lawrence Y. Sherman

Another notable person who spoke at the 1915 Chautauqua was Senator Lawrence Y. Sherman of Illinois. Sherman was already well known in Jefferson County, and the August 10 *Mt. Vernon Daily Register* headline was "Sherman Coming to Mt. Vernon Chautauqua." This article was much bigger than the story about Helen Keller next to it. Part of the excitement for Sherman's appearance was his interest in running for president in the 1916 Republican primary. Most of the article was about his presidential prospects and about his refusal to accept a fee for his speech. He spoke at the Chautauqua on August 20, 1915. He did not win the Republican nomination in 1916, which went to Charles Evans Hughes.[287]

Charles S. Deneen

From September 23 to 27, 1915, Mt. Vernon hosted a Methodist Episcopal Church Conference. There were front page stories each day and large crowds in attendance. Ex-Governor Charles S. Deneen delivered an address for McKendree College at the conference on September 24. Since the governor was a member of a Moose lodge in Chicago, he spoke to the local lodge while he was in Mt. Vernon.[288]

Bohumir Kryl

On November 26, 1915, the Mt. Vernon M. E. Church was again the host for a notable visitor. Bohumir Kryl and his band provided musical entertainment at the church. Kryl was a former circus acrobat and sculptor who became a protégé of John Philip Sousa. After playing with Sousa and other bands he formed his own organization in 1906. His group was called Bohumir Kryl's Bohemian Band because Kryl was born in Bohemia. They became one of the most popular bands on the Chautauqua circuit. One of his featured numbers was the "Anvil Chorus" with four men in leather aprons hammering on anvils with sparks flying.[289]

Cal Stewart

On February 7th and 8th, 1916, Cal Stewart appeared in person at the Gem Theater (102 S. 9th). He was a well-known vaudevillian who developed a comic character called "Uncle Josh from Way Down East." He became a friend of Mark Twain and Will Rogers who shared his style of humor. In the late 1800s the Thomas Edison Company hired him to make "cylinder" recordings of his famous speeches. These best-selling recordings included titles such as: "Uncle Josh's Arrival in New York" (1898), "I'm Old But I'm Awfully Tough" (1898), "Uncle Josh's Huskin Bee Dance" (1901), and "Uncle Josh on an Automobile" (1903). The ad for his visit said that Stewart was "Uncle Josh of Graphophone fame," and that in addition to seeing and hearing him at the Gem, the people of Mt. Vernon could hear some of his records on the Victrola at the Compton and Appleman Furniture Store.[290]

Opera House Visitors

The June 19, 1916, *Mt. Vernon Daily Register* announced that the Grand Opera House had been dismantled. The front page article said: "Such well known celebrities as Walter Whiteside, the eminent Shakespearean actor and Charles Murray, the famous screen comedian have interested and amused many audiences …" in the old opera house. Charlie Murray started his career in the circus and vaudeville. In 1911 he started his film career with the Mack Sennett Company. In the 1920s he gained new fame in the silent film series the "Cohens and the Kellys." His career in films continued well into the early "talkies" era in the 1930s.[291]

Grand Opera House

Political Visitors

The year 1916 was to be a very important political year, and in July and August many early political figures arrived. On July 5, 1916, Col. Frank Smith, Republican candidate for Illinois governor, visited and stayed overnight at the Colonial Hotel. On July 10, 1916, Col. Frank O. Lowden, another Republican candidate for governor, came to Mt. Vernon and spoke at the Mahaffy House. On July 21 Morton D. Hull, still another Republican candidate for governor, was in Mt. Vernon. On July 24 Medill McCormick, the Republican candidate for Illinois Representative-at-large, was in town. McCormick was back on August 12 for a speech at the Mt. Vernon Chautauqua. And on August 17 Helen Ring Robinson, "Colorado's famous woman senator," came to Jefferson County. (She was one of the first women ever elected to a state legislature.)[292]

Religious Leaders

In August of 1916 two significant religious leaders spoke to the Mt. Vernon Chautauqua. Charles Sheldon was a Congregational minister and a leader of the Social Gospel movement. He developed a series of sermons based on the question, "What would Jesus do?" These ideas were explained further in a novel, *In His Steps*. Sheldon's novel was brought back into print in the late Twentieth Century—which brought the "What would Jesus do?" question back into public discussion. Sheldon's liberal Christianity inspired Walter Rauschenbusch and the Social Gospel movement. Sheldon's ideas also supported the women's movement and its struggle for equal rights for women. The second religious figure at the Chautauqua was Charles Reign Scoville, an evangelist of the Christian Church (Disciples of Christ). As an evangelist he toured the United States and the world with the largest company of any Christian Church leader of the time.[293]

Harvey W. Wiley

Another famous figure who spoke to the Chautauqua in August of 1916 was Dr. Harvey W. Wiley, "The Father of the Pure Food and Drugs Act." Wiley received a medical degree from Indiana Medical College and a science degree at Harvard. In 1883 he became the chief chemist at the federal Department of Agriculture and began testing foods and drugs produced and sold in the United States. He found that many products were made with cheap or even dangerous materials. Some companies even put morphine in "soothing syrups" given to babies. He induced Congress to introduce pure food bills in the 1880s and 1890s, but they were always blocked by powerful interests. Finally in 1906 Congress passed and President Theodore Roosevelt signed the Pure Food and Drugs Act. By the time Dr. Wiley came to Mt. Vernon in 1916, he was working for *Good Housekeeping* magazine and continuing his crusade for tougher inspection of meat, flour, and other foods. Because of his work, the Good Housekeeping Seal of Approval became the important consumer symbol it is today.[294] While in Mt. Vernon Dr. Wiley visited the home of Mrs. O. L. Record, a childhood friend from his school days in Indiana.[295]

Frank O. Lowden

On October 5, 1916, Frank O. Lowden (1861–1943), the Republican candidate for Illinois governor, came to Mt. Vernon. Lowden was a United States congressman from Illinois from 1907 to 1911. In 1916 he was elected governor of Illinois. In the 1920 Republican Convention in Chicago he was a serious candidate for the nomination for president. At that convention he actually led the vote on the eighth ballot but couldn't get the majority needed for victory. Because of the stalemate between Lowden and General Leonard Wood of Missouri, the convention turned to Warren G. Harding of Ohio as a compromise candidate picked in the classic "smoke-filled room" by party leaders. Most historians agree that Lowden, or any of the other leading candidates, would have been a better president. Harding had a scandal-plagued presidency and died in office. Lowden never ran for public office again.

Lowden's campaign stop in Mt. Vernon in 1916 was a thirty minute visit on a special train with three Pullmans (Lowden was married to Pullman Car Company president George Pullman's daughter.) and a decorated flat car at the rear. Also on board were other Republican candidates and "Chin Chin" the baby elephant. The meeting was chaired by Louis L. Emmerson of Mt. Vernon who was running for Illinois secretary of state. Lowden and the other candidates spoke from the flat car and praised the GOP candidates for president and vice president, Hughes and Fairbanks. They criticized Democratic President Woodrow Wilson for his policy in Mexico and his claim that he "kept us out of the war in Europe." One candidate said: "It is all bunk that Wilson kept us out of war."[296]

William B. Wilson

The *Mt. Vernon Weekly News* of October 11, 1916, had a story with the headline "Wilson in Mt. Vernon Saturday Afternoon." But this was not President Woodrow Wilson. This was Secretary of Labor William B. Wilson. He was a former coal miner from 1871 to 1898, the secretary-treasurer of the United Mine Workers of America from 1900 to 1908, and a member of the United States House of Representatives from 1907 to 1913. In 1913 he was appointed the first-ever secretary of labor by President Woodrow

Wilson. When he came to Mt. Vernon, he was dusty and tired as a result of a hard ride in a Ford automobile. He had missed his train in Altamont and was on the way to speak to six thousand coal miners in Marion.

Hughes Article

Charles Evans Hughes

On October 13, 1916, the Republican nominee for president, Charles Evans Hughes (1862–1948) came to Mt. Vernon. Hughes was a major political figure in the first half of the Twentieth Century. He was governor of New York from 1907 to 1910, associate justice of the United States Supreme Court from 1910 to 1916, Republican nominee for president in 1916, United States secretary of state from 1921 to 1925, and chief justice of the United States Supreme Court from 1930 to 1941. When he visited Jefferson County in 1916, he was running against the Democrat, President Woodrow Wilson. Many people thought he would win. The *Mt. Vernon Daily Register* had a large, front-page picture of Hughes with the caption "Next President Went Through Mt. Vernon Early this Morning." The Hughes' special train arrived unannounced at 6:45 in the morning and was in Mt. Vernon for only twenty minutes. Few people saw Mr. Hughes, and he did not give a speech. His train was headed for St. Louis for a campaign stop. When the election was held in November, all indications were that Hughes had indeed been elected. Woodrow Wilson went to bed that night thinking he had lost. But the next day California unexpectedly came in for Wilson, and he was elected for a second term.[297]

Political Visitors

Also on October 13, 1916, another presidential candidate, J. Frank Hanly, was in Mt. Vernon. Hanly, a former governor of Indiana, was the Prohibition Party candidate for president. Also on the special train was Ira Landreth, the party candidate for vice president. Both men had been in Mt. Vernon before as Chautauqua speakers.[298]

Illinois Governor Edward F. Dunne was in Mt. Vernon three times in one week – October 20, 21, and 27, 1916. The October 20 visit was accidental and unnoticed as the governor missed connections and had to board a freight train to his speaking engagement in Benton. He was back in town on the morning of the 21st and met with some of Jefferson County's Democratic Party leaders. The *Mt. Vernon Daily Register* noted, however, that "some of the high moguls were conspicuous by their absence …." The governor was back on the 27th campaigning with William Jennings Bryan.[299]

William Jennings Bryan

William Jennings Bryan gave his last political speech in Mt. Vernon on October 27, 1916. Bryan had resigned his position as secretary of state in Wilson's cabinet in 1915 but nevertheless was campaigning hard for his re-election over Hughes in 1916. He arrived on a special train on the C.& E. I. (3rd and Main) just after 11 o'clock along with Governor Dunne, Illinois Secretary of State Stevenson (son of former VP Adlai Stevenson, and father of Illinois Governor Adlai Stevenson), and Congressman M. D. Foster. According to a 1952 *Mt. Vernon Register-News* article by Edwin Rackaway, an enormous crowd had gathered, but the train was late and local Democrats were very worried that they would leave. "We've got to hold this crowd until Bryan gets here. It means hundreds of votes," the county chairman, Charles Keller, said. In desperation he found Bruce Campbell, an East St. Louis attorney and young rising politician. "Get up and hold'em, Bruce," Keller pleaded. Campbell jumped on the platform and talked for nearly three hours without a note. Here's how Rackaway described it: "Campbell sailed with the Pilgrims at Plymouth rock. He cried for liberty or death with Patrick Henry. He shot down Redcoats at Bunker Hill. He trudged with bloodstained feet in the snows of Valley Forge with Washington's ragged heroes. He opened the great West with Daniel Boone. He died at the Alamo. He charged with Pickett at Gettysburg. He sailed into Manila Bay with Dewey." The crowd stayed until Bryan arrived and Rackaway said it was the "best speech against time you ever heard."[300]

Bryan Article

The *Mt. Vernon Daily Register* of October 27 gave a very negative, partisan view of the Bryan visit stating: "Mr. Bryan spoke to what was probably the smallest and undoubtedly the least enthusiastic gathering he ever addressed in Mt. Vernon." The article also said: "The Great Commoner is making but a feeble contribution to the Wilson campaign as he devotes his time almost exclusively to the 'He kept us out of war' slogan with which the Democratic Party is trying to blindfold the uninformed."

The *Mt. Vernon Weekly News* of November 1 gave an equally partisan, but positive report on the Bryan visit. This article stated that an enthusiastic crowd of four thousand heard the "Great Commoner" praise President Wilson for not sending American boys to die in Mexico or Europe. Bryan was quoted as saying: "Our boys are safe while Wilson is President." Upon Bryan's death in July of 1925 the *Mt. Vernon Register-News* article was also more positive about this 1916 Bryan visit. It reported that he spoke only a few minutes from the rear of a train at the C. & E. I. depot, but it was a "masterly speech ..." It further reported that he told a great crowd: "I tell you my friends that a vote for Hughes is a vote for war, and a vote for Wilson is a vote for peace." It said local party leaders credited Bryan's campaigning with helping Wilson win Jefferson County and re-election as president in an extremely close vote.[301]

Richard Yates

The United States entered World War I in April of 1917. On May 25 Mt. Vernon had a huge Liberty Bond parade to support the war. In addition to the parade down Main Street local women entered the Appellate Court by the west stairs and exited by the winding front stairs with little American flags. Later some important people came to Mt. Vernon to promote Liberty Loan Drives, the Red Cross, or patriotism in general. Ex-Governor Richard Yates came to town on August 1, 1917, to support the Red Cross. Governor Yates, who was state chairman of the Red Cross, was to speak from the band platform on the square. The band was to give its weekly concert featuring patriotic numbers before and after the speech. Red Cross booths were placed at each corner of the square to receive membership dues and give out Red Cross buttons. This plan was ruined by threatening weather that forced the governor, the band, and a much smaller-than-expected crowd indoors. Despite this setback the governor gave an "eloquent and witty" patriotic speech, which "went straight to the hearts of his audience ...," and the Red Cross recruited over fifty new members. The *Mt. Vernon Daily News* lamented: "Had the weather conditions been favorable and Governor Yates spoke from the band stand as was planned, a record breaking crowd would no doubt have been present."[302]

Liberty Bond Parade

Liberty Bond Parade

Adolph Eberhart

In spite of the war, the 1917 Mt. Vernon Chautauqua was held as usual. Former Minnesota Governor Adolph Eberhart gave the opening lecture on August 10. Eberhart was governor from 1909 to 1915. By the time he came to town his political career was on the decline. He was defeated for the nomination for governor in 1915 and for senator in 1916. His speech was about rural school consolidation and other measures to keep young people from moving to the big cities.[303]

Clyde Lee Fife

Well-known evangelist Clyde Lee Fife came to Mt. Vernon on November 25, 1917, for services that lasted until December 14. The local papers were filled with headlines and stories for over two weeks. Fife was referred to as the "famous union evangelist from the Southland," the "most effective and noted southern preacher since the days of Sam Jones," and "one of the foremost religious leaders, writers and thinkers of the present day." In addition to his preaching he brought with him a concert violinist and a choir of five hundred people. They put up a tent at 9th and Harrison, which seated over two thousand people. According to one newspaper account, "the streets were black with people ...," and thousands heard his opening sermon.[304]

Henry Riggs Rathbone

On February 12 and August 11, 1918, Henry Riggs Rathbone spoke in Mt. Vernon. Rathbone was an attorney from Chicago who became a United States representative from 1922 to 1928. But his greatest fame came from an event that occurred before his birth. His parents to be, Major Henry Reed Rathbone and Clara Harris, were the guests of President and Mrs. Lincoln at Ford's Theater on the night of Lincoln's assassination by John Wilkes Booth. Major Rathbone tried to restrain Booth and received a knife wound to his arm. In 1883 while consul to Germany Major Rathbone murdered his wife and attempted to kill himself. Young Henry, then about thirteen, was brought back to the United States and raised by his uncle. On his

February 12 visit to Jefferson County Henry Riggs Rathbone spoke at the Masonic Hall. He was chairman of the War Committee of the Chicago Bar and gave a patriotic speech about the war effort. His August 11 visit was to deliver another patriotic lecture titled "A Plea for National Harmony and Co-operation" at the Mt. Vernon Chautauqua at 9th and Harrison.[305]

The Sousa Jackie Band

On February 25, 1918, the Sousa Jackie Band came to Mt. Vernon. These musicians were Marines or "Jackies" from the Great Lakes Naval Training Station who were chosen and trained by the famous John Philip Sousa. Sousa, himself, was not with them. They were led by Sousa's protégé, Harry Raschig. The band with a drill squad, color guard, and vocalists was touring Illinois with a speaker, Julian S. Nolan, to raise patriotism and sell U.S. Savings Stamps. The event was held at the Jefferson County Courthouse.[306]

George Edmund Foss and Medill McCormick

Two rivals for the U.S. Senate came to Jefferson County in the summer of 1918. George Edmund Foss, U.S. representative from 1895 to 1913 and 1915 to 1919, was in Mt. Vernon on June 22, 1918, campaigning for the Republican nomination. The *Mt. Vernon Daily Register* called him the "father of the modern navy" because of his work as chairman of the Committee on Naval Affairs. On June 27, 1918, Medill McCormick, also seeking the Republican senate nomination, spoke at the Jefferson County Courthouse. McCormick was the owner and publisher of the *Chicago Tribune* and was in Mt. Vernon with Theodore Roosevelt in 1914. He was in the U.S. House of Representatives from 1917 to 1919. He had been on the World War I battlefields in France for three months and titled his speech the "Over There Message." A third candidate for the Senate, Mayor "Big Bill" Thompson of Chicago did not come to a meeting at the Gem Theater on August 24, 1918, but sent a representative. McCormick received the nomination and was elected in 1918.[307]

The 1918 Chautauqua

The 1918 Mt. Vernon Chautauqua was held from August 11 to 18 but not at its usual location at Chautauqua Park on West Broadway. In order to keep costs down and donate the savings to the war effort the Chautauqua Committee decided to have the meetings at the Warren Lots at the corner of 9th and Harrison. The *Mt. Vernon Daily Register* urged readers to "Buy War Savings Stamps with what you save on the Mt. Vernon Chautauqua." The headline speaker was Lieutenant Pat O'Brien, a World War I fighter pilot and author of "Outwitting the Hun." He told exciting stories of fighting air battles with the Germans, being shot down, and escaping from a German POW camp. He described a sky full of blue tracer bullets and said: "I dodged and maneuvered to keep them off my tail, but the first thing I knew I was hit. It was like a sledge-hammer blow. I remember thinking 'I am dead', and that was all until I woke up in a Hun hospital the next morning."[308]

William E. Mason

On August 24, 1918, U.S. Representative William E. Mason appeared at the Gem Theater. He was a candidate for re-nomination, and a representative for Chicago Mayor Thompson who was running for the U.S. Senate. Mason was first elected to the U.S. House in 1887, the U.S. Senate in 1897, and the U.S. House again in 1916. Mason, who had been in Mt. Vernon many times, was sixty-eight years old in 1918 and died in office in 1921.[309]

The "Blind" Boone Concert Company

On January 7, 1919, "Blind" Boone and his Concert Company came to Mt. Vernon. Boone was born in 1864 to a slave mother and white father. He lost his sight early in life but was soon recognized as a musical prodigy. He learned to play the piano, composed complex pieces of music, and in spite of the prejudice of the times began to tour the country. He became such a famous entertainer that he was asked to cut piano rolls. He is honored today at a ragtime festival in Columbia, Missouri. When he came to Jefferson County, Boone was about fifty-six years old and his career was beginning to decline. His concert was at the Majestic Theater at 226 South Ninth Street.[310]

Ernestine Schumann-Heink

Known as the world's greatest contralto, Ernestine Schumann-Heink visited Mt. Vernon May 2, 1919. She first gained fame in Europe and came to the United States in 1898. She performed at the Metropolitan Opera in New York for many years. Her recordings were very popular and can still be found today. During World War I she toured the country to raise funds for the war effort, even though she had sons in the armies of both sides. In 1926 she sang *Silent Night* over the radio on Christmas Eve. It became a Christmas tradition through 1935. Eventually she had her own weekly radio show and appeared in movies.

By the time she came to Mt. Vernon her name was a household word. The headline in the *Mt. Vernon News* was "Nation's Most Popular Singer Visitor in Mt. Vernon." According to the article Madame Schumann-Heink was traveling from Herrin, where she had a concert, to Evansville. She spent the night at Mt. Vernon before taking the L. & N. to her next concert. She delighted local people by walking around the public square and greeting people. She walked into a meeting at the Jefferson State bank. Thinking it was a Victory Loan committee meeting, she contributed two hundred dollars to the cause. She didn't just walk in and out. She told the committee about her sons in the German army and in the American army, and about her daughter whom she was worried about in Germany. The newspaper report stated: "The secret of the popularity of this singer aside from her wonderful voice is her splendid personality and she makes friends wherever she goes, whether it is in a great city or a small town. She is what is known as a 'good mixer' which is the reason she is so immensely popular all over the country."[311]

Edwin B. Winans

On July 18, 1919, Brigadier General Edwin B. Winans was the featured speaker at the Chautauqua. General Winans was a career military officer who had participated in all the major conflicts from the Indian Wars in the 1890s to World War I. Among many honors, he received the Distinguished Service Medal and the French Croix de Guerre. The local newspaper called him the hero of Chateau Thierry, Argonne, and other World War I battles. He retired in 1933. The Chautauqua was back at Casey's Grove "at the west end of Broadway" when Winans spoke. The *Daily Register* wrote: "The patrons of the Mt. Vernon Chautauqua seem universally glad that the assembly is to be held in the old grounds instead of town." The general spoke about the war and how unprepared we were. He said the United States needed to have universal military training to be ready for any future conflicts.[312]

Branch Rickey, Rogers Hornsby, and the St. Louis Cardinals

The St. Louis Cardinals baseball team came to Mt. Vernon on September 24, 1919. The Cardinals weren't very good that year, but they had a new manager, Branch Rickey, and a young infielder, Rogers Hornsby, who would later make the Hall of Fame. Rickey was a player with the St. Louis Browns in 1905–1906 and 1914 and with the New York Highlanders in 1907. He was the manager of the St. Louis Browns from 1913 to 1915 and the St. Louis Cardinals from 1919 to 1925. But his real achievement and fame came as the general manager of the St. Louis Cardinals from 1925 to 1942 and the Brooklyn Dodgers from 1943 to 1950. As a Cardinal he developed the modern minor league farm system. And while with Brooklyn in 1947, he made baseball history by integrating the "national pastime" when he hired Jackie Robinson, the first African-American to play in the major leagues.

Mt. Vernon Car Builders Baseball Team

Rogers Hornsby was one of the greatest players in baseball history. He played with the Cardinals from 1915 to 1926 and later with the Giants, Braves, Cubs, and Browns. He was an excellent fielder and maybe the best hitter in the history of baseball. His career batting average was .358. He won seven batting titles, two home run titles, and four RBI crowns. Hornsby's .424 batting average in 1924 was the highest in the National League in the Twentieth Century.

There is very little information about the game. The local newspaper simply noted: "A baseball game has been booked for the Mt. Vernon club against the St. Louis National League club." Later it was reported: "The Mt. Vernon Car Builders defeated the St. Louis Cardinals here yesterday afternoon by a score of 3 to 1."[313] In February of 1920 an article stated: "Fans can still remember that tremendous drive from Rogers Hornsby's bat that Elders turned into a put out in the Cardinals game here last fall."[314] However, this probably is the same game described in *Mt. Vernon Remembers* from the memory of local resident, Joe Torregrossa. If so, the game was played on the ball field where Precision National was located later. Branch Rickey was so impressed with the local team that he signed three of its players—Ray Blades, Jim McLaughlin, and Walter Shultz to major league contracts.[315]

Santa Claus

The most important visitor of all came to Jefferson County every year in December. Santa Claus, so famous that he needs no introduction, visited every home in Jefferson County during these years bringing joy to children and adults. Since there isn't enough space to document all of his visits, a few examples will have to suffice. On December 23, 1885, he arrived at D. H. Wise's on the Crews' Block, south side of the square with "loads of valuable presents." On December 24, 1902, Santa made his headquarters at J. N. Johnson's on the northeast corner of the square. That same year he was also seen at the Boston Store handing out gifts to children. On December 22, 1916, he was at the Leader (Carps) with free gifts for children. On Christmas Day of that same year at 2:30 p.m. Santa arrived at the Jefferson County Courthouse "to distribute presents and confections to about 400" of the city's poor children. No doubt Santa was the most famous and most welcome of all of the visitors to Jefferson County.[316]

SANTA CLAUS

HAS ARRIVED AT

D. H. WISE'S

WITH LOADS OF VALUBLE PRESENTS.

EVERYTHING THAT IS

SENSIBLE. USEFUL, ORNAMENTAL

Can be found in our stock of

HOLIDAY GOODS!

DON'T FAIL TO AVAIL YOURSELF OF THIS GREAT OFFER

WISHING YOU ALL

A MERRY CHRISTMAS

I am very respectfully,

D. H. WISE,

YOUR CLOTHIER,

Crews' Block, South Side of Square, - - Mt. Vernon, Ill.

D. H. Wise Christmas Ad

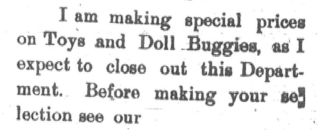

Headquarters for
Santa Claus

All Regular
Holiday Goods
Carried In
Stock.

I am making special prices on Toys and Doll Buggies, as I expect to close out this Department. Before making your selection see our

Game Boards

Fine Paintings

Bisc Ware and

Elegant Furniture

J. N. JOHNSON,
Northeast Corner Square.

J. N. Johnson Christmas Ad

CHAPTER VI

Close But No Cigar

Some famous visitors missed Jefferson County but came very close. They may have been in the county but the evidence does not support it at this time. However, for some there is proof that they visited nearby counties. They also may have been scheduled to be in the county but cancelled for various reasons. Traveling close to Jefferson County, or being scheduled to be in Mt. Vernon both come under the category "Close But No Cigar."

Tecumseh

One example of a close visit came in 1811, before Jefferson County officially existed. In 1811 and 1812 the great Indian chief, Tecumseh, came to southern Illinois. He was a Shawnee leader who—along with his brother, the Prophet—tried to organize the various tribes to resist the western expansion of the Americans. After an 1811 conference with William Henry Harrison in Vincennes, Indiana, he traveled through Bone Gap in Edwards County to Frankfort in Franklin County and then to the area near Marion in Williamson County. He continued south to speak with the "Five Civilized Tribes" of the South. Tecumseh's visit to southern Illinois didn't gain him many followers but may have led to the death of Andrew Moore and the kidnapping of his son in Jefferson County. The well-known killing of Moore in 1812 was linked to the Tecumseh visit by John W. Allen of Southern Illinois University.[317] Tecumseh himself was killed the next year at the Battle of Thames in October of 1813.

Lorenzo Dow

In the 1820s the famous preacher, Lorenzo Dow (1777–1834), was in Marion County and other southern Illinois counties. He was a major figure in the Second Great Awakening and one of the best-known ministers of his day. He was a Methodist but after 1799 was not an official of the church. Known for his unkempt appearance and his eccentric ways, he traveled alone all over the country by foot or horseback. He had long hair and a beard that never saw a comb. He owned only one suit, and it was worn and tattered. He would suddenly appear in public places and announce, "Lorenzo Dow will speak here in 365 days." Then he would disappear, only to re-appear in exactly that time. He often would climb through windows rather than use the door of a building. He spoke in barns, town halls, fields, and frontier camp meetings—where he often drew crowds of ten thousand or more. His preaching style was very different from the usual, conservative ministers of the time. He screamed, shouted, made jokes, told stories, and usually kept the audience spellbound.

Dow came to southern Illinois on a number of occasions. He visited Lawrence County in 1820 and again in 1830. He preached on a platform at the courthouse in Lawrenceville and attracted a large crowd from forty miles around. He remained seated the entire sermon, except sometimes knelt down and crawled around the platform.[318] In Marion County he was reported to be in Raccoon Township and Salem Township. Samuel Huff who settled in Raccoon Township in 1822 offered his home for traveling preachers. According to a Marion County history, "One of these itinerant preachers who stopped at Huff's was the celebrated Lorenzo Dow, who preached from a wagon on the text 'The End of All Things Is At Hand, Be Ye Therefore Sober and Watchful Unto Prayer.'" In the same county history under Salem Township it states, "The celebrated Lorenzo Dow, Thomas Cole, Leonard Maddux, and Elder Patterson were among the first preachers, and often the funeral sermon of a deceased friend was preached a year or more after interment."[319] Actually these Marion County visits may have been in Jefferson County since it extended north into that area until 1823. Marion County was created out of Jefferson and Fayette Counties in 1823.

Dow may have been in Clinton County in the 1820s. One of the older residents of Jefferson County, Martha Maddox Short, who died in 1902, told stories of camp meetings conducted by Lorenzo Dow and Peter Cartwright. She lived in Clinton County from 1825 to the mid-1830s and then moved to Jefferson County.[320] Dow himself reported that he traveled by steamboat to St. Louis in 1827 and then across Illinois to Vincennes, Indiana. In 1830 he moved from Vincennes to St. Louis and then to Pike, Green, and Morgan counties. The overland route from St. Louis to Vincennes would probably be north of Jefferson County, but close.[321] Lorenzo Dow could easily have come into Jefferson County. Crenshaw's place on the Goshen Road in Moore's Prairie was an emigrant campground and a preaching place for wandering ministers. Pleasant Grove, four miles north of Mt. Vernon, became well known all over southern Illinois as a "religious rendezvous." Thomas Casey's home was a headquarters for pioneer circuit riders and wandering evangelists in the 1820s and 1830s.[322]

Henry Clay Warmoth

On May 9, 1842, Henry Clay Warmoth, the future governor of Louisiana, was born in a log cabin on the public square in McLeansboro, Illinois. He served in the Civil War and was wounded in the Battle of Vicksburg. After the war he stayed in the South and was elected to Congress with the support of the newly freed black men. These were the times of Reconstruction where so-called "carpetbaggers" (white northern Republicans) ruled the South with black support. In 1868 Warmoth was elected governor of Louisiana, at age twenty-six possibly the youngest ever. After great political turmoil and corruption Warmoth was impeached and removed from office. This brought the lieutenant governor, P.B.S. Pinchback, into office as the first black governor in the United States. Warmoth continued to be involved in politics but was never elected to such high office again. In 1921 at age seventy-nine Mr. Warmoth, his wife, and his daughter visited McLeansboro. This was his first time back since he left as a child.[323]

Peter Cartwright

In the fall of 1844 Peter Cartwright came to Nashville, Illinois, to attend a Methodist Conference. By this time he was about fifty-nine years old and a well established leader of the church. He was involved in politics but had not yet made his failed run for the U.S. Congress against Abraham Lincoln. While riding to Nashville he became very sick. He described it this way in his autobiography: "On my way to Nashville in the fall of 1844, I was suddenly taken ill with a real shaking ague …."[324]

Visitors of the 1850s

A number of very famous figures were in nearby counties in the 1850s. The famous western lawman, William "Bat" Masterson, may have been born near Fairfield, Illinois, in 1855.[325] (Other sources say he was born November 23, 1853, near Golden Gate in eastern Wayne County, Illinois.) However, some sources disagree and state he was born in Canada and moved to some unspecified point in Illinois. John A. Logan was elected prosecuting attorney for the Jefferson County area and moved to Benton, Illinois, in the mid-1850s to be more centrally located. Lincoln and Douglas were both in Salem, Illinois, September 22, 1856.[326] They were both in Centralia for the fair on September 16, 1858. They had just debated in Anna and were traveling north to the next debate in Charleston. George McClellan was in Centralia in the late 1850s while working for the Illinois Central Railroad.[327]

The Fremont Rally

A "Fremont for President" rally was apparently scheduled for October of 1856 in Mt. Vernon. It never happened. The *Mt. Vernon Sentinel*, a Democratic newspaper, gleefully reported that: "Monday came; we looked anxiously for the rushing crowds … Not a single man of their party here! Wasn't it a glorious 'fizzle' …?" The article used harsh, racist language toward both John C. Fremont and candidate for governor, William H. Bissell, both Republicans, calling Fremont a "Nackass" and Bissell a "government plunderer." The article did not name any of the Fremont or Bissell men who might have come to Jefferson County. But Abraham Lincoln was one political leader who campaigned for Fremont. He gave over fifty speeches, most in central and southern parts of Illinois.

Maybe the Fremont supporters were wise to stay away from Jefferson County in 1856. The Republican Party was first organized in the county in that year, and it didn't have much support. When the election was held, Fremont received either twelve or sixty votes—depending on which source you believe. A county-by-county vote tally published in the *Alton Courier* of November 4, 1858, reports sixty votes for Fremont in Jefferson County in 1856. But an article on an old county resident in the *Mt. Vernon Register* of February 14, 1900, states that he "was one of the twelve men in this county that voted for John C. Fremont."

Bryan, Grant, and Borah

There were also famous figures in nearby towns and counties in the 1860s. William Jennings Bryan was born in Salem in 1860. Ulysses S. Grant was in Mattoon, Anna, and Cairo in 1861 as part of his military duties during the Civil War.[328] Also in the 1860s a very famous future U.S. senator was born near Fairfield. William E. Borah was born in 1865 and attended Black Oak school in Fairfield and the Southern Illinois Academy in Enfield. He was a United States senator from Idaho from 1907 to 1940. He was a progressive Republican and an "Irreconcilable" who opposed and helped defeat Woodrow Wilson's Treaty of Versailles in 1919. Later he became chairman of the Senate Foreign Relations Committee and ran unsuccessfully for the Republican nomination for president in 1936. He was a major figure in U.S. politics in the first half of the Twentieth Century.[329]

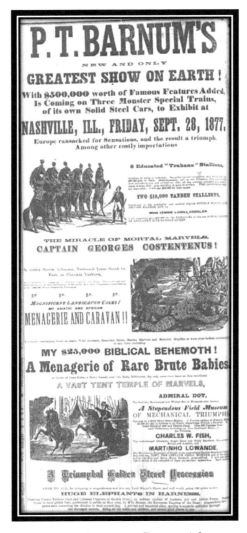

P. T. Barnum Circus Ad

P. T. Barnum's Circus

P.T. Barnum's Greatest Show on Earth exhibited in Nashville, Illinois, on September 28, 1877. They brought with them a "menagerie" of elephants, lions, camels, baboons, and many other animals. They also had Captain Georges Costentenus, "a Greek Albanian tattooed from head to foot in Chinese Tartary," and Charles W. Fish, the "unchallenged champion single horse and trick bareback equestrian." All of this and more cost fifty cents, or you could get free admission by buying Barnum's autobiography.[330]

Geronimo

The famous Apache, Geronimo, was sent to Florida via the southern route. If he had been with his tribe on the northern route, he would have been in Mt. Vernon on September 15, 1886. Geronimo surrendered on September 4, and on September 8 he and his band were sent east on a special train of three cars. General Miles went with them to Albuquerque to meet the train containing the other Indians from the Apache reservation "who will be taken to Florida via Kansas City, St. Louis, and Atlanta." Actually Geronimo did come to Mt. Vernon—Mt. Vernon Barracks in Alabama in 1887. Although he remained a prisoner the rest of his life, he became an even greater national figure by appearing in Wild West shows and at the 1904 St. Louis World's Fair. He died February 17, 1909.[331]

"Casey" Jones

The famous railroad engineer, "Casey" Jones (1863–1900) came to Centralia in the winter of 1892–1893. His fame came from his courage in sacrificing his own life to save passengers when his train collided with a freight train at Vaughan, Mississippi, in 1900. The story of his death was spread by newspaper headlines and by a song sung by his friend, Wallace Saunders, an African-American engine wiper. Jones loved trains and began working on railroads in the 1870s as a very young man. In 1888 he took a job with the Illinois Central Railroad. He developed a reputation as a good engineer who was always on time. He had a distinctive train whistle; so everyone along the tracks knew it was him. He looked the part of a hero. He was over six-feet tall and very strong. Most of Jones' work for the Illinois Central was in the South. But extra help was needed in Illinois. So he moved to Centralia in 1892, where he was assigned to take freight trains north and south. He was only there for several months when the company asked for volunteers to work at the Chicago World's Fair. At this point Casey left Centralia and spent the summer of 1893 carrying passengers to and from the fair.[332]

Benjamin Harrison

President Benjamin Harrison (1833–1901) was scheduled to be in Centralia for the Seventeenth Annual Soldiers' Reunion—which was held October 3, 4, and 5 of 1893. Harrison was a grandson of President William Henry Harrison. After service in the Civil War he went into politics and was elected U.S. senator from Indiana in 1880. He was elected president in 1888 and served one term from 1889 to 1893. He was defeated for re-election by Grover Cleveland. So when he was scheduled to come to southern Illinois, he was a former president, having left office about six months before his possible visit.[333]

Dr. Andy Hall

General Howard and General Sickles

Two very famous Civil War generals were in Fairfield, Illinois, in 1896. They were Oliver O. Howard and Daniel Sickles. Howard participated in many of the important Civil War battles including Bull Run, Gettysburg, and Sherman's March to the Sea. He was wounded, lost his right arm to amputation, and eventually was awarded the Medal of Honor for heroism at the Battle of Fair Oaks. After the war he headed the Freedmen's Bureau and helped establish a school for ex-slaves, which today is called Howard University. By the time he came to Fairfield he was two years into retirement with the rank of major general.

While Howard was known as the "Christian general," General Sickles had quite the opposite reputation. In the 1850s while a member of Congress, Sickles shot and killed a man who was having an affair with his wife. In a sensational trial he was acquitted after using temporary insanity as a defense—the first person ever to use that tactic. During the Civil War Battle of Gettysburg he created enduring controversy by moving his troops against orders. They were destroyed and he lost a leg to a cannonball. But he always insisted he did the right thing, and many years later he was awarded the Medal of Honor. He donated his leg and the cannonball to the National Museum of Health and Medicine where it is on display today. After the war Sickles was again involved in politics and served in Congress from 1893 to 1895, leaving office the year before coming to Fairfield. The 1896 Howard and Sickles visit to Fairfield was for a McKinley rally in the campaign for president against William Jennings Bryan. Dr. Andy Hall of Mt. Vernon attended the meeting and recalled that both men spoke but were interrupted by yells of "Jefferson Davis." The hard feelings over the Civil War still had not disappeared.[334]

"Buffalo Bill" Cody

Buffalo Bill's Wild West was in Carmi, Carterville, and probably other southern Illinois towns in 1898. An October 4, 1898, note in the *Mt. Vernon Register* tells of a Mt. Vernonite who traveled to Carmi to see the show. Later Cody was in Benton. A man from Ina reported, "In 1905 I saw Buffalo Bill Cody in Benton at the ball park. He had 40 Indians with him."[335]

William "Buffalo Bill" Cody (1846–1917) was one of the most famous Americans in history. After service in the Civil War he became a buffalo hunter for the railroads and a scout for the U.S. Army. He received a Medal of Honor for "gallantry in action" while serving as a civilian scout. In 1883 he created his show and toured with it or other shows for the rest of his life. At one time his show employed such famous figures as Sitting Bull and Annie Oakley.

Annie Oakley

Annie Oakley was with Buffalo Bill's show in 1898. So she would have been in southern Illinois at that time. She was not with Cody in his 1905 visit to Benton. However, she joined a different show (Young Buffalo Wild West Show) in 1911 and gave her very last Wild West show performance on October 4, 1913, in Marion, Illinois.[336] Oakley was a talented sharpshooter who was probably America's first female entertainment "superstar." By the time she came to southern Illinois she had already toured the U.S. and Europe with Buffalo Bill for over ten years. Nicknamed "Little Sure shot" by Sitting Bull, she performed before Queen Victoria and shot the ashes off a cigarette held by the future Kaiser Wilhelm II of Germany. She left the Buffalo Bill show in 1901 after a serious train accident but continued working until her death in 1926.

William Jennings Bryan

William Jennings Bryan visited the Jefferson County area just before and after 1900. On June 5, 1899, he spoke to a large crowd in Walnut Hill. He was there for a family reunion. His mother was raised in Walnut Hill and his father practiced law there. Shortly after the turn of the century William Jennings Bryan came to McLeansboro and Broughton in Hamilton County. He arrived via the L. & N. Railroad, so he may have come through Mt. Vernon. While in McLeansboro he toured in an open automobile, gave a speech at the Stelle Opera House, and attended a formal dinner. Unfortunately one of the hostesses spilled food into his lap while serving him. He was, however, very gracious about the incident.[337] On another occasion Bryan accepted an invitation to visit Broughton. Although no date was given, it also was probably soon after the turn of the century. He arrived in a black suit and high hat. Some little boys saw the hat as a target and couldn't resist throwing rocks at it as Bryan passed in an open vehicle.[338]

Octave Chanute

The famous engineer and pioneer aviator, Octave Chanute, may have been in Jefferson County during the time when he owned the Chicago Tie Company plant that was located in Mt. Vernon. The local plant was built in the 1890s under the direction of Mr. Chanute.[339] However, that doesn't prove he was in town. A *Mt. Vernon Register* article from 1909 gives the impression that the local reporter had spoken with Chanute. But there are other explanations. Octave Chanute designed and constructed the Chicago Stock Yards and the Hannibal Bridge, the first to cross the Missouri River. He also invented a system for pressure treating rail ties and telephone poles with creosote to preserve them. But he is most famous as an aviation pioneer. The *Mt. Vernon Register* article is titled "Father of Aviation." He wrote books about flying, organized conferences, invented gliders, and encouraged the Wright Brothers. The Chanute Air Force base near Rantoul was named after him.

Mr. Chanute's son, Charles D. Chanute, was the manager of the local plant—which was located at various places including South Fourth Street and the 900 block of Shawnee Street.[340] Charles Chanute and his family lived in Mt. Vernon at 312 Jordan Street from April to December of 1899. Charles Chanute continued to manage the plant from his home in Chicago until his death in 1911. He passed away in Mt. Vernon at the Egyptian Hospital at the age of forty-six. He was in town inspecting the tie plant and seemed in good health. But a cigarette burn on his arm caused his entire system to become infected. His father had died just about one year before him in 1910.[341]

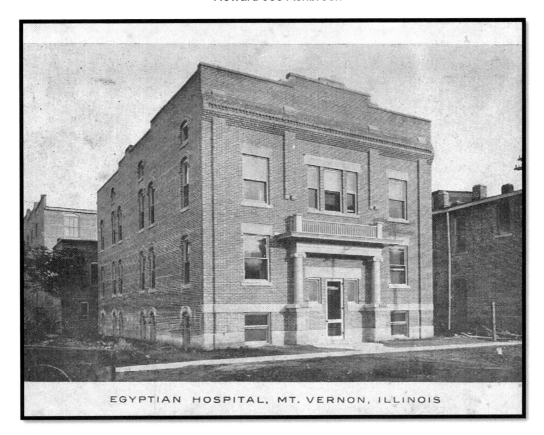

EGYPTIAN HOSPITAL, MT. VERNON, ILLINOIS

Egyptian Hospital

Chautauqua Visitors

A number of well-known figures were scheduled for the Mt. Vernon Chautauqua but could not come for various reasons. Governor Bob Taylor of Tennessee was signed for the 1910 Chautauqua but cancelled.[342] Governor Herbert Hadley of Missouri was supposed to be in town in August of 1913 but became ill and was replaced by Congressman William E. Mason. Emil Seidel, the first socialist mayor of a major American city and the Socialist Party candidate for vice president on the Eugene Debs ticket in 1912, was scheduled to debate socialism with James A. Bede at the 1914 Chautauqua. He cancelled his engagement in Mt. Vernon to attend the International Convention of Socialists in Vienna, Austria. This was unfortunate timing for him as the bullets were beginning to fly in World War I that same month. One of the local newspapers joked that he might be in a much "hotter debate" there than in Mt. Vernon.[343]

John Bunny and Elbert Hubbard

The 1915 Chautauqua had to make changes for an unusual reason—the deaths of two invitees—John Bunny and Elbert Hubbard. Bunny was a vaudeville comedian who became a silent movie star. In 1910 he began to work for Vitagraph Studios and by 1915 had starred in over one hundred extremely popular comedies. His death of Bright's disease in April of 1915 was front page news in Europe as well as the United States. He has a star on the Hollywood Walk of Fame.

The Chautauqua Committee scheduled Elbert Hubbard to take his place on the program. Hubbard was a writer, editor, and lecturer. He founded an arts and crafts community called Roycraft that produced fine books, furniture, and leather and copper goods. The community became a meeting place for radicals, free thinkers, and reformers. Hubbard's lectures were a mixture of socialism and free enterprise. Some of his best-known sayings include: "Responsibility is the price of freedom", "Life is just one damned thing after another", and "Don't take life too seriously. You will never get out of it alive." In 1912 when the Titanic went down, he praised Mr. and Mrs. Isidor Straus for voluntarily going down together. Little did he know that he would have the same opportunity. He and his wife were on the Lusitania on May 1, 1915, when it was torpedoed by a German submarine. A survivor wrote a letter to Hubbard's son describing what happened: "Your father and Mrs. Hubbard linked arms …. I called to him, 'What are you going to do?' … then he did one of the most dramatic things I ever saw done. He simply turned with Mrs. Hubbard and entered a room on the top deck, the door of which was open, and closed it behind him."[344]

Dwight Hillis

Dr. Dwight Hillis was scheduled for the 1917 Chautauqua. The June 26, 1917, *Mt. Vernon News* called him "one of the most famous preachers in all America." As World War I heated up in Europe, Hillis spoke forcefully in favor of U.S. entry into the fight. When the U.S. did join the Allies in the war, he became an enthusiastic "Liberty Loan" speaker. He told lurid atrocity stories that helped promote hatred of the German enemy. He often stated: "When the syphilitic German has used a French or Belgian girl, he cuts off her breasts as a warning to the next German soldier." On August 8, it was announced that he had broken his contract and sailed for Europe. When the Chautauqua opened on August 11, he was replaced by Governor Eberhart of Minnesota.[345]

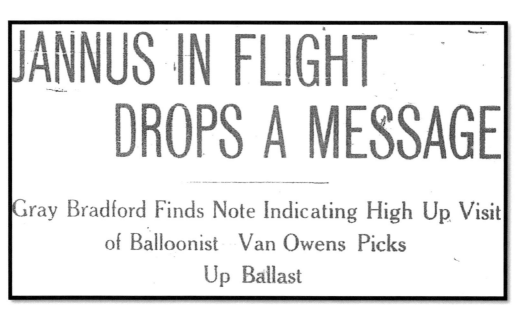

Jannus Article

Tony Jannus and Ruth Law

Two famous flyers, Tony Jannus and Ruth Law, were supposed to be in Mt. Vernon but cancelled. Jannus was to be in town for the September, 1913, King City Fair with the Benoist Aerialists. But due to a schedule error, Jannus was to be at the Centralia Fair on the same date. Jannus kept his job in Centralia, and a different flyer came to Jefferson County. Jannus also came close on November 6, 1914, when he flew over Mt. Vernon in a balloon. He dropped two bags and a note that landed near Eighth and Broadway. The note said: "Passing over this city at 8 o'clock. Going south. Altitude 1400 feet. Tony Jannus."[346]

Jannus was a well-known early pioneer aviator. He was the pilot for the first test of airborne machine guns, for the first parachute jump from an airplane, and for the world's first commercial airline flight. Because of his good looks and charming personality as well as his aviation exploits, he was idolized by the general public, especially women. He dated movie actresses and was the center of attention wherever he went. He was killed on October 12, 1916, over the Black Sea in Russia while testing a plane for the Czar. If he had not died at the age of twenty-seven, he might be even more famous today.

Law Article

Ruth Law was scheduled to be in Jefferson County for a Liberty Loan Rally of the Red Cross on August 3, 1917. The front page headline of the July 27, 1917, *Mt. Vernon Register* said: "Ruth Law Will Fly To Mt. Vernon Next Week." The story stated that she was the "world's most famous aviatrix" and that her appearance "will bring a huge crowd to Mt. Vernon on this day as Ruth Law is known from coast to coast as one of the most daring aeroplane operators in the world …." However, the next day the appearance was cancelled because her plane had been "broken beyond repair."[347]

Law started flying in 1912 and was well known for doing exhibition stunts such as the "loop the loop." In 1916 she set a new record of five hundred ninety miles by flying non-stop from Chicago to New York. President Wilson and other dignitaries held a dinner in her honor in December of 1916. After being rejected for service in the army, she helped the World War I Liberty Loan Drives. After the war she organized a barnstorming group called the "Ruth Law Flying Circus." She died in 1970.

William "Big Bill" Thompson

William "Big Bill" Thompson, the notorious mayor of Chicago, couldn't come to a political meeting for U.S. Senate candidates in Mt. Vernon on August 24, 1918. The meeting at the Gem Theater drew a number of candidates but only a representative of the mayor. The *Mt. Vernon Register* editorialized: "It will be a disappointment to the voters not to see the mayor in person as all other candidates for the U.S. Senate have been here."[348] (The mayor was in Mt. Vernon in 1911.) Thompson, mayor from 1915 to 1923 and again from 1927 to 1931, was an entertaining but corrupt character. He once "debated" two live rats that he used to represent his opponents. The *Chicago Tribune* once wrote about him: "He has given the city an international reputation for moronic buffoonery, barbaric crime, triumphant hoodlumism, unchecked graft, and a dejected citizenship." After his death in 1944 nearly $1.5 million in cash was found in two of his safe deposit boxes.

Index

Notes

[1] John A. Wall, *Wall's History of Jefferson County* (Indianapolis, Indiana: B.F. Bowen & Company, 1909), 21–22

[2] Linda Mick Short, ed., *Jefferson County Historical Society Early Papers 1946–1965* (Mt. Vernon, Illinois: Jefferson County Historical Society, 2006) iv, 3; *Mt. Vernon Register-News Special Edition*, May 27, 1929

[3] Susannah Johnson, *The Recollections of the Rev. John Johnson and His Home*, Adam Clarke Johnson, ed., (Nashville, Tennessee: Southern Methodist Publishing House, 1869), 253

[4] Linda Mick Short, ed., *Jefferson County Historical Society Early papers 1946–1965* (Mt. Vernon, Illinois: Jefferson County Historical Society, 2006), 33

[5] Jefferson County Circuit Court Record Book A, 1–77; William H. Perrin, ed., *History of Jefferson County* (Chicago: Globe Publishing Co., 1883), 171

[6] Wikipedia at www.wikipedia.com

[7] Jefferson County Circuit Court Record Book A, 1–77

[8] Charles Wallis, ed., *Autobiography of Peter Cartwright* (New York: Abindgon Press, 1956), 167

[9] Perrin, 124

[10] Jefferson County Circuit Court Record Book A, 45

[11] Jefferson County Circuit Court Record Book B, 58; Perrin, 171

[12] Jefferson County Circuit Court Record Book B, 199–484

[13] McClernand letter to Lincoln, May 26, 1847, Lincoln Papers, Library of Congress

[14] Perrin, 174

[15] Earl Schenck Miers, ed., *Lincoln Day-by-Day* (Dayton, Ohio: Morningside Press, 1991), 143

[16] This church was built by the Methodists in 1835–1836. In 1853 it was purchased by Harvey T. Pace for the use of the Christian Church. When Mr. Pace died in the 1870s, it was briefly used as a carpenter shop and a billiard room. From 1880 until 1906 it was used by the Trinity Episcopal Church. Starting in 1906 it was used as an office for the Mt. Vernon Lumber Company.

[17] *Mt. Vernon Register-News Special Edition*, May 25,1929

[18] *Illinois State Register*, September 11, 1840, and October 16,1840

[19] Jefferson County Circuit Court Record Book B, 261–262

[20] Jefferson County Circuit Court Record Book B, 37–171; Wall, 107

[21] John Y. Simon, *Abraham Lincoln in Southern Illinois*, xviii; This article was included in the reprint of *When Lincoln Came to Egypt* (Herrin, Illinois: Crossfire Press, 1993), by George W. Smith.

[22] Miers, 321

[23] *Kellogg v. Crain* at www.lawpracticeofabrahamlincoln.org

[24] Perrin, 174

[25] Shelby M. Cullom, *Fifty Years of Public Service: Personal Recollections of Shelby M. Cullom* (Chicago: A.C. McClurg & Co., 1911), 182

[26] John Dean Caton, *Early Bench and Bar of Illinois* (Chicago: Chicago Legal News Company, 1893), 153–159

[27] Perrin, 176

[28] *Illinois Supreme Court Reports*, 11:7, 12:14, 13:30, 14:66

[29] Carlton J. Corliss, *Mainline of Mid-America: The Story of the Illinois Central* (New York: Creative Age Press, 1950), 22

[30] Perrin, 155–159

[31] *Mt. Vernon Register-News*, unknown date, Wheeler Scrapbook at Jefferson County Historical Society

[32] *Illinois Supreme Court Reports*, 11:27

[33] Ibid., 11:7; 23:38,59

[34] Ibid., 15: 8

[35] Ibid., 15:8; 17:63; 20:771

[36] Eva Ingersoll Wakefield, ed., *The Letters of Robert G. Ingersoll* (New York: Hallmark-Hubner Press, 1951), 18

[37] Wall, 177

[38] *Mt. Vernon Weekly News,* February 25, 1920

[39] Supreme Court Order, November 20, 1849, *Dorman v. Lane,* authored by Finney D. Preston, clerk of the First Grand Division at Mt. Vernon; Agreement, November 15, 1850, *Dorman v. Lane*

[40] *Illinois Supreme Court Reports,* 13:127

[41] Samuel D. Marshall to Lincoln, April 20, 1849, Lincoln Papers, Library of Congress

[42] Transcript, *Casey v. Casey* at www.lawpracticeofabrahamlincoln.org; Jefferson County Circuit Court Record Book D, 34, 67, 82, 106, 127, 178, 272, 297, 306, 346, 366, and 430; *Mt. Vernon Register-News Special Edition,* May 25, 1929; Adam Clarke Johnson, *Recollections of Jefferson County and Its People* (Mt. Vernon, Illinois: Jefferson County Historical Society, 2000), 34

[43] Judge's Docket, November, 1852, and Transcript 11–8–1852 to 12–15–1852 for *Casey v. Casey* at www.lawpracticeofabrahamlincoln.org; *Illinois Reports,* December Term 1852, 14:112; John Long, *The Law of Illinois, Lincoln's Cases Before the Supreme Court* (Shiloh, Illinois: Illinois Company, 1996), 2: 119–124

[44] *People v. Illinois Central RR* at www.lawpracticeofabrahamlincoln.org

[45] Charles Leroy Brown, "Lincoln and the Illinois Central Railroad, 1857-1860," *Journal of the Illinois State Historical Society,* 36, No. 2, 1943, 122–153; Corliss, 115; *Illinois Supreme Court Reports,* 27: 64

[46] Jack Flood of the Fifth District Appellate Court first discovered this.

[47] William K. Alderfer to Lowell Dearinger, October 26, 1977, Jefferson County Historical Society files; Robert W. O'Brian to Lowell Dearinger, January 19, 1978, Jefferson County Historical Society files; *People v. Illinois Central RR* at www.lawpracticeofabrahamlincoln.org

[48] David and Joseph Gillespie to Lincoln, August 16, 1859, Lincoln Papers, Library of Congress

[49] Michael G. Dale to Lincoln, November 4, 1859, Lincoln Papers, Library of Congress

[50] Roy P. Basler, ed., *The Collected Works of Abraham Lincoln* (8 Volumes; New Brunswick, New Jersey: Rutgers University Press, 1953–55), 3:494

[51] The *Mt. Vernon Register-News,* August 5, 1930, Obituary of Dr. J.II. Watson

[52] Sidney Breese Opinion, *People v. Illinois Central RR,* January, 1860; Brown, 153–156

[53] Corliss, 115, 121; Brown, 124,132; Sidney Breese Opinion, *People v. Illinois Central RR,* January, 1860; Official Plaque at the Fifth District Appellate Court in Mt. Vernon

[54] George W. Smith, *When Lincoln Came to Egypt* (Herrin, Illinois: Crossfire Press, 1993), 57–59, 110

[55] Basler, 3:135

[56] Smith, 57

[57] The Lincoln Log, March 31, 1864, at www.thelincolnlog.org

[58] Wall, 177

[59] *Mt. Vernon Register-News,* September 16, 1932

[60] Smith, 105

[61] Ibid., 130

[62] Ibid., 145–146

[63] A June 6, 1930, *Mt. Vernon Register-News* article states that Judge William S. Partridge had found an old assessment roll of Jefferson County certified to in 1841 by Stephen A. Douglas, then Illinois Secretary of State. Strangely, the article states that Douglas' handwriting "resembles that of a woman more than that of a man."

[64] Wall, 138; Marriage license, Jefferson County Clerk's Office

[65] *The Jeffersonian,* May 7, 1852

[66] *Mt. Vernon Register-News,* September 9, 1954

[67] Wakefield, 15-17

[68] *Mt. Vernon Register-News,* October 20, 1952

[69] Ibid., August 5, 1930; *Mt. Vernon Weekly News,* December 25, 1912

[70] Wakefield, 18

[71] *Mt. Vernon Weekly News,* December 25, 1912, quoting the *St. Louis Chronicle,* December 4, 1886

[72] *Mt. Vernon Daily Register*, August 11, 1914; *Mt. Vernon Weekly News,* August 12, 1914

[73] *Mt. Vernon Register-News*, April 6, 1961

[74] Wheeler Scrapbook at Jefferson County Historical Society quoting Mildred Warren

[75] Jon Musgrave, *Slaves, Salt, Sex, and Mr. Crenshaw* (Marion, Illinois: Illinois History.com, 2004), 350

[76] James P. Jones, "John A. Logan, Freshman In Congress, 1859-1861," *Journal of the Illinois State Historical Society,* 56: 40, (Volume 56, No. 1, Spring, 1963)

[77] *St. Louis Chronicle,* December 3, 1886

[78] James P. Jones, *Black Jack: John A. Logan and Southern Illinois in the Civil War Era* (Carbondale, Illinois: Southern Illinois University Press, 1995), 83; *Mt. Vernon Weekly News,* December 25, 1912

[79] Gary Ecelbarger, *Black Jack Logan: An Extraordinary Life in Peace and War* (Guilford, Connecticut: Lyon's Press, 2005), 152–158; *Nashville Journal*, August 28, September 4, 1863; *Centralia Sentinel*, August 20, 1863

[80] Civil War Archive of Illinois Governor Richard Yates at www.historicamericana.com

[81] John Y. Simon, ed., *The Papers of U.S. Grant* (16 volumes, Carbondale, Illinois: Southern Illinois University Press, 1969), 2: 349

[82] *The War of the Rebellion,* Series 2, Volume 2 (Washington, D.C., U.S. Government Printing Office, 1897) 240–249; http://digital.library.cornell.edu; These men may have been guilty only of speaking out against President Lincoln and his war with the Confederacy. Dodds was the sheriff of Jefferson County both before and after the Civil War. Green had a long and important career in Jefferson County. Pace became the first mayor of Mt. Vernon.

[83] Ecelbarger, 188–197; *Centralia Sentinel*, October, 1864

[84] Wall, 274

[85] Edwin Rackaway, *The Boswells* (n.p., n.d.), 32–33; *Mt. Vernon Register-News*, August 13, 1953

[86] Collom, 184

[87] *Burlington Iowa Hawkeye,* November 12, 1864; *Nashville Journal,* November 3, 1864; Ecelbarger, 194

[88] *Mt. Vernon Register-News,* September 8, 1926, article on the social season of 1864 quoting from old newspapers

[89] Hamilton County Historical Society, *Goshen Trails* (18 volumes, McDowell Publications, 2005), 2:16 (January, 1966, Volume 2, #1); *Alton Telegraph,* November 4, 1864; *Fairfield War Democrat,* November 30, 1864

[90] Ecelbarger, 208-211; *Centralia Sentinel*, November 17, 1864

[91] Wakefield, 140

[92] *Mt. Vernon Register-News,* October 20, 1952

[93] Wakefield, 151

[94] *Mt. Vernon Register*, August 27, 1890

[95] Sidney Breese to Abraham Lincoln, September 11, 1863, Lincoln Papers, Library of Congress

[96] *Illinois Supreme Court Reports*, 42: 366, 44: 492

[97] Ibid., 44: 479, 47: 327

[98] *Mt. Vernon Register*, February 18, 1891

[99] Glenn J. Sneed, *Ghost Towns of Southern Illinois* (Johnston City, Illinois: A.E.R.P. Publishing, 1977), 101

[100] *Mt. Vernon Register-News,* February 4, 1926

[101] *US News & World Report*, June 24, 2007 (story based on the book, *The Plot to Steal Lincoln's Body* by Thomas Craughwell)

[102] *Mt. Vernon Register*, September 25, 1889

[103] Cullom, 201

[104] *Mt. Vernon News*, October 15, 1872

[105] *Illinois Supreme Court Reports*, 67: 561, 94: 123

[106] Ibid., 67: 569, 78: 172

107 Ibid., Volume 79 (The summary of this special meeting upon the death of William H. Underwood was placed at the beginning of the volume. It was not included in all copies of Volume 79.)

108 Ibid., 92: 503

109 Poster at Jefferson County Historical Society

110 William Jennings Bryan and Mary Baird, *The Memoirs of William Jennings Bryan* (Chicago: The John C. Winston Company, 1925), 97

111 Fly scrapbook at Jefferson County Historical Society (*Mt. Vernon Register-News,* no date but probably 1920s)

112 *Mt. Vernon News,* September 6 and October 21, 1876

113 Karen Mills Hales, *A Place Some Call Home* (Poplar Bluff, Missouri: Stinson Press, 2006), 14

114 *Mt. Vernon News*, January 3, 1877

115 www.circusinamerica.org; *Nashville Journal*, September 20, 1877; M.R. Werner, *Barnum* (New York: Harcourt, Brace and Company, 1923), 309–329; Although P.T. Barnum was probably never in Jefferson County, his great grandniece, Ruth Lee Barnum, gave a recital at the First Baptist Church in Mt. Vernon on May 4, 1938. See *Mt. Vernon Register-News,* April 29, 1938.

116 Wall, 277; *Mt. Vernon Daily Register*, May 18, 1915

117 The *Washington Post*, August 17, 1878

118 *Mt. Vernon Register-News*, April 7, 1962

119 Cullom, 185

120 *Mt. Vernon News*, September 12, 1909

121 Stanley Hirshson, *The White Tecumseh* (New York: J. Wiley and Sons, 1997), 343, 352, 356

122 *Mt. Vernon Daily Register*, May 18, 1915 (Sherman's letter of June 30, 1878, reprinted.)

123 Hirshson, 343, 352, 356

124 Ibid., 365; Lynn Hoogenboom, *William Tecumseh Sherman: The Fight to Preserve the Union* (New York: PowerPlus Books, 2004), 92

125 Cullom, 200; Logan won the Senate seat in 1879 by defeating Oglesby in the legislature.

126 Ecelbarger, 239

127 *Decatur Republican*, August 15, 1878; *The Golden Era* (McLeansboro, Illinois), August 23, 1878 (from the *Mt. Vernon Free Press*); The dispatch from Mt. Vernon which was included in the *Decatur Republican* of August 15, 1878, reports that General McClernand was scheduled to speak on the second day of the reunion. So, he may have been in Mt. Vernon on August 15, 1878.

128 *The Golden Era* (McLeansboro, Illinois), August 23, 1878; *Mt. Vernon Register-News*, April 7, 1962; *Washington Post*, August 17, 1878

129 Perrin,.337; Wall, 157

130 Short, 60–61

131 *Mt. Vernon Register-News*, October 9, 1920

132 The Ingersoll Chronology by Doug Schiffer at www.funygroup.org

133 *Outdoor Illinois*, February, 1972

134 *Mt. Vernon Weekly Exponent*, August 29, 1883

135 *Mt. Vernon Weekly Register*, October 15, 1884

136 Ibid., October 29, 1884

137 Ibid., October 15, and October 22, 1884

138 Stephen O'Connor, *Orphan Trains: The Story of Charles Loving Brace and the Children Saved and Failed* (Chicago: University of Chicago Press, 2001), 342

139 *Mt. Vernon Register*, March 25, 1885

140 The *New York Times*, September 10, 1886

141 *Mt. Vernon Weekly Register*, September 22, 1886

142 The *St. Louis Globe-Democrat* article, as reprinted in the *Mt. Vernon Weekly Register*, September 22, 1886

143 *Mt. Vernon Weekly Register*, October 27, 1886

[144] Ibid., July 13, 1887

[145] Ibid., September 21, 1887

[146] He was known to hunt pigeons from the roof of the State House with a shotgun. See www.ilstatehouse.com.

[147] Thomas A. Puckett, *Mount Vernon Remembers* (St. Louis: G. Bradley Publishing, 2000), 16–17

[148] The *New York Times*, February 20 and 21, 1888

[149] *Mt. Vernon Register*, March 14, 1888; *Mt. Vernon Register-News Special Edition,* May 27, 1929

[150] Ishbel Ross, *Angel of the Battlefield* (New York: Harper & Brothers, 1956), 168

[151] The *New York Times*, March 18, 1888; *Mt. Vernon Register-News Special Edition,* May 27, 1929

[152] *Mt. Vernon Register*, March 7, 1888; Marshall W. Fishwick, *Illustrious Americans: Clara Barton* (Morristown, New Jersey: Silver Burdett Co., 1966), 212–214

[153] Elizabeth Brown Pryor, *Clara Barton: Professional Angel* (Philadelphia: University of Pennsylvania Press, 1987), 243

[154] *Mt. Vernon Register-News*, July 28, 1934

[155] *Mt. Vernon Register*, October 17, 1888

[156] Ibid., July 31, 1889

[157] *Illinois Supreme Court Reports*, 101: 334; 104: 435; 105: 309; 110: 611; 114: 326; 117: 399; 119: 233; 122: 336; 125: 578

[158] Ibid., 110: 456

[159] Ibid., 114: 425

[160] Ibid., 103: 460; 104: 456; 110: 605

[161] *Mt. Vernon Register*, August 27, 1890

[162] Ibid., February 18, 1891

[163] Ibid., June 17, 1891

[164] Ibid., June 10 and July 8, 1891

[165] Ibid., October 19, 1892

[166] Ibid., June 13, 1894

[167] H. Allen Smith, *To Hell in a Hand-Basket* (Garden City, New York: Doubleday & Company, 1962), 33–34

[168] *Mt. Vernon Register*, October 3, 1894

[169] Ibid., October 17, 1894

[170] After the last of the Green family died in 1935 Green Lawn Place was torn down to make way for the National Guard Armory. In 1936 stories (which had apparently circulated for years) about a non-marriage pact among the Green family children, suicides, and eccentric behavior were published in the December 7, 1936, *St. Louis Post-Dispatch.*

[171] *Mt. Vernon Register*, October 24, 1894; *McLeansboro Leader,* October 25, 1894

[172] Ibid., October 24, 1894

[173] Ibid., October 31, 1894

[174] Ibid., March 18, 1896

[175] The *Nashville Journal*, July 21, 1921; Mt. Vernon Register-News, October 21, 1924

[176] *Mt. Vernon Weekly Register*, July 1 and 8, 1896

[177] The *St. Louis Post-Dispatch*, October 22, 2007 (article by Paul Krugman)

[178] *Mt. Vernon Register*, September 9, 1896

[179] Ibid., September 16, 1896

[180] Ibid., September 16, 1896

[181] Ibid., September 23, 1896

[182] The old cannon built for the McKinley campaigns of 1896 and 1900 was sold to a collector from Springfield, Illinois, in 1966. See *Mt. Vernon Register-News,* March 17, 1966

[183] *Mt. Vernon Register*, September 30, 1896

[184] Ibid., October 7, 1896; Harry Barnard, *Eagle Forgotten: The Life of John Peter Altgeld* (Secaucus, New Jersey: Lyle Stuart, Inc., 1973), 379–381; *Mt. Vernon Register-News,* As you Were 30 Years Ago, October 5, 1926

[185] Linda Mick Short, "The Jeffersonian" (newsletter of the Jefferson County Historical Society), vol. XVIII, No. 1, Spring 2008, p. 6, quoting a 1952 *Register-News* article by Edwin Rackaway

[186] The Continental Historical Bureau, *History of Jefferson County* (Mt. Vernon, Illinois: Continental Historical Bureau, 1962), D-4

[187] *Mt. Vernon Register-News,* As you Were 30 Years Ago, September 27 and November 4, 1926

[188] Ibid., As You Were 35 Years Ago, November 5, 1931

[189] *Mt. Vernon Register*, December 16, 1896

[190] *Mt. Vernon Register-News*, As You Were 30 Years Ago, January 24, 1927; Wakefield, 587

[191] Ibid., January 27, 1953

[192] *Mt. Vernon Register*, May 26 and July 7, 1897; *Mt. Vernon Register-News*, May 28, 1927; *Mt. Vernon Register-News*, January 27, 1953

[193] *Mt. Vernon Register-News*, As You Were 25 Years Ago, September 28 and 29, 1922

[194] *Mt. Vernon Weekly Register*, November 17, 1897

[195] *Mt. Vernon Register-News*, As You Were 25 Years Ago, July 9, 1923

[196] Ibid., As You Were 30 Years Ago, March 1, 1927

[197] Paul M. Angle, *Bloody Williamson* (Urbana, Illinois: University of Illinois Press, 1992), 92

[198] Puckett, 77

[199] Angle, 96

[200] *Mt. Vernon Register-News*, As You Were 25 Years Ago, June 13, 1924

[201] Angle, 99-105

[202] *Mt. Vernon Register-News*, As You Were 25 Years Ago, October 19, 1923

[203] *Mt. Vernon Register*, October 26, 1898

[204] *Mt. Vernon Register-News*, As You Were 25 Years Ago, November 3, 1923

[205] Ibid., As You Were 25 Years Ago, December 21 and 22, 1923

[206] Ibid., As You Were 25 Years Ago, March 1, 1924

[207] *Mt. Vernon Register*, July 12, 1899

[208] *Mt. Vernon Register*, August 23, 1899; *Mt Vernon Register-News*, As You Were 25 Years Ago, August 24, 1923; *Mt. Vernon Register-News*, As You Were 25 Years Ago, August 24, 1924

[209] *Mt. Vernon Register-News*, As You Were 35 Years Ago, January 26, 1935

[210] Ibid., As You Were 30 Years Ago, April 26, 1930; *Mt. Vernon Register*, October 5, 1892; *Salem Republican,* October 25, 1900; Yates came to the Appellate Court as an attorney for the St. Louis, Springfield, and Peoria Railroad in April of 1913 and July of 1914. See *Illinois Appellate Court Reports, Fourth District*, 1913, 180:84, 1914, 188:323

[211] *McLeansboro Leader,* September 20, 1900

[212] *Mt. Vernon Register*, October 30, 1903

[213] Ibid., September 14, 1904

[214] Ibid., November 18, 1903

[215] Ibid., July 30, 1904; *Mt Vernon Weekly News,* August 3, 1904; Fran Grace, *Carry A. Nation: Retelling the Life* (Bloomington, Indiana: Indiana University Press, 2001), *237–240*

[216] Grace, 237–240

[217] *Mt. Vernon Register*, September 20, 1904

[218] Ibid., October 21, 1904

[219] Ibid., February 8, 1905; Louis W. Koenig, *Bryan: A Political Biography* (New York: G.P. Putnam's Sons, 1971), 400

[220] *The St. Louis Globe-Democrat*, April 5, 1905; *The New York Times*, April 5, 1905

[221] *Mt. Vernon Register*, April 5, 1905

[222] Edmund Morris, *Theodore Rex* (New York: Random House, 2001), 215

[223] Ibid., 696

[224] *Mt. Vernon Register*, September 14, 1905

[225] Ibid., December 5, 1905

[226] Ibid., March 20, 1906

[227] Ibid., April 13, 1906

[228] Leslie Heaphy, "Bloomer Girls" at www.baseballguru.com

[229] *Mt. Vernon Register*, May 1, 1906; *Mt. Vernon Register-News*, As You Were 20 Years Ago, May 22, 1928

[230] *Mt. Vernon Register*, May 26, June 2, July 26 & 27, 1906; Linda Mick Short, *The Preserver*, Vol. III, No. 3 & 4, May/Aug. 1996, 1-3

[231] *Mt. Vernon Register*, July 30, 1906

[232] *Mt. Vernon Weekly News,* October 10 and October 17, 1906; *Mt. Vernon Daily Register,* October 17, 1906

[233] *Mt. Vernon Register-News*, As You Were 25 Years Ago, October 18, 1923; *Mt. Vernon Register,* May 3, 14, 1907

[234] *Mt. Vernon Register*, March 18, and June 17, 1907

[235] Ibid., March 18, and June 17, 1907; Steven L. Piott, "Holy Joe" at www.umsystem.edu

[236] Ibid., September 23, 1907; *Mt. Vernon Weekly News,* September 18, 25, and October 2, 1907

[237] Ibid., December 12, 1907

[238] Ibid., March 10, 1908; September 25, 1916

[239] Ibid., April 13, 1908

[240] Ibid., April 27, 1908

[241] Ibid., June 10, 1908; June 16, 1908; June 15, 1911

[242] Ibid., July 7, 1908; October 10, 1908

[243] Ibid., October 2 and 3, 1908; *Mt. Vernon Weekly News,* October 7, 1908

[244] Ibid., October 7, 10, 1908; *Mt. Vernon Weekly News,* October 7, 1908; www.baseballhalloffame.org

[245] *Mt. Vernon Register-News*, August 17, 1920

[246] *Mt. Vernon News*, June 19 and 21, 1909; and July 18, 29, 30, and 31, 1909; *Mt. Vernon Register*, July 31, 1909; Roger A. Bruns, *Preacher: Billy Sunday and Big-Time Evangelism* (New York: W.W. Norton, 1992), 82–111

[247] *Mt. Vernon News*, August 18, 1910

[248] Ibid., August 22, 1910

[249] Ibid., August 26, 1910

[250] *Mt. Vernon Register*, May 13, 1911; http://library.ferris.edu

[251] *Ibid.*, June 16, 1911

[252] *Ibid.*, October 17, 1911

[253] *Mt. Vernon Weekly News,* January 3, 1912

[254] *Mt. Vernon Register-News*, As You Were 15 Years Ago, December 30, 1926

[255] *Mt. Vernon Register*, February 9, 1912

[256] Ibid., February 20 and March 22, 1912

[257] Ibid., April 6, 1912

[258] *Mt. Vernon Weekly News,* April 10, 1912

[259] *Mt. Vernon Register*, April 20 and 22, 1912; *Mt. Vernon News*, April 20, 1912

[260] *Mt. Vernon News*, July 3, August 11, 19, 20, and 21, 1912; *Mt. Vernon Register*, August 19 and 20, 1912

[261] *Mt. Vernon Register*, August 21, 1912; *Mt. Vernon News*, September 7, 1912; *Mt. Vernon Weekly News,* September 4, 1912; *Mt. Vernon Register-News,* September 9, 1937, As You Were 25 Years Ago

[262] *Mt. Vernon News*, September 17, 1912; *Mt. Vernon Weekly News,* September 18, 1912

[263] David McCullough, *Truman* (New York: Simon & Schuster, 1992), 214; *Mt. Vernon Register-News*, As You Were 10 Years Ago, September 20, 1922 and As You Were 15 Years Ago, September 19, 1927; *Mt. Vernon Weekly News,* September 25, 1912

[264] *Mt. Vernon News*, October 1, 1912

[265] Ibid., October 23 and 28, 1912; *Mt. Vernon Weekly News,* November 6, 1912

[266] *Mt. Vernon Register*, February 14, 1913

[267] *Mt. Vernon Register*, June 17, 1913 and August 7 and 12, 1913

[268] Ibid., September 19 and 22, 1913

[269] Ibid., May 2, 1914

[270] Ibid., May 15, 1914

[271] *Mt. Vernon Register-News*, November 12, 1926

[272] *Mt. Vernon Register*, June 16, July 31, August 2, 10, 11, and 12, 1914; Someone mistakenly labeled the photo of Speaker Cannon at the Chautauqua with the date of Aug. 5, 1909. He actually came to Mt. Vernon on Aug. 11, 1914.

[273] Ibid., August 13, 1914

[274] Ibid., August 2, 1914

[275] Ibid., September 23, October 31, 1914; *Mt. Vernon Weekly News,* September 30, 1914

[276] Ibid., September 11, 15, 24, 25, and 26, 1914; Kathleen Dalton, *Theodore Roosevelt: A Strenuous Life* (New York: Alfred A. Knopf, 2002), 438–443

[277] *Mt. Vernon Register-News*, As You Were 10 Years Ago, October 14, 1924; *Mt. Vernon Weekly News,* October 28, 1914

[278] *Mt. Vernon Register*, October 10 and 17, 1914

[279] www.nps.gov

[280] *Mt. Vernon News*, October 25, 1914; *Mt. Vernon register-News*, As You Were 10 Years Ago, October 27, 1924

[281] *Mt. Vernon Register*, November 12, 1914

[282] Ibid., April 7, 1915

[283] In 1905 Anne Sullivan married John Macy and was referred to as Mrs. Anne Macy in the 1915 Mt. Vernon newspapers. In the 1962 film, *The Miracle Worker*, Anne Bancroft won an Academy Award for her portrayal of Anne Sullivan.

[284] Dorothy Herrmann, *Helen Keller, A Life* (Chicago: University of Chicago Press, 1999), 180–189, 194, 223, 228

[285] *Mt Vernon Register.*, July 13, 19, 25, August 3, 10, 17, 18, 1915

[286] Ibid., July 13 and 19, 1915

[287] Ibid., August 10, 1915

[288] Ibid., September 24, 1915

[289] Ibid., November 26, 1915

[290] Ibid., February 4, 1916

[291] Ibid., June 19, 1916

[292] Ibid., July 10, 18, 24, 25, and 27, 1916

[293] Ibid., July 31, 1916

[294] Ibid., July 31, 1916; www.fda.gov

[295] *Mt. Vernon Weekly News,* August 23, 1916

[296] Ibid., October 7, 1916

[297] Ibid., October 13, 1916

[298] Ibid., October 13, 1916

[299] Ibid., October 21 and 27, 1916

[300] Linda Mick Short, "The Jeffersonian" (newsletter of the Jefferson County Historical Society), Vol. XVIII, No. 1, 7

[301] *Mt. Vernon Register*, October 16 and 17, 1916; *Mt. Vernon Register-News*, July 27, 1925

[302] *Mt. Vernon News*, August 2, 1917; *Mt. Vernon Register*, August 1, 1917

[303] Ibid., July 26, August 11, 16, 1917

[304] *Mt. Vernon Register*, November 21, 28, December 3, 7, 11, and 12, 1917

305 Ibid., February 13 and July 17, 1918

306 Ibid., February 20 and 27, 1918

307 Ibid., June 19, 26, July 3, August 24, 1918

308 Ibid., March 13, July 17, and August 14, 1918 (O'Brien committed suicide in Los Angeles in 1920, leaving a note blaming a woman for breaking up his marriage.)

309 Ibid., August 24, 1918

310 Ibid., January 4, 1919

311 *Mt. Vernon News, May 7, 1919*

312 *Mt. Vernon Register*, July 5, 18, and 19, 1919

313 *Mt. Vernon Register-News*, As You Were 5 Years Ago, September 19, and 25, 1924

314 *Mt. Vernon Weekly News,* February 18, 1920

315 Puckett, 100–101; Jefferson County Historical Society files.

316 *Mt. Vernon Register*, December 23, 1885; December 24, 1902; and December 23, 1916

317 John W. Allen, *Legends and Lore of Southern Illinois* (Johnston City, Illinois: A.E.R.P. Publishing, 1985), 113; *Mt. Vernon Register-News*, October 15, 1953

318 W. R. Brink, *Atlas of Lawrence County* (Evansville, Indiana: UNIGRAIC, 1875), 1–45

319 J. H. G. Brinkerhoff, *History of Marion County* (Indianapolis, Indiana: B.F. Bowen & Company, 1909), 166, 172

320 www.rootsweb.com/iljeffer/obits (Obituary of Martha Maddox Short)

321 Lorenzo and Peggy Dow and John Dowling, *The Dealings of God, Man, and the Devil; As Exemplified in the Life and Travels of Lorenzo Dow* (New York: Cornish, Lamport & Co., 1850), 178, 181

322 Perrin, 124; Wall, 500

323 Hamilton County Historical Society, *Goshen Trails* (18 volumes, McDowell Publications, 2005), 1:8–9 (October 1965, Vol. 1, No.5) and 12:11 (January 1976, Vol. 12, No.1)

324 Wallis, 425

325 John W. Allen, *It Happened in Southern Illinois* (Johnston City, Illinois: A.E.R.P. Publishing, 1985), 23

326 Smith, 105; The website, thelincolnlog.org, doesn't have Lincoln in Salem that day. They have him in Olney September 20 and Vandalia September 23. The date September 22 is blank.

327 Bill Nunes, *Southern Illinois, An Illustrated History* (n.p., 2001), 245

328 John Y. Simon, *The Papers of U.S. Grant* (16 volumes, Carbondale, Illinois: Southern Illinois University Press, 1969), 2:32

329 *Mt. Vernon Register-News*, December 16, 1935; Borah had a long affair with Alice Roosevelt Longworth and was the father of her only child, Paulina Longworth.

330 *The Nashville Journal*, September 20, 1877

331 *The New York Times*, September 10, 1886

332 Corliss, 303

333 *Mt. Vernon Weekly Register*, August 23, 1893

334 *Mt. Vernon Register-News*, April 6, 1961 (article on Dr. Andy Hall's speech to the Jefferson County Historical Society)

335 *Mt. Vernon Register-News*, As You Were 30 Years Ago, October 4, 1928; Byford Campbell, *History of Ina, Illinois* (n.p., 1998), 29

336 www.pbs.org

337 Hamilton County Historical Society, *Goshen Trails* (18 volumes, McDowell Publications, 2005), 1: 9 (June 1965); John D. Shaw, *History of Walnut Hill: A Chronology* (n.p., 2009), 55

338 Ibid., July 1972, 15

339 Puckett, 138

340 Ibid., 139

341 *Mt. Vernon News*, April 23, December 7, and 29, 1899; *Mt. Vernon Register*, October 11, 1909; *Mt. Vernon News*, September 18, 1911

[342] *Mt. Vernon News*, September 11, 1909

[343] *Mt. Vernon Register*, August 12, 1913; *Mt. Vernon Weekly News,* August 12, 1914

[344] Ibid., May 27, 1915

[345] *Mt. Vernon News*, June 26, August 8 and 11, 1917

[346] *Mt. Vernon Register*, November 7, 1914

[347] *Mt. Vernon News*, September 27 and 28, 1917

[348] *Mt. Vernon Register*, August 24, 1918